Better **Wordpower**

Janet Whitcut is an experienced lexicographer and has written widely on English usage. Her previous publications include *The Little Oxford Guide to English Usage* (with Edmund Weiner and Andrew Delahunty) and Sir Ernest Gowers' *Complete Plain Words* (revised edition, with Sidney Greenbaum).

Oxford Paperback Reference

The most authoritative and up-to-date reference books for both students and the general reader.

Abbreviations
ABC of Music
Accounting
Archaeology*
Architecture
Art and Artists
Art Terms*
Astronomy
Bible
Biology
British Women Writers
Buddhism*
Business
Card Games
Chemistry
Christian Church
Classical Literature
Classical Mythology*
Colour Medical
Colour Science
Computing
Dance*
Dates
Earth Sciences
Ecology
Economics
Engineering*
English Etymology
English Folklore*
English Grammar
English Language
English Literature
English Place-Names
Euphemisms
Film*
Finance and Banking
First Names
Food and Nutrition
Fowler's Modern English
   Usage
Geography
Handbook of the World*
Humorous Quotations
Irish Literature*
Jewish Religion
Kings and Queens*
King's English
Law
Linguistics

Literary Quotations
Literary Terms
London Place Names*
Mathematics
Medical
Medicines
Modern Design
Modern Quotations
Modern Slang
Music
Nursing
Opera
Paperback Encyclopedia
Philosophy
Physics
Plant-Lore
Plant Sciences
Political Biography
Political Quotations
Politics
Popes
Proverbs
Psychology*
Quotations
Sailing Terms
Saints
Science
Shakespeare
Ships and the Sea
Sociology
Statistics*
Superstitions
Synonyms and Antonyms
Theatre
Twentieth-Century Art
Twentieth-Century Poetry
Twentieth-Century World
   History
Weather Facts
Who's Who in Opera
Who's Who in Twentieth
   Century
Word Games
World History
World Mythology
World Religions*
Writers' Dictionary
Zoology

*forthcoming

Better Wordpower

Janet Whitcut

OXFORD
UNIVERSITY PRESS

OXFORD

UNIVERSITY PRESS

Great Clarendon Street, Oxford OX2 6DP

Oxford University Press is a department of the University of Oxford.
It furthers the University's objective of excellence in research, scholarship,
and education by publishing worldwide in

Oxford New York

Athens Auckland Bangkok Bogotá Buenos Aires Calcutta
Cape Town Chennai Dares Salaam Delhi Florence Hong Kong Istanbul
Karachi Kuala Lumpur Madrid Melbourne Mexico City Mumbai
Nairobi Paris São Paulo Singapore Taipei Tokyo Toronto Warsaw

with associated companies in Berlin Ibadan

Oxford is a registered trade mark of Oxford University Press
in the UK and in certain other countries

Published in the United States
by Oxford University Press Inc., New York

British Library Cataloguing in Publication Data

Data available

Library of Congress Cataloging in Publication Data

Data available

ISBN 0-19-280108-2

10 9 8 7 6 5 4 3 2

Printed in Great Britain
on acid-free paper by
Cox & Wyman, Reading, Berkshire

Contents

List of Illustrations

Introduction

The size of one's general vocabulary is a rough indication of the extent and quality of one's reading. 'General' is to be emphasized here, since an expert in any specialized subject will also have a specialized vocabulary in that subject—plumbing, entomology, palaeontology—which the rest of the world neither has nor needs, and we may each have one or more of such specialisms. Again, there are words such as the latest slang which we 'know' from picking them up orally, but may never have seen written down, and so perhaps are uncertain about their spelling; and a final, important, distinction must be made between those words which we can actually use, and those which we can 'decode' when we encounter them in context but would be unlikely to think of spontaneously and perhaps cannot pronounce.

An unfamiliar word is often pretty well defined by its context:

> He . . . began to whistle a dance tune . . . still whistling his estampie at intervals—Ellis Peters, *The Leper of St Giles* (1981)

That gives a rough definition of the strange word 'estampie', which the *Oxford Companion to Music* explains more fully:

> **estampie** (Fr.) or **estampita** (Provençal). A type of tune for dancing (with or without words—more properly, perhaps, without). In its alternation of several little strains, each followed by the same refrain, it resembles the rondeau. It belonged to the life of southern Europe in the twelfth to fifteenth centuries, and was, apparently, one of the forms associated with the art of the Troubadours. Boccaccio calls it *stampita*.

Again, in Thomas Love Peacock's *Melincourt* (1817), Sir Oran Haut-Ton walks past the window:

> Sir Oran's mode of progression being very vacillating, indirect, and titubant; enough so, at least, to show that he had not completely danced off the effects of the Madeira.

A rare word, this 'titubant'; in fact according to the *Oxford Dictionary*, Peacock seems to have made it up himself, from the Latin *titubare*. But we can see, first that it is an adjective, since it describes his 'mode of progression', and then that it goes with 'vacillating' and 'indirect' as describing someone's walk after drinking too much Madeira. In fact it means 'staggering, reeling, unsteady', which is exactly what one might expect.

Or consider the episode in Act IV, scene vi, of *King Lear*, in which Edgar pretends to Gloucester that they are standing at the top of Dover Cliff:

> How fearful
> And dizzy 'tis to cast one's eyes so low!
> The crows and choughs that wing the midway air
> Show scarce so gross as beetles: half way down
> Hangs one that gathers samphire, dreadful trade!

Those of us who are not botanists may never have met the word 'samphire'; yet we can at once see that it is a noun—the object of a verb—and that one 'gathers' it. It is therefore presumably a plant. That is all we need to make tolerable sense of the passage, but if we wish to pursue the matter further the *Concise Oxford Dictionary* will tell us more:

> **samphire** *n.* **1** an umbelliferous maritime rock plant, *Crithmum maritimum*, with aromatic fleshy leaves used in pickles.

So it grows on maritime rocks such as Dover Cliff, where it is gathered for pickle-making.

That may well be enough. As for that difficult word 'umbelliferous', it is certainly the business of dictionaries to define things as simply as possible, but they must also be reasonably concise. To avoid this technical term, it would have been necessary to explain what an 'umbel' is: 'a flower cluster in which stalks nearly equal in length spring from a common centre and form a flat or curved surface, as in parsley'. So to get a full picture of what samphire looks like, one may have to look up more than one word in the dictionary.

In certain situations the context gives very little help:

> Those clients [of a bank] who own more than a quarter of the £70 billion of assets DMG manages, stayed partly thanks to Mrs Horlick's talent for schmoozing—*The Economist*, 18 January 1997

This tells us no more about 'schmoozing' than that it was something Mrs Horlick 'did'—a verb, in fact. If we are bewildered, we must turn to the *Supplement to the Oxford Dictionary*:

schmooze *v. US colloq.* To chat, gossip, engage in a long and intimate conversation.

So Mrs Horlick kept her clients by the charm with which she 'chatted them up'.

This book suggests various strategies for tackling unknown words, both for comprehension and for the further stage of using them correctly and with confidence. We begin by discussing various sorts of wordbooks, and how best to use them. Then come sections dealing with some pitfalls of spelling, some 'Confusable' words, and a list of 'Foreign Phrases', followed by two powerful ways of building one's vocabulary: a list of 'Antonyms', and another of the 'Word Elements' from which so many English words have been constructed and go on being formed today. The rest of the book consists of a number of specialized 'Topics', and a 'Lexicon of Hard Words'.

Part 1

The Basic Toolkit

Dictionary or Encyclopedia?

The first decision in tracking down an unknown item is whether we need a dictionary or an encyclopedia. Both are primarily for 'decoding', in the sense of finding the meaning of a word that has occurred in some context. (The exception is that when we want a foreign word we are 'encoding', as when an English speaker uses the English–French or English–Swedish half of a bilingual dictionary.)

But dictionaries are different from encyclopedias. Very roughly a dictionary is about 'words', while an encyclopedia is about 'things'; but the distinction is subtle, and there is considerable overlap. There are only nouns in an encyclopedia; it is to the dictionary that we look for *establish, ethical,* or *ever.* Both dictionaries and encyclopedias include such 'common' nouns as *iron* (the encyclopedia of course at much greater length) but the first—not the second—has *irony,* and the second—but probably not the first—has *Ironmongers Company.* In this matter of proper names, though, the policy varies. French and American dictionaries include by tradition more names of people and places than is usual in Britain. Users mostly prefer whichever style is the more familiar.

Finding a Word

Ordering of Words

To use a dictionary or encyclopedia (or indeed to use a cookery book, gazetteer, or telephone directory) one must grasp the principle of alphabetical order. There are two ways of alphabetizing, with minor variations within each: 'word-by-word' and 'letter-by-letter', and it is quite important to notice which method is used in one's own particular dictionary. As regards single words, the policy is the same. A root word precedes the same word with an added suffix:

>**jail**
>**jailer**.

There is some variation even here as to whether capitalized items are to precede or follow lower-case ones. One may find either:

>**Polish** (=of Poland)
>**polish** (=for shoes, etc.)
>or: **polish**
>   **Polish**.

Thereafter, the variation is wider. The word-by-word system alphabetizes multi-word items up to the first word space, with hyphenated and open compounds usually treated under their first word. So the 1990 edition of the *Concise Oxford Dictionary*, with a modified word-by-word system, has:

>**water**
>**water jump** (at *water*)
>**waterfall**.

In contrast, the letter-by-letter system ignores word spaces. The American *Webster's Ninth New Collegiate Dictionary*, accordingly, has:

> **water**
> **waterfall**
> **water jump**.

The Oxford shows the phrasal verb **work out** at **work**, and the noun **workout** as a separate item, whereas Webster treats both as separate items, in the order of solid compounds before open ones:

> **workout**
> **work out**.

Both systems have their relative advantages. The letter-by-letter one produces a more open layout on the page, in contrast with the long paragraphs demanded by the word-by-word. But word-by-word gives more semantic coherence:

> **law**
> **law of nature** (at *law*)
> **lawn**

rather than:

> **law**
> **lawn**
> **law of nature**.

Users are probably happier with whichever system is the more familiar. In any case, of course, one finds a word in its alphabetical place by looking, not only at the first letter, but at all subsequent ones; so that **plutonic**, for instance, precedes **plutonium** because its final **-c** comes before the final **-um**. In flipping rapidly through a dictionary, one should look at the 'guidewords' at the tops of the pages: **plutonium** and **plutonic** may come on a page which runs from **plump** to **ply**.

The two remaining problems in finding an unfamiliar word are, first, its 'part of speech', and second, the ordering of the senses in one's dictionary.

Parts of Speech

The English parts of speech are:

noun a word (other than a pronoun) used to name or identify any of a class of persons, places, or things, or a particular one of these: *novelist, city, potato, Tuesday, Edward*.

article *a* and *the*.

pronoun a word used instead of and to indicate a noun already mentioned or known, especially to avoid repetition: *we, this, ourselves.*

adjective a word or phrase naming an attribute, added to or grammatically related to a noun to modify it or describe it: *sleepy, dangerous, Swiss.*

adverb a word or phrase that modifies or qualifies another word (especially an adjective, verb, or other adverb) or a word-group, expressing a relation of place, time, circumstance, manner, cause, degree, etc.: *gently, quite, then, there.*

verb a word used to indicate an action, state, or occurrence, and forming the main part of the predicate of a sentence: *hear, become, happen.*

preposition a word governing (and usually preceding) a noun or pronoun and expressing a relation to another word or element: the man *on* the platform, came *after* dinner, what did you do it *for*?

conjunction a word used to connect clauses or sentences or words in the same clause: *and, but, if.*

interjection an exclamation: *ah! dear me!*

But an unknown word is almost certainly a noun or verb, or just possibly an adjective or adverb. Mother-tongue speakers of English know all the prepositions, pronouns, and conjunctions, since these constitute a 'closed set' which is never added to. One might, just possibly, hear a new interjection?

Some dictionaries treat each different part of speech as a new headword. So, to return to **water**, Oxford combines the noun and the verb in one long entry, while Webster treats the noun **water** separately from the verb **to water**.

Ordering of Senses

As for the ordering of senses, there are again two systems. Where a word has several meanings, some dictionaries treat them in the historical order in which they entered the language, while others show them with the commonest meaning first. Thus the *Concise Oxford Dictionary*, which is ordered by frequency, gives as its first sense of **fowl** 'any domestic cock or hen of various gallinaceous birds, kept for eggs and flesh', while the massive and scholarly *Oxford Dictionary* itself begins with the oldest meaning, 'bird'. It is a common failing of inexperienced dictionary users to look only at the first meaning, and then to conclude that it does not match the context in which the unknown word appears, and so to give up. This can equally apply to the rarer senses of fairly common words. The reader, perhaps, might be confronted with the following sentence by Charles Darwin: '[The stigmas] form two protuberant, almost horn-shaped processes on each side of the mouth.' Most of us know the word **process**, in the sense of something like 'a course of action, a proceeding, something going on'. We must look through the senses of even such a moderate-sized dictionary as the *Concise* as far as sense **5**, 'a natural appendage or outgrowth on an organism' in order to make out what Darwin was talking about.

When the Word is Found

It is well worthwhile to study the introductory section of the dictionary one uses. It will explain the dictionary's policy over the foregoing matters, and also list the abbreviations employed. These concern parts of speech, such as *v.tr.* for transitive verb (one that takes a direct object); inflections, such as *pl.* for plural; geographical restrictions, such as *US* for American English; levels of formality, such as *sl.* for slang; subject areas, such as *Anat.* for Anatomy; and languages referred to in the etymologies, such as *Afrik.* for Afrikaans. Dictionaries for the foreign learner of English must necessarily include far more detailed grammatical information, telling the user for instance that the verb **put** needs not only a direct object but something more—one **puts** *something somewhere*. We said at the outset that a monolingual—one-language—dictionary is primarily intended for decoding, but we approach now the area of 'encoding', whereby the dictionary advises on how actually to use the word.

Pronunciation and Stress

Probably the first item in any dictionary, after the headword itself, is its pronunciation. One may have merely read a word and be uncertain how to say it, and there are two ways of representing this: by means of the International Phonetic Alphabet (IPA), or by the use of a 'respelling' system which confines itself more or less to the letters of the ordinary alphabet. Thus the word **cleavage** will be represented phonetically as /ˈkliːvɪdʒ/, or respelt as /ˈkleevij/. Both systems have their advocates, and for an English dictionary for English speakers there may not be much to choose between them, provided that whatever system is used is clearly set out and easy to find, ideally in a 'running foot' at the bottom of each page. A foreigner, naturally, would find the respelling system useless, having no preconceptions about how the 'respelt' version should be pronounced either. But the native speaker, anxious to know how to say a word, may need not much more than some indication of where the stress should fall: is it CLEMatis or cleMATis?

The IPA symbols relevant to the English language are:

Consonants

b, d, f, h, k, l, m, n, p, r, s, t, v, w, z, which have their usual English values.

g as in get	x as in lo*ch*	ð as in *this*	j as in *yes*
tʃ *chip*	ŋ *ring*	ʃ *she*	
dʒ *jar*	θ *thin*	ʒ *decision*	

Vowels

SHORT VOWELS		LONG VOWELS		DIPHTHONGS	
æ	as in c*a*t	ɑ:	as in *a*rm	eɪ	as in d*ay*
e	b*e*d	ɛ:	h*air*	ʌɪ	m*y*
ə	*ago*	i:	as in s*ee*	ɔɪ	b*oy*
ɪ	s*i*t	ɔ:	s*aw*	əʊ	n*o*
i	cos*y*	ə:	h*er*	aʊ	h*ow*
ɒ	h*o*t	u:	t*oo*	ɪə	n*ear*
ʌ	r*u*n			ʊə	p*oor*
ʊ	p*u*t			ʌɪə	f*ire*
				aʊə	s*our*

(There is some minor variation here between dictionaries.)

The main stressed syllable of a word is shown by the mark '
        'paper   be'cause.
Any secondary stress, in longer words, is shown by
        'irri,tate   ,irri'tation.
(A few dictionaries place these stress marks after, rather than before, the syllable to be stressed. The question can be sorted out by looking at any one really familiar word.)

Where there are two possible ways of pronouncing a word, or alternative places to put the stress, a dictionary may give advice on the matter. Stress and pronunciation do change with time, and the accomplished speaker will wish to be up to date, not lagging too far behind or straying too far ahead of received opinion, or pronouncing British English in too 'American' a manner. For instance, the *Concise Oxford* advises 'harass rather than ha'rass, but allows both 'applicable and ap'plicable, centri'fugal and cen'trifugal. It prefers the long diphthong of d*ay* in the first syllable of 'status, although one may also hear the word pronounced with the short vowel of c*at*. But pronunciation is a fluid matter, and although British dictionaries describe educated southern British English there is now far less prejudice against the pronunciations of regional speech.

There are also, of course, pitfalls in the pronunciation of names, which are not included in many dictionaries, and it is beyond the scope of this book to give much advice. The BBC have their own recommendations for place names: Blaenau Festiniog /'blaɪnaɪ fes'tɪnjɒg/. Note that British and American standards may vary over proper names; the British pronounce Oedipus as /'iːdɪpəs/, the Americans as /'edəpəs/.

Levels of Formality

Perhaps one of the most useful pieces of advice a dictionary may give about actually using a word is its level of formality. We may know the word perfectly well, but the dictionary may still help us to use it with confidence. In writing a formal job application, for instance, we probably realize that instead of asking for a **job** it is more suitable to call it a **post** or **position**. We know that **kids** (which the *Concise Oxford* calls *slang*) is less formal than **children**, and choose the right one for our needs. But we may think first of a slang word, perhaps in such a context as 'Her sudden resignation caused a lot of **hoo-ha**', and the dictionary will usefully suggest the more suitable alternatives 'commotion, row, uproar, trouble' for **hoo-ha**, and may even comment that **'a lot of'** is somewhat colloquial and might be replaced by 'a great deal' or 'a considerable amount'. Conversely it may say that **commence** is a formal word, and propose the less stuffy alternatives **begin** and **start**. It will take us from **bog** (*British slang*) and **loo** (*British colloquial*) to **lavatory** and **toilet**, from **cock** (*British slang*) to **nonsense**, from **clink** (*slang*) to **prison**. Even where the distinction of formality is less sharp, it offers such synonyms as **afterwards** for **subsequently**, **enough** for **sufficient**, **take away** for **remove**, **tired** for **fatigued**, **whole** for **entire**, **only** for **exclusively**, **lucky** for **fortunate**, **like** for **similar**, **go down** for **descend**, **put up** for **erect**, and a choice between **articles**, **items**, and just **things**.

The dictionary may be even more helpful in pointing out which near-synonyms are actually coarse or offensive. Of the various words for **penis**, the *Concise* regards **prick** and **tool** as *coarse slang*, **willy** as just *British slang*, and **pecker** as *US coarse slang*. More importantly it advises, as any good dictionary will, over racial slurs: the use of **jew** as a verb 'get a financial advantage over' is *offensive slang*, and so is **darky**, while **nigger** is just *offensive*.

The Thesaurus

But in all this matter of synonyms we reach the territory of another sort of wordbook, the thesaurus, from the Greek word for 'treasure house'. In contrast to the dictionary this is designed for 'encoding', and is therefore specifically for writers. Thesaurus users have thought of a meaning, so to speak, and are groping for the right word to express it. To find that right word, one looks up a word that is near to it in meaning, in the index at the back—if there is one—or in the general A–Z word list if there is not, and runs through the list of synonyms.

One may do this to avoid repetition: perhaps we used the word **progressive** in our last sentence, so we seek for variation and the thesaurus suggests **avant-garde**. Or we may simply be unable to think of the exact word: **rude** is not quite right, but when we look it up, the thesaurus provides such near synonyms as **discourteous, churlish**, and **insolent**.

The original *Roget's Thesaurus*, first published in 1852 and now long out of copyright, is based on a hierarchy of philosophical concepts such as 'Prominence, Multiformity, Exertion, Rashness' for each of which are provided the English words necessary to express them. Strictly speaking, then, Roget is different from the more usual 'dictionary of synonyms', since he starts from an idea rather than from a word. He is consequently not constrained by the grammatical parts of speech: **pride**, **proud**, and **show off** are grouped together, and are followed by their negatives: **humility, unassuming**, and so on. This fluid approach may help the writer to recast a sentence in the negative, or to convey an idea by a verb rather than a noun.

But most thesauruses today are arranged in A–Z order, with or without a separate index. This makes for a more approachable kind of book; although, unlike Roget, they cannot cover a concept for which there is only one word in the same part of speech, where Roget might offer some circumlocution. They may or may not, and Roget does not, advise about formality, regional variation, and so on, in the way that dictionaries do, and they may or may not provide example sentences to display the words in use. The *Oxford Thesaurus* gives such examples: at **lawful**, for instance, 'I am the lawful heir.'

There are virtually no exact synonyms in the language, though words may differ only in their degree of formality or in being perhaps British and American equivalents. What no conventional thesaurus can do is to discuss the delicate distinctions between its listed near-synonyms, since that would be impossibly space-consuming. Thus, for **fleeting**, the *Concise Oxford Thesaurus* lists 'rapid, swift, brief, short-lived, short, momentary, transient, transitory, ephemeral, fugitive, evanescent, fugacious, vanishing, flying, passing, flitting, here today and gone tomorrow, temporary, impermanent'. A conventional dictionary might indeed offer some of these as definitions of each other! But users of either thesauruses or dictionaries must discover for themselves that hotel guests are **transient** (but not momentary or fugitive), that a prefabricated wooden structure is **temporary** (but not evanescent or ephemeral), and that one may catch a **fleeting** or **momentary** glimpse of something (but not a temporary or flying one). For one sense of **mean**, the thesaurus proposes 'base, dishonourable, ignoble, disreputable, vile, sordid, foul, nasty, despicable, contemptible, abominable, odious, hateful, horrible'. But **mean** people are chiefly petty, ungenerous, and small-minded, while **ignoble** emphasizes the lack of higher qualities, and **sordid** adds a suggestion of corruption and squalor.

Some thesauruses, of the kind usually called dictionaries of synonyms, also suggest antonyms—opposites—of the listed words where appropriate. This can be extremely useful, overcoming as it does Roget's advantage of listing **humility** next to its near opposite, **pride**. Some dictionaries have a few opposites too; the *Concise Oxford* gives **perigee** as the opposite of **apogee**. But as the provision of antonyms is fairly uncommon, and is a powerful mechanism for enlarging one's vocabulary, we include a selected list on pages 47–56 of this book.

Part 2

Reference Section

Spelling

Sound and Spelling

Some difficulties in spelling arise because, if one does not know the first letter of a word, one cannot either look it up in a dictionary or use the word processor's spellcheck. The following may help:

SOUND		OTHER SPELLINGS
i as in *bite*	may be spelt as in	*aye, eye, aisle*
our as in *sour*		*hour, sauerkraut*
ch as in *cheer*		*cello, Czech*
f as in *few*		*physics, cough*
n as in *no*		*gnaw, know, mnemonic, pneumonia*
r as in *red*		*rhubarb, wriggle*
s as in *sit*		*schism, psychology*
t as in *top*		*pterodactyl*
w as in *we*		*one, while*

British and American Spellings

The main differences are:

	BRITISH	AMERICAN
ae and **oe**	gynaecology, diarrhoea	gynecology, diarrhea
-ce or **-se**	(nouns) licence, defence, offence, pretence	license, defense, offense, pretense
double letters	appal, skilful, traveller, worshipped, woollen	appall, skillful, traveler, worshiped, woolen
silent **e**	axe, programme	ax, program

	BRITISH	AMERICAN
-oul- or **-ol-**	mould, smoulder	mold, smolder
-our or **-or**	colour, humour	color, humor
-re or **-er**	centre, theatre	center, theater
-yse or **-yze**	analyse, paralyse	analyze, paralyze

See also those words marked *, for 'American', in the following spelling list. It includes only words in fairly general use. For the more technical, see the various Topics discussed later.

Difficult Spellings

A
abattoir
aberration
abrogate
abscess
abysmal
accelerate
accessory
accommodation
accrue
acknowledge
acolyte
acquaintance
acquiesce
acquire
acquit
acrylic
acumen
acupuncture
adenoids
adieu
adjourn
admissible
adolescence
advantageous
adviser
aegis
aerial
affidavit
aficionado

aghast
agitator
agoraphobia
aisle (church)
alimentary
allege
allegiance
alleluia (Heb.
  hallelujah)
alliteration
almanac (also
  almanack)
amanuensis
ambidextrous
ambience (also
  ambiance)
amoeba *ameba
amok (also amuck)
amphibious
anachronism
anaemia *anemia
anaesthetic
  *anesthetic
analgesic
analyse *analyze
ancillary
androgynous
anemone
annihilate
anomalous
antecedent

antechamber
antediluvian
antirrhinum
antitype
Apennines
apophthegm
apostasy
appal *appall
appreciate
appurtenance
aqueduct
archetype
archipelago
arpeggio
artefact (also artifact)
ascendancy
asinine
asphalt
asphyxiate
aspidistra
assassin
asthma
attendant
aubergine
aubrietia
auxiliary
avocado

B
bacillus
baguette

bargain
baroque
battalion
behove *behoove
benefited *benefitted
bitumen
bivouacking
blancmange
blond (man)
blonde (woman)
bouillabaisse
bourgeois
Brittany
broccoli
budgerigar

C

cadaver
caffeine
calibre *caliber
callipers
calypso
camellia
carcass
Caribbean
cataclysm
catarrh
cemetery
chancellor
charismatic
chauffeur
chauvinism
cheque *check
chiaroscuro
chihuahua
chilblain
chilli *chili
chlorophyll
cholesterol
chromosome
chrysalis
chrysanthemum
coalesce
colander
colloquial

colonnade
colossal
commemorate
committee
competent
concede
connoisseur
conscientious
consensus
coolly
corollary
corpuscle
correspondence

D

dachshund
dahlia
decrepit
definite
descendant
desiccated
deteriorate
dialogue *dialog
diaphragm
diarrhoea *diarrhea
dilettante
diphtheria
disappoint
dissect
duly
dungeon
dysentery

E

ebullient
eccentric
ecstasy
effervescence
eisteddfod
eligible
embarrass
embryo
enrol *enroll
enthral *enthrall
epitome

erogenous
erroneous
eucalyptus
exaggerate
exhilarate
expedite
eyrie

F

facetious
Fahrenheit
fallible
fiasco
fiery
fiord (also fjord)
fluorescent
forebode
foreign
foresight
foretell
forty
fuchsia
fulfil *fulfill
fulsome
furore *furor
fuselage
fusillade

G

gases
gauge *gage
gazpacho
gazump
geriatric
gherkin
ghoul
gigolo
glycerine *glycerin
gnome
goulash
government
granddaughter
grievance
guerrilla (also guerilla)
guillotine

Gurkha
gymnasium
gynaecology
  *gynecology

H

habeas corpus
haemoglobin
  *hemoglobin
haemorrhage
  *hemorrhage
hara-kiri
harangue
harass
hashish
hausfrau
heinous
herbaceous
hirsute
holocaust
homeopathy
humorous
hyacinth
hydrangea
hypochondria
hypocrisy
hysteria

I

ichthyosaurus
icicle
idiosyncrasy
impeccable
impromptu
incandescent
incur
indefatigable
indefensible
independent
indigenous
indigestible
indispensable
initial
innocuous
innovate

inoculate
instalment *installment
instil *instill
intercede
internecine
inveigle
irascible
iridescent
irresistible

J

jamb (of door)
jardinière
jeopardy
jeweller *jeweler
jodhpurs
juggernaut
juxtapose

K

kaleidoscope
khaki
kleptomania

L

labyrinth
lachrymose
lackadaisical
lacquer
languor
laryngitis
lascivious
leisure
leprechaun
liaison
library
liquefy
loathsome
longevity
loofah (also luffa)
loquacious
luncheon
Luxembourg

M

macabre
maelstrom
maestro
manoeuvre *maneuver
maraschino
marquis
Marylebone
massacre
mayonnaise
medicine
mediocre
Mediterranean
merely
meringue
mezzanine
migraine
milieu
millennium
minuscule
misogynist
misspell
mistakable
mnemonic
moustache *mustache
myrrh
myxomatosis

N

necessary
neighbour *neighbor
neuralgia
nickel
niece
nuptial

O

oasis
obeisance
obsequious
occasionally
occurred
odyssey
oesophagus
  *esophagus

oppressor
opprobrium
orangeade
orang-utan
oscillate
overrun

P

paid
papier mâché
paraffin
parakeet
paralleled
paralyse *paralyze
paraphernalia
parenthesis
pariah
parliament
paroxysm
parquet
partisan (also partizan)
pavilion
peaceable
peccadillo
pejorative
Peloponnese
pencilling *penciling
penicillin
perceive
perennial
periphery
permanent
permissible
personnel
persuade
pettifogging
Philippines
phlegm
phlox
phonetic
phosphorescence
physique
Piccadilly
picnicking
playwright

plebeian
plenitude
politician
polythene
Portuguese
possession
posthumous
precede
precipice
predecessor
pretentious
privilege
proceed
promiscuous
promissory
promontory
pronunciation
propeller
pseudonym
psychedelic
pursue
pusillanimous
pyjamas *pajamas

Q

quarrelled *quarreled
quatercentenary
questionnaire
queue
quotient

R

recede
receipt
recommend
recompense
recondite
reconnoitre
  *reconnoiter
relevant
remedy
reminiscence
repellent
repertory
reprehensible

rescind
resplendent
restaurateur
resuscitate
rhetoric
rheumatism
rhinoceros
rhododendron
rhubarb
rhythm
ricochet
riveting
rotisserie

S

sacrilege
salutary
sanatorium
sanctimonious
sarsaparilla
sauerkraut
schizophrenic
schnapps
sciatica
scimitar
scurrilous
scythe
secateurs
secede
secretary
seize
separate
sepulchre
Shakespearian (also
  -rean)
shanty
sheikh (also shaikh,
  sheik)
shibboleth
sibyl
siege
simultaneous
skiing (also ski-ing)
snorkel (also schnorkel)
solemnly

soliloquy
soufflé
soupçon
spontaneous
strategy
strychnine
stupefy
stymie (also stimy)
subtle
succeed
succinct
sufficient
sulphur *sulfur
sumptuous
supercilious
supersede
surgeon
surprise
surreptitious
surveillance
suspicious
sycophant
syllabus
symmetry
syncopation
synthesis

T

tacit
tattooing

taxiing
Teheran
tenant
tendentious
Tennessee
tête-à-tête
thesaurus
thief
threshold
thyroid
titbit *tidbit
titillate
toboggan
tonsillitis
tourniquet
transcendent
transferred
traveller *traveler
triptych
trousseau
truly
truncheon
tunnelling *tunneling
tyranny

U

ubiquitous
umbrella
unctuous
unguent

V

vaccination
vacillate
vacuum
valuable
variegated
vehicle
vendor
venereal
vermilion
verruca
veterinary
victuals
vigorous
vinaigrette
violoncello
viscous
voluptuous

W

warranty
Wednesday
welfare
werewolf
whisky* & Irish whiskey
wisteria (also wistaria)
withhold

Y

yashmak
Yom Kippur

Confusables

Here is a short list of those words which, being similar in sound or spelling, are most commonly confused.

A

advice is the noun; **advise** the verb.

affect and **effect** can both be verbs. To *affect* is to have an influence on: *affected his health*. To *effect* is to bring about: *effect changes*. There is a noun *effect* meaning result or (in the plural) property, but no noun *affect* except in the technical language of psychology.

alternate means every other, happening in turns: *on alternate days*; in American use it sometimes replaces **alternative**, which chiefly means available instead of another or others: *an alternative route*.

To **amend** something is to improve it, to **emend** (a text) is to remove errors from it.

annex is the verb, **annexe** the noun.

To **appraise** is to estimate the value of: *appraised her skills*. To **apprise** is to inform: *apprised him of the facts*.

An **auger** is a sort of large corkscrew; to **augur** is to portend a particular outcome.

autarchy is despotism; **autarky** is economic self-sufficiency.

B

One **bails out** a prisoner, and *bails* water out of a boat. One **bales** hay, and *bales out* of an aircraft.

bait is for fish, or is rat poison; but **bated** breath.

balmy means fragrant, **barmy** means crazy.

bass and **base** both mean low, but *bass* is for music and *base* is inferior or ignoble.

benzene is a hydrocarbon C_6H_6 found in coal tar; **benzine** is a mixture derived from petroleum.

A **beret** is a hat; a **berry** is a fruit.

A **berth** is for sleeping in; **birth** is being born.

beside is by the side of, or compared with; **besides** is as well as, or other than.

A **bloc** is a combination of parties, governments, or groups. Use **block** for all other meanings.

A **boar** is a male pig; a **bore** is a dull person or thing, or a tidal wave. The verb is *bore*.

bogey is a golf score, **bogey** or **bogy** is a goblin, a **bogie** is a wheeled truck.

A child is **born; borne** means carried, or given birth to: *She has borne two sons.*

A **breach** is a gap or a breaking, but **breech** for a gun or for *breech birth*.

A **bridle** is for horses; **bridal** concerns brides and weddings.

by is the adverb or preposition; **bye** is a term in cricket or golf, or is short for goodbye.

C

A **caddie** carries golf clubs; a **caddy** is a container for tea.

A **calendar** is for dates, but a **calender** is a mangle.

A **cannon** is a gun or a stroke in billiards; a **canon** is a clergyman, a law, or a term in music.

canvas is cloth, but to **canvass** votes.

carousal is noisy celebration; a **carousel** is at an airport for luggage, or else it is a merry-go-round.

A **censer** contains incense; a **censor** examines books, films, etc. before public release; to **censure** is to disapprove.

chord is for music, mathematics, and engineering; **cord** is any kind of string, including such anatomical 'strings' as the *spinal cord* and *vocal cords*.

complaisant means politely acquiescent; **complacent** is self-satisfied.

A **complement** makes something complete; to **compliment** is to praise.

A **confidant** is someone in whom you confide; **confident** means bold and trusting.

A **corps** is a body of people, especially troops; a **corpse** is a dead body.

A **council** is an assembly, whose members are **councillors; counsel** is advice, and a **counsellor** is either an adviser or a senior diplomat.

crape is a black fabric; **crêpe** is either a thin fabric, a kind of rubber, or a pancake.

A **crevasse** is a hole in ice; a **crevice** is any small fissure.

crochet is rather like knitting; a **crotchet** is a musical note.

A **curb** is a restraint, and to *curb* is to restrain; the edge of a pavement is a curb or a **kerb**.

A **cygnet** is a young swan, but a **signet** is a seal, often set in a ring.

Cyprus is an island, but a **cypress** is a tree.

D

dependant is the noun, **dependent** the adjective.

To **deprecate** something is to deplore it; to **depreciate** it is to belittle it or reduce its value.

To **desert** is to abandon, and a *desert* is a dry sandy place; but the sweet course of a meal is **dessert**.

device is a noun, **devise** a verb.

A **dinghy** is a boat; **dingy** means grimy.

discreet means judicious; **discrete** means separate.

To **douse** is to quench; to **dowse** is to use a divining rod.

A **draft** is a military party, a money order, or a sketch; as a verb it means to prepare a document, the work of a **draftsman**. A **draught** is a current of air, a drink, a ship's depth, while a **draughtsman** either draws plans or is one of the pieces in the game of *draughts*. (But the Americans sensibly use draft for both.)

E

etymology is about words, **entomology** is about insects.

F

A **faun** is a rural deity; a **fawn** is a young deer, and to **fawn** is to flatter.

To **flaunt** something is to display it ostentatiously; to **flout** a rule is to break it contemptuously.

To **forbear** is to abstain, but a **forebear** is an ancestor.

foregoing and **foregone** mean preceding, complete; but to **forgo** something is to relinquish it.

fortuitous means accidental, **fortunate** means lucky.

G

Gallic means French; **Gaelic** means the Celtic languages or peoples.

A **geezer** is an old man, but a **geyser** is a hot spring or a bathroom water heater.

To **gibe** or **jibe** is to jeer; to **gybe** is what a sail does.

A **gourmet** is a connoisseur of food, but a **gourmand** is just greedy.

grisly means horrible; a **grizzly** is a bear.

A **groin** is a kind of arch, or an anatomical part; a **groyne** is a breakwater.

H

To **hail** is to greet or summon someone; to **hale** is to drag someone, but a person may be *hale and hearty*.

A **hangar** is for aircraft; one hangs things on a **hanger**.

A **hoard** is a store; a **horde** is a tribe.

homogeneous means all the same; **homogenous** means of common descent.

hummus (or **hoummos**) is ground chickpeas; **humus** is soil.

I

immanent means inherent; **imminent** means impending.

To **indict** is to accuse; to **indite** is to write.

its means of it; **it's** means it is, or it has.

L

A **lama** is a Buddhist monk, but a **llama** is a South American animal.

A **ledger** is an account book, but it is a **leger** line in music.

In British spelling, **licence** is the noun and **license** the verb.

lightening is making light; **lightning** accompanies thunder.

linage is the number of printed or written lines, but **lineage** is ancestry.

lineaments are features, **liniment** is embrocation.

A **liqueur** is a sweet alcoholic spirit; **liquor** is any alcoholic drink.

lumbar refers to the lower back; **lumber** is either disused junk or timber.

M

A **magnate** is a rich influential person; a **magnet** attracts iron.

A **mannequin** is a dressmaker's model; a **manikin** or **mannikin** is a dwarf, or an artist's lay figure.

A **mantel** is a mantelpiece, a **mantle** is a cloak.

A **marten** is a kind of weasel, but a **martin** is a kind of swallow.

matt means without lustre; **matte** is a smelting product, or a mask used in filming.

metal is gold, iron, etc.; **mettle** is a person's spirit or courage.

A **meter** is a measuring instrument; a **metre** is a metric unit, or any form of rhythm in poetry.

A **moat** is a ditch; a **mote** is a speck of dust; a **motte** is a castle mound.

O

To **omit** something is to leave it out. To **emit** it is to send it out: *emitted a scream.*

An **ordinance** is a decree; **ordnance** is weaponry; **ordonnance** is systematic arrangement.

An **outcast** is a rejected or homeless person, but an **outcaste** is a casteless Hindu.

P

A **paean** is a song of praise; a **paeon** is a metrical foot; a **peon** is various sorts of worker.

The **palate** is the roof of one's mouth; an artist uses a **palette**; a **pallet** is a tool, platform, or mattress.

parricide is the killing of any near relative; **patricide** is specifically killing one's father.

A **pastel** is a crayon, but a **pastille** is a lozenge.

A **pedal** is a foot lever; to **peddle** is to sell things as a **pedlar**, but a seller of drugs is a **peddler**.

A **peer** is a noble, or one's contemporary; a **pier** is in the sea, or it supports an arch.

pendant is a noun, **pendent** an adjective.

As nouns, a **plain** is flat land, while a **plane** is a level surface, an aircraft, a tree, or a tool.

A **plaintiff** brings a case in a law court; **plaintive** means mournful.

One may **pore** over a book, but **pour** liquids.

In British spelling, **practice** is the noun and **practise** the verb.

principal means chief, or a chief; a **principle** is a basis of behaviour.

programme is the usual British spelling, but **program** in the US and in computer language.

R

A **rabbet** is not a rabbit but a groove in woodwork.

One may **rack** one's brains, things may be *nerve-racking* or go to *rack and ruin*, and it is *rack* of lamb; **rack** or **wrack** is driving clouds, but only *wrack* is seaweed.

racket is the only spelling for all its senses except that of tennis, where **racquet** is an alternative.

radical is both the chemical and the general word, **radicle** only in botany.

reverend is deserving reverence, **reverent** is showing it.

A **review** is a survey or report, a **revue** is a musical show.

rhyme is the matching of sounds in verse; **rime** is frost.

A **rout** is a disorderly retreat, and to *rout out* is to fetch or force out of somewhere; a **route** is the way to somewhere, and *routeing* is sending by a particular route.

S

saccharin is a noun, **saccharine** an adjective.

satire is sarcasm in literature; a **satyr** is a woodland deity.

A **scull** is an oar, but the bone of the head is a **skull**.

A **sergeant** is in the army, airforce, or police; a **serjeant** is in the law.

A **sestet** is part of a sonnet; a **sextet** is a musical work for six parts.

You **sew** with a needle and **sow** seeds.

A **sole** is a fish or the underneath of one's foot, but the **soul** is one's spiritual part.

stationary means unmoving; **stationery** is writing materials.

A **stile** is steps; **style** is shape or manner.

A **storey** is one level of a house, but a **story** is a narrative.

It is **straight-faced** and *straightforward*; but **strait-laced**, *strait-jacket, dire straits, straitened circumstances.*

One may **swat** flies, but to **swot** is to study.

T

A **troop** is a company of people, soldiers, or animals; a **troupe** is a company of performers.

V

A **villain** is an evil-doer; a **villein** was a medieval serf.

W

To **waive** is to forgo rights; otherwise the word is **wave**.

wreath is the noun, **wreathe** the verb.

To **write** something *off* is to damage it irreparably; *right off* means immediately.

Y

It is the **yolk** of an egg, but **yoke** for a crossbar or the top of a garment.

Foreign Phrases

The following words and expressions are not fully naturalized in English. Some of them may appear in italics in printed matter. (An item that does not feature here may occur in one of the specialized 'Topics' later in the book.)

A

à bas down with.

ab initio from the beginning.

ab ovo from the very beginning.

absit omen may what is threatened not happen.

accouchement childbirth.

accoucheur a male midwife.

acharnement 1 bloodthirsty fury; ferocity. 2 gusto.

à deux for or between two.

ad fin. at or near the end.

ad hoc for a particular purpose.

ad hominem 1 relating to a particular person. 2 (of an argument) appealing to the emotions and not to reason.

ad infinitum without limit, for ever.

ad interim meanwhile.

ad libitum, ad lib freely, at pleasure, improvised.

ad nauseam to an excessive or disgusting degree.

ad personam to the person, personally.

aet., aetat, aetatis of or at the age of.

affairé busy, involved.

affaire de cœur a love affair.

à fond completely, thoroughly.

a fortiori with the stronger reason, more conclusively.

agent provocateur someone employed to tempt suspected offenders into incriminating action.

à huis clos in private.

aide-mémoire something to remind, a memorandum.

à la after the manner of.

à la carte ordered separately from a menu.

à la mode 1 fashionable. **2** (of beef) braised in wine. **3** US with ice cream.

à l'anglaise in the English style.

alter ego 1 a trusted friend **2** one's secondary or alternative personality.

amende honorable an open apology, perhaps with reparation.

amoretto (pl. **amoretti**) a Cupid.

amour propre self-respect.

ancien régime 1 the French political and social system before 1789. **2** any superseded regime.

anno aetatis suae in the (specified) year of his/her age.

annus mirabilis a remarkable or auspicious year.

anschluss unification, especially the annexation of Austria by Germany in 1938.

aperçu 1 a summary or survey. **2** an insight.

a posteriori (of reasoning) inductive, proceeding from effects to causes.

appellation contrôlée a label guaranteeing the quality of French wine.

a priori 1 (of reasoning) deductive, proceeding from causes to effects. **2** not derived from experience; conjectural.

arcus senilis a narrow opaque band commonly encircling the cornea in old age.

arrière-pensée 1 an undisclosed motive. **2** a mental reservation.

artel a Russian association of craftsmen, peasants, etc.

auberge an inn.

au courant knowing what is going on, well-informed.

au fait having current knowledge, conversant.

au fond basically, at bottom.

au gratin cooked with a crisp crust of breadcrumbs or melted cheese.

au naturel raw, or cooked in the simplest way.

au revoir goodbye (until we meet again).

avant-garde innovators, especially in art or literature.

B

bagarre a scuffle or brawl.

ballon d'essai an experiment to test out a new policy.

barège a silky gauze made from wool or other material.

beau geste a noble gesture.

beau idéal the highest type of excellence or beauty.

beaux arts the fine arts.

bel esprit a witty person.

belle époque the settled and comfortable period before 1914.

belle laide a fascinatingly ugly woman.

ben trovato well invented; characteristic even if not true.

bête noire one's particular aversion; a bugbear.

bijou a jewel; a trinket.

bijouterie jewellery; trinkets.

Bildungsroman a novel dealing with one person's early life and development.

blague humbug, claptrap.

blagueur a pretentious talker.

bombe a dome-shaped dish or confection, frequently frozen.

bona fide genuine, sincere.

bondieuserie church ornaments or devotional objects, especially those of little artistic merit.

bon mot a witty saying.

bon vivant someone indulging in good living.

borné narrow-minded; limited.

bouilli stewed or boiled meat.

C

cabotin a second-rate actor; a strolling player.

café au lait white coffee.

café noir black coffee.

calzoni breeches; drawers.

canaille the rabble; the populace.

carabiniere (pl. **carabinieri**) an Italian gendarme.

carte blanche full discretionary authorization to act.

casus belli a justification or cause of war.

cause célèbre a lawsuit attracting much attention.

causerie an informal article or talk, especially on a literary subject.

caveat emptor the buyer alone is responsible.

chacun à son goût everyone to his/her own taste.

chansons de geste medieval French epics.

chapeau-bras a three-cornered flat silk hat often carried under the arm.

chasse a liqueur taken after coffee.

chassé a gliding step in dancing.

chef-d'œuvre a masterpiece.

cherchez la femme there's a woman at the bottom of it.

ci-devant (of someone's name or status) former; that has been.

cinéma-vérité, ciné-vérité realistic films avoiding artistic clichés.

cloqué a fabric with an irregularly raised surface.

clou 1 the point of greatest interest; the chief attraction. **2** the central idea.

cogito the philosophical principle establishing the existence of a being from the fact of its thinking or awareness.

cognoscente (pl. **cognoscenti**) a connoisseur.

coiffeur (fem. **coiffeuse**) a hairdresser.

coiffure a hairstyle.

comme ci, comme ça so so, middling.

commedia dell'arte popular Italian comedy of the sixteenth–eighteenth centuries.

comme il faut (of behaviour) correct.

compos mentis sane.

compte rendu a report, statement.

con amore zealously.

condottiere (pl. **condottieri**) a leader or member of a troop of mercenaries once prevalent in Italy etc.

confrère a fellow member of a profession, scientific body, etc.

congé an unceremonious dismissal; leave-taking.

conte 1 a short story (as a form of literary composition). **2** a medieval narrative tale.

convenances the conventional proprieties.

conversazione a social gathering held by a learned or art society.

coram publico in public.

cordon sanitaire a buffer zone.

corps de ballet the company of ensemble dancers in a ballet.

corps d'élite a select group.

corps diplomatique a diplomatic corps.

coup de foudre love at first sight.

coup de grâce a finishing stroke, to kill a wounded creature.

coup de main a sudden vigorous attack.

coup de maître a master stroke.

coup d'état a violent seizure of power.

coup d'œil a comprehensive view.

court bouillon stock usually made from wine, vegetables, etc., often used in fish dishes.

cri de cœur a heart-felt appeal or protest.

crime passionnel a crime, especially murder, provoked by sexual jealousy.

cru 1 a French vineyard or wine-producing region. **2** the grade of wine produced there.

cui bono? who stands to gain? (implying that this person is responsible).

cum grano salis with a pinch of salt.

curriculum vitae an account of one's education, qualifications, and previous career.

D

danse macabre a medieval dance in which Death leads all to the grave.

de facto in fact, whether by right or not.

de haut en bas in a condescending or superior manner.

Dei gratia by the grace of God.

déjà vu a sense of having already experienced something before.

de jure rightful.

démarche a political step or initiative.

démenti an official denial of a rumour etc.

demi-mondaine a woman of the demi-monde.

demi-monde a class of women of doubtful morality, on the fringes of respectable society.

demi-pension hotel accommodation with breakfast and one main meal a day.

démodé out of fashion.

de nos jours of the present time.

de nouveau, de novo starting again; anew.

Deo gratias thanks be to God.

Deo volente God willing.

dépaysé removed from one's habitual surroundings.

de profundis a cry from the depths (of sorrow).

de règle customary, proper.

de rigueur required by custom or etiquette.

dernier cri the very latest fashion.

déshabillé a state of being only partly or carelessly dressed.

désœuvré out of work, unemployed, unoccupied; languidly idle.

de trop unwelcome, in the way.

deus ex machina an unexpected power or event that saves the situation.

dévot (fem. **dévote**) a devotee.

Dies irae day of wrath.

dies non a day on which no legal business can be done.

Ding an sich a thing in itself.

diseuse (masc. **diseur**) a female artiste entertaining with spoken monologues.

disjecta membra scattered fragments.

distingué (fem. **distinguée**) having a distinguished air, features, manner, etc.

dolce far niente pleasant idleness.

dolce vita a life of pleasure and luxury.

donnée, donné 1 the subject or theme of a story etc. **2** a basic fact or assumption.

dos-à-dos 1 (of two books) bound together with a shared central board and facing in opposite directions. **2** a seat whose occupants sit back to back.

dot a woman's dowry.

doublure an ornamental lining, usually leather, inside a book-cover.

durchkomponiert (of a song) having different music for each verse.

E

echt authentic, genuine.

éclaircissement an enlightening explanation of something hitherto inexplicable (e.g. conduct etc.).

editio princeps the first printed edition.

eiusdem generis of the same kind.

embarras de choix, embarras de richesse(s) more choices than one needs.

éminence grise someone who exercises power without holding office.

en bloc in a block, wholesale.

en brosse (of hair) cut short and bristly.

en cabochon (of a gem) polished but not faceted.

en clair (of a message) in ordinary language; not in code.

en effet in fact, indeed.

en famille at home, with one's family.

enfant gâté a spoilt child.

enfant terrible an embarrassingly indiscreet or unruly person.

en fête celebrating a holiday.

engagé (of a writer etc.) morally committed.

en masse all together.

en passant 1 by the way. **2** *Chess* used of the permitted capture of an opponent's pawn in certain circumstances.

en pension as a boarder or resident.

en prise (of a chess piece) exposed to capture.

en rapport in harmony.

entente cordiale a friendly understanding between States.

entrain enthusiasm, animation.

entrechat a leap in ballet, with one or more crossings of the legs while in the air.

entremets 1 a sweet dish. **2** any light dish served between two courses.

entre nous between you and me.

esprit sprightliness, wit.

esprit de corps proud devotion to one's group.

esprit de l'escalier a clever remark that comes to mind too late.

estaminet a small French café etc. selling alcoholic drinks.

ex cathedra (especially of a papal pronouncement) with full authority.

exeunt omnes all leave the stage.

ex gratia as a favour rather than from obligation.

ex hypothesi according to the hypothesis proposed.

ex-libris (on a bookplate) among the books of.

ex nihilo out of nothing.

ex officio by virtue of one's office.

ex post facto with retrospective action or force.

ex silentio by the absence of contrary evidence.

F

fait accompli something that has been done and is past altering.

famille jaune/noire/rose/verte Chinese enamelled porcelain predominantly yellow/black/pink/green.

faubourg a suburb, especially of Paris.

faute de mieux for want of a better alternative.

fauteuil a kind of wooden seat in the form of an armchair with open sides and upholstered arms.

faux pas a tactless blunder or indiscretion.

favela a Brazilian shack, slum, or shanty town.

felo de se suicide.

feng-shui in Chinese mythology, a system of good and evil spirit influences which inhabit the natural features of landscapes, and must be taken account of on determining sites for houses and graves.

fête champêtre an outdoor entertainment or festival.

fête galante a fête champêtre, especially of the kind depicted by Watteau.

feu de joie a ceremonial salute by gunfire.

fidus Achates a devoted friend or follower.

figura a person or thing representing or symbolizing a fact etc.

figurant (fem. **figurante**) a ballet dancer appearing only in a group.

fille de joie a prostitute.

fils (added to a surname to distinguish a son from a father) the son, junior (compare PÈRE).

fin de siècle characteristic of the (decadent) end of the nineteenth century.

fine champagne old liqueur brandy.

fines herbes mixed herbs used in cooking, especially to flavour omelettes.

flânerie idling, idleness.

flâneur an idler; a lounger.

force majeure unforeseeable compulsion.

frappé iced, cooled.

fritto misto a mixed grill.

G

garçon a waiter in a French restaurant, hotel, etc.

Gastarbeiter a foreign worker in Germany.

gasthaus a small inn or hotel in German-speaking countries.

gasthof a German hotel, usually larger than a gasthaus.

gemütlich 1 pleasant and comfortable. 2 genial, agreeable.

giaour *derog. or literary* a non-Muslim, especially a Christian.

gîte a furnished holiday house in France, usually small and in the country.

Gleichschaltung the standardization of political, economic, and social institutions in authoritarian States.

grande dame a dignified lady of high rank.

grand mal a serious form of epilepsy.

grand monde fashionable society.

grand siècle the seventeenth century in France.

gran turismo a touring car, with plenty of room for passengers and luggage.

gratiné cooked au gratin.

gravitas solemn demeanour, seriousness.

H

hakenkreuz a swastika, especially as a Nazi symbol.

haute couture high fashion; the leading fashion houses.

haute cuisine French traditional cookery of a high standard.

haute école the art of training horses in advanced classical deportment.

haut monde fashionable society.

Herrenvolk 1 the German nation, characterized by the Nazis as born to mastery. 2 a group regarding itself as naturally superior.

Homo any primate of the genus *Homo*, including modern humans and various extinct species.

Homo sapiens modern humans as a species.

honnête homme an honest and decent man.

honoris causa (especially of a degree awarded without examination) as a mark of merit.

hors concours 1 unrivalled. 2 not competing for a prize.

hors de combat out of the action, disabled.

hortus siccus a collection of dried plants.

I

idée fixe an obsession that dominates the mind.

idée reçue a generally accepted opinion.

in absentia in (his, her, their) absence.

in extenso in full, at length.

in extremis 1 at the point of death. **2** in great difficulties.

infra below, further on (in a book or writing).

infra dig beneath one's dignity, unbecoming.

in loco parentis in the position of a parent.

in medias res into the middle of things.

in propria persona in his or her own person.

in re in the matter of.

in situ in its (original) place.

in statu pupillari in the position of a pupil; under authority.

inter alia among other things.

in toto completely.

in utero in the womb; before birth.

in vacuo in a vacuum.

in vitro (of biological processes) taking place in a test-tube or other laboratory environment.

in vivo (of biological processes) taking place in a living organism.

ipse dixit a statement resting merely on the speaker's authority.

ipsissima verba the precise words.

ipso facto by that very fact or act.

J

j'adoube *Chess* 'I adjust', used when touching a piece that one does not intend to move.

je ne sais quoi an undefinable something.

jeu de mots a pun.

jeu d'esprit a witty trifle.

jeunesse dorée rich fashionable young people.

joie de vivre high spirits.

jolie laide a fascinatingly ugly woman.

jongleur a medieval itinerant minstrel.

K

kultur German civilization and culture, seen derogatorily as racist, authoritarian, militaristic, etc.

kulturkampf the conflict in nineteenth-century Germany between the civil and ecclesiastical authorities, especially as regards the control of schools.

L

lacrimae rerum the tragedy of life.

laissez-aller unconstrained freedom.

laissez-passer a permit allowing the holder to pass.

langue de chat a very thin finger-shaped biscuit or piece of chocolate.

lapsus calami a slip of the pen.

lapsus linguae a slip of the tongue.

Lebensraum the territory which a State or nation believes is needed for its natural development.

lèse-majesté treason, or presumptuous insult to a ruler.

lex talionis the law by which a punishment resembles the offence in kind and degree.

locus classicus the best-known or most authoritative passage on a subject.

locus standi a recognized (especially legal) status.

longueur 1 a tedious passage in a book etc. **2** a tedious stretch of time.

loquitur (he or she) speaks (with the speaker's name following, as a stage direction or to inform the reader).

Luftwaffe the former German Air Force.

lusus naturae a freak of nature.

lycée a State secondary school in France.

M

Machtpolitik power politics.

magnum opus 1 a great work. **2** the major work of an artist, writer, etc.

mal de mer seasickness.

mañana in the indefinite future (especially to indicate procrastination).

maquillage make-up; cosmetics.

mariage de convenance a marriage for financial or political reasons.

matelote a dish of fish etc. with a sauce of wine and onions.

matériel available means, especially materials and equipment in warfare.

mauvais quart d'heure a short but nasty experience.

mea culpa 'My fault', acknowledging an error.

membrum virile the penis.

memento mori a reminder of death.

ménage à trois a household of three people, usually a couple and the lover of one of them.

mensch a person of integrity and honour.

mésalliance a marriage with someone of a lower social position.

Messeigneurs pl. of Monseigneur.

métier 1 one's trade, profession, or department of activity. **2** one's strong point.

millefeuille a rich confection of puff pastry split and filled with jam, cream, etc.

mirabile dictu astonishing to relate.

mirepoix sautéed chopped vegetables, used in sauces etc.

mise en scène 1 the scenery and properties of a play. **2** the setting of an event.

modus operandi the way in which a task is performed or a thing works.

modus vivendi a compromise by which parties of differing interests can carry on.

Monseigneur a title given to an eminent Frenchman, especially a prince, cardinal, or bishop.

mot a witty saying.

mot juste the most appropriate expression.

multum in parvo a great deal in a small space.

mutatis mutandis with the necessary alterations having been made.

N

nem. con. with no one dissenting.

ne plus ultra 1 the furthest attainable point. **2** the culmination, perfection.

nihil obstat an official authorization, especially that a book is acceptable to the Roman Catholic Church.

nil desperandum never give up hope.

noblesse the nobility, especially of a foreign country.

noblesse oblige privilege entails responsibility.

nolens volens willy-nilly.

nom de guerre an assumed name under which someone fights, plays, etc.

nom de plume an assumed name under which someone writes.

non placet a negative vote in an assembly.

non possumus a statement of inability to act.

non sequitur an illogical conclusion.

nostalgie de la boue a hankering for degradation and squalor.

nota bene observe what follows, take notice (usually drawing attention to a following qualification of what has preceded).

nouveau riche someone newly and ostentatiously rich.

nouvelle cuisine a modern style of cookery, light and elegantly presented.

nouvelle vague a trend in French film-making of the early 1960s.

O

obiter dictum a judge's incidental expression of opinion.

objet d'art a small decorative object.

omertà a code of silence, as practised by the Mafia.

on dit a piece of gossip.

opéra comique a light-hearted, especially French opera with spoken dialogue.

P

pace (in stating a contrary opinion) with due deference to (the person named).

papabile suitable for high office (originally to be Pope).

par avion by airmail.

par excellence being the supreme example of its kind.

pari-mutuel 1 a form of betting in which the losers' stakes are shared among those backing the first three places. 2 a totalizator.

pari passu 1 with equal speed. 2 simultaneously.

parti pris prejudice, prejudiced.

pas de chat a leap in dancing, especially in classical ballet, in which each foot in turn is raised to the opposite knee.

pas de deux a dance for two people.

pas glissé a glissé; a sliding step in which the flat of the foot is often used.

pas seul a solo dance.

passim (of allusions or references in a published work) to be found at various places throughout the text.

pâté de foie gras a paste of fatted goose liver.

pavé 1 a paved street, road, or path. 2 a setting of jewels placed closely together.

paysage a rural landscape.

pensée a thought or reflection put into literary form; an aphorism.

pension a Continental, especially French, boarding-house providing full or half board at a fixed rate.

per annum for each year.

per capita for each person.

père (added to a surname to distinguish a father from a son) the father, senior (compare FILS).

per pro. through the agency of (used in signatures).

per se in itself.

persona grata a person (especially a diplomat) acceptable to certain others.

persona non grata an unacceptable person.

pétanque a game like bowls, played originally and chiefly in the south of France.

petitio principii the logical fallacy of begging the question.

petit-maître a dandy, coxcomb.

petit mal a mild form of epilepsy.

pièce de résistance the most important item.

pied-à-terre a small dwelling for occasional use.

pis aller a course of action followed as a last resort.

pissoir a public urinal.

placet an affirmative vote in an assembly.

plat du jour the special dish on a day's menu.

plus ça change the true nature of a thing never changes.

poilu a French private soldier, especially as a nickname.

pons asinorum any difficult problem that defeats the slow-witted.

porte-cochère a roofed porch at an entrance, where vehicles discharge passengers.

poste restante a direction that a letter is to be kept at a post office until collected.

post-partum after childbirth.

pot-au-feu a traditional thick French soup.

pourboire a gratuity or tip.

predikant a minister of the South African Dutch Reformed Church.

prima facie on a first impression, on the face of it.

primum mobile 1 the main source of motion or action. **2** in medieval astronomy, an outermost sphere believed to revolve round the earth in 24 hours and cause the inner spheres to revolve.

primus inter pares a first or most important among equals.

pro forma as a matter of form (especially of an invoice sent in advance).

pro hac vice for this occasion only.

proneur a person who extols; a flatterer.

pro rata in proportion.

prosit an expression used colloquially in drinking someone's health.

pro tempore for the time being.

proxime accessit the person who comes second in an examination.

Q

quid pro quo something given in fair exchange.

quod vide (in cross-references) which see.

R

raison d'être the purpose that justifies a thing's existence.

rangé (fem. **rangée**) domesticated, orderly, settled.

rara avis a rare kind of person or thing.

réchauffé 1 a warmed-up dish. **2** a rehash.

reductio ad absurdum a method of disproving a premiss by showing that the logical consequence is absurd.

Regina the reigning queen (after a name or in the titles of lawsuits, e.g. *Regina v. Jones* the Crown versus Jones).

reliquiae remains.

requiescat in pace (on tombstones) may he/she rest in peace.

Rex the reigning king (after a name or in the titles of lawsuits, e.g. *Rex v. Jones* the Crown versus Jones).

roman-à-clef a novel giving invented names to real people or events.

roman-fleuve a novel, or series of novels, recounting the lives of one family.

rouge-et-noir a gambling game in which players place stakes on a red and black table.

rus in urbe the country in the city (used of a pleasant suburb).

S

sang-froid composure in agitating circumstances.

sans-gêne without constraint.

sauve qui peut everyone for himself.

savoir faire the quality of knowing what to do.

schadenfreude the malicious enjoyment of another's misfortunes.

Sehnsucht yearning, wistful longing.

sensu stricto in a narrow sense.

shul a synagogue.

sic (usually in brackets) used, spelt, etc. as written (confirming, or drawing attention to, the form of quoted or copied words).

siffleur (fem. **siffleuse**) a professional whistler.

sine die (of business) adjourned indefinitely.

sine qua non an indispensable requirement.

skol, skoal used as a toast in drinking.

slainte a Gaelic toast; good health!

soi-disant self-styled.

soigné (fem. **soignée**) carefully finished or arranged; well-groomed.

soixante-neuf mutual stimulation of two people's genitals.

son et lumière an entertainment by night at a historic place, recounting its history by means of lighting effects and recorded sound.

sotto voce in an undertone.

souteneur a pimp.

Spätlese a white wine made (especially in Germany) from grapes gathered later than the general harvest.

sportif **1** interested in sports. **2** suitable for informal wear.

status quo the existing state of affairs.

Sturm und Drang a late eighteenth-century German artistic and literary movement expressing violent emotion.

sub rosa (of consultation etc.) in secrecy.

succès de scandale a book, play, etc. made successful by its scandalous content.

sui generis of its own kind; unique.

summum bonum the highest good.

supra above, earlier on (in a book or writing).

suprême a dish served in a rich cream sauce.

T

tableau vivant a silent and motionless group of people arranged to represent a scene.

taedium vitae weariness of life, especially as leading to suicide.

tant mieux so much the better.

tant pis so much the worse.

terminus ad quem the finishing-point of an argument, policy, etc.

terminus ante quem the finishing-point of a period.

terminus a quo the starting-point of an argument, policy, etc.

terminus post quem the starting-point of a period.

terra incognita unknown territory.

terra sigillata clay, or pottery, from Lemnos or Samos.

terza rima *Prosody* an arrangement of especially iambic pentameter triplets rhyming *aba bcb cdc*, etc.

tête-à-tête an intimate conversation.

tête-bêche (of a postage stamp) printed upside down or sideways.

thé dansant an afternoon tea with dancing.

ton 1 a prevailing fashion. **2** fashionable society.

tour de force a feat of strength or skill.

tous-les-mois food starch from tubers of a canna, *Canna Indica.*

tout court without addition, simply.

tout de suite at once, immediately.

trahison des clercs the betrayal of standards by intellectuals.

trente-et-quarante rouge-et-noir.

tristesse sadness, grief, melancholy.

trouvaille a lucky find; a windfall.

U

Übermensch a superman.

ujamaa a village community in Tanzania.

ultima Thule a distant unknown region.

Untermensch a racially inferior person in Nazi terms.

V

vendeuse a saleswoman, especially in a fashionable dress-shop.

ventre à terre at full speed.

verboten forbidden, especially by an authority.

verkrampte conservative or reactionary as regards South African apartheid.

verligte progressive and enlightened as regards South African apartheid.

vers libre irregular or unrhymed verse.

via media a compromise.

victor ludorum a sports champion.

vide (as an instruction in a reference to a passage in a book etc.) see, consult.

vieux jeu old-fashioned, hackneyed.

vingt-et-un the card-game pontoon.

vin ordinaire cheap (usually red) French wine.

vin rosé light pink wine.

vis-à-vis in relation to, compared with.

viva (cried as a salute etc.) long live.

Völkerwanderung a migration of peoples, especially that of Germanic and Slavic peoples into Europe from the second to the eleventh centuries.

volte-face a complete reversal of position.

vox populi public opinion.

W

Wehrmacht the German armed forces, especially the army, from 1921 to 1945.

Weltanschauung a particular philosophy or view of life; a conception of the world.

Z

zollverein a customs union, especially of German States in the nineteenth century.

Antonyms

We here suggest the approximate 'opposites' of some words. Omitted are the simple negatives, such as *active* and *inactive*, and the very common ones such as *good* and *bad* or *up* and *down*. Note that a word with several senses will necessarily have several opposites. Thus, when *dear* means 'lovable', the opposite might be *disagreeable*, but when it means 'expensive' the opposite is obviously *cheap*. When *present* is a noun meaning 'gift' it really has no opposite, and when it means 'now' the opposite is *past*, while the opposite of one of its adjective senses is probably *absent*. There is space here only for the opposites of words with one meaning, or at any rate with one chief meaning. If there should be any doubt, it is easy to look up the 'new' word in a dictionary.

A

abandon – retain
abase – exalt
abbreviate – amplify
abiding – transitory
ability – incapacity
abolish – maintain
abortive – fruitful
abrogate – ratify
abrupt – gradual
absolute – conditional
absolve – censure
abstract – concrete
abundant – scanty
accept – reject
accidental – planned
accommodating – disobliging
accuse – absolve

acme – nadir
acquiesce – dissent
acquit – convict
active – dormant
acute – dull
add – deduct
admiration – abhorrence
adorn – disfigure
adroit – clumsy
adulation – obliquy
advent – disappearance
adventurous – unenterprising
adversary – ally
adverse – favourable
affected – genuine
affirm – deny
affirmative – negative
alert – oblivious

alleviate – aggravate
allow – prohibit
ally – opponent
altogether – partially
amass – disperse
amateur – professional
ambiguous – unequivocal
amenable – inflexible
amicable – inimical
ample – meagre
analysis – synthesis
antipathy – rapport
apocryphal – authenticated
applicable – irrelevant
apposite – inappropriate
appreciate – disparage
approve – condemn

arbitrary – reasoned
archaic – up-to-date
ardent – apathetic
arduous – effortless
aromatic – fetid
arrogant – modest
ascetic – sybaritic
assemble – disperse
assent – dissent
assist – impede
assurance – diffidence
astute – ingenuous
athletic – puny
attentive – remiss
attract – repel
augment – diminish
authentic – fake
avid – apathetic

B

balmy – noxious
banal – original
baneful – salutary
bankrupt – solvent
barbarous – cultured
barren – fertile
bawdy – decent
bearable – insufferable
beautify – disfigure
beefy – scrawny
befitting – inappropriate
beggarly – liberal
believer – sceptic
belittle – magnify
benediction –
    malediction
beneficial – detrimental
benevolent –
    malevolent
benign – malignant
bewitch – disenchant
bizarre – normal
blameable –
    praiseworthy

bland – spicy
blatant – subtle
blemish – enhancement
bliss – misery
blunt – subtle
boastful – unassuming
boisterous – quiet
boorish – refined
boundless – restricted
bountiful – stingy
boycott – support
brash – reserved
brawny – flabby
brevity – prolixity
brief – lengthy
brisk – sluggish
brusque – courteous
brutal – humane
bulky – slim
bury – exhume

C

cacophonous –
    harmonious
cadaverous – ruddy
calamity – boon
calculated –
    spontaneous
callous –
    compassionate
callow – experienced
calumny –
    commendation
cancel – confirm
candid – secretive
capable – incompetent
capacious – cramped
carefree – worried
carnal – chaste
casual – systematic
catastrophe – blessing
categorical – qualified
catholic – bigoted
caustic – mild
cautious – reckless

celebrity – nonentity
celestial – earthly
censorious –
    appreciative
censure –
    commendation
ceremonious – informal
changeable – constant
changeless – variable
chaotic – ordered
charm – repel
chaste – promiscuous
chatty – taciturn
cheerful – melancholy
chic – inelegant
chivalrous – boorish
chubby – skinny
churlish – pleasant
circuitous – direct
circumspect –
    imprudent
civilized – barbarous
clandestine – above-
    board
clarity – obscurity
clemency – harshness
clumsy – graceful
coarse – refined
coerce – persuade
cogent – unconvincing
colossal – diminutive
comatose – alert
comedy – tragedy
comfortable –
    cheerless
comic – serious
commend – criticize
commodious – cramped
communal – individual
compendious – diffuse
complex – simple
complicate – simplify
composure – agitation
compound – simple

comprehensive –
limited
compunction –
impenitence
concave – convex
conceited – modest
concise – wordy
concord – discord
concrete – abstract
concupiscent – ascetic
condemn – acquit
condense – dilute
confidence – distrust
confirm – deny
conflict – harmony
confront – avoid
congratulate – condole
congregate – disperse
conscientious –
slapdash
conservative –
progressive
considerable –
negligible
conspicuous –
unobtrusive
construction –
demolition
contemptible –
honourable
contiguous – distant
continuous – sporadic
contract – expand
converge – diverge
convict – acquit
copious – sparse
cordial – frigid
corporeal – spiritual
corroborate – disprove
corrupt – honest
cosmopolitan –
provincial
counterfeit – genuine
counterpart – antithesis
covert – overt

coy – brazen
crafty – ingenuous
creditable –
dishonourable
credulity – scepticism
crisp – flaccid
cross – good-humoured
crude – refined
culpable – blameless
cumbersome –
convenient
cunning – ingenuous
current – out-of-date
cursed – blessed
cursory – thorough
curtail – extend
customary – unusual
cynical – optimistic

D

dainty – coarse
daunt – encourage
deadly – innocuous
dearth – plenty
debt – credit
debut – swansong
deceit – candour
decided – hesitant
declivity – ascent
decorous – unseemly
decorum – impropriety
decry – commend
dedicated – apathetic
defeat – victory
defective – adequate
defer – expedite
deference – disrespect
defiance – submission
deficit – surplus
definite – inconclusive
deflate – inflate
defunct – extant
delectable – revolting
delete – insert

deliberate – accidental
delirious – coherent
delude – enlighten
demure – shameless
denigrate – extol
departure – arrival
deplorable – admirable
depraved – upright
deranged – rational
dereliction –
observance
derogatory –
appreciative
descend – ascend
deserted – populous
designing – artless
desirous – averse
despicable –
commendable
despondency – elation
destitute – prosperous
destructive –
constructive
desultory – systematic
detached – passionate
deter – encourage
deteriorate – improve
determination –
indecision
determined – hesitant
deterrent – incentive
detrimental –
advantageous
deviant – normal
devout – impious
diabolic – angelic
diaphanous – opaque
diastole – systole
difference – similarity
diffidence – self-
confidence
diffuse – concentrated
dignify – degrade
dilate – contract
dilatory – expeditious

diligent – lazy
diminution – increase
diminutive – gigantic
diplomatic – indiscreet
disadvantageous –
  favourable
disastrous – fortunate
disclose – conceal
discord – harmony
discreet – imprudent
discursive – concise
disembodied –
  corporeal
disfigure – adorn
dishearten – encourage
disinclination –
  willingness
disingenuous – frank
disinterested – biased
dismantle – assemble
disown – acknowledge
disparage – overrate
disperse – assemble
display – conceal
disputatious –
  conciliatory
disreputable –
  respectable
disrupt – organize
dissension –
  agreement
dissipate – conserve
dissolute – temperate
dissonance – harmony
distend – contract
distinct – vague
distinguished – obscure
diverge – converge
diverse – similar
divide – combine
docile – intractable
dominant – subservient
dour – cheerful
dowdy – fashionable
drab – gaudy

drastic – moderate
dreamy – practical
drivel – coherence
drowsy – alert
dulcet – harsh
duplicity – candour
durable – ephemeral
dwarf – giant

E

eager – apathetic
earnest – frivolous
earthly – heavenly
easy-going – intolerant
economical –
  spendthrift
economize – squander
ecstasy – anguish
edible – noxious
effeminate – virile
effete – vigorous
egotism – altruism
elaborate – simple
elastic – inflexible
elementary – advanced
élite – rabble
eloquent – inarticulate
embellish – deface
embolden – dishearten
emigration –
  immigration
eminent – obscure
emphasize –
  understate
emphatic – tentative
empirical – theoretical
encomium – censure
endear – estrange
endless – finite
enduring – short-lived
enforced – optional
enigmatic – lucid
enjoyable –
  disagreeable

enlighted – narrow-
  minded
enmity – goodwill
enormous – diminutive
enrich – impoverish
entangle – unravel
enterprising –
  unadventurous
entertaining – boring
enthusiastic –
  apathetic
entire – partial
ephemeral – lasting
equable –
  temperamental
equitable – unjust
equivocal – definite
erect – demolish
erratic – consistent
erudite – illiterate
essential – superfluous
eternal – temporal
eulogy – censure
euphonious –
  discordant
evasive – direct
exacerbate – soothe
exact – inaccurate
exaggerate – minimize
exceptional – normal
excess – dearth
exempt – liable
exhale – inhale
exhaustive –
  perfunctory
exonerate – implicate
exorbitant – moderate
expand – contract
expedite – hinder
expert – maladroit
explicit – ambiguous
export – import
extant – extinct
extempore – prepared
extenuate – aggravate

exterior – interior
extraneous – intrinsic
extraordinary – commonplace
extravagant – thrifty
extrovert – introvert

F

face – evade
facetious – grave
factitious – genuine
faith – scepticism
fake – authentic
famine – plenty
fantastic – realistic
fashionable – dated
fastidious – sloppy
fatigue – energy
fatuous – sensible
faulty – correct
favourite – *bête noire*
fearless – craven
feasible – impracticable
fecund – sterile
feeble – robust
felicitate – condole
ferocious – gentle
fervour – apathy
fickle – steadfast
fictional – real
fictitious – genuine
fidelity – perfidy
fiendish – angelic
figurative – literal
filthy – spotless
finite – unbounded
fitful – steady
flabby – firm
flagrant – slight
flawless – defective
fleeting – permanent
flexible – rigid
flimsy – sturdy
flippant – serious

florid – pale
flout – obey
flowery – unadorned
fluent – hesitant
following – preceding
foment – allay
foolhardy – cautious
foppish – slovenly
forbid – permit
foreign – native
former – latter
forthright – reticent
fortuitous – calculated
fractious – tractable
fragile – tough
fragrant – malodorous
frank – reticent
frequent – rare
friendship – enmity
frighten – reassure
frugal – improvident
fruitful – fruitless
frustrate – stimulate
fundamental – incidental
furtive – open

G

garish – sober
garrulous – taciturn
gather – disperse
gaunt – obese
genius – dolt
genuine – spurious
germane – irrelevant
gigantic – puny
glamorous – dowdy
glaring – inconspicuous
glib – tongue-tied
glum – jovial
glut – dearth
goad – pacify
godless – pious
goodwill – ill will

graceful – ungainly
gradual – abrupt
grand – humble
graphic – vague
grave – flippant
greedy – altruistic
gregarious – unsociable
groundless – justified
grubby – spotless
guileless – sly
guilt – innocence
gullible – astute
gusto – distaste

H

habitual – unaccustomed
haggard – sleek
hallowed – desecrated
hamper – facilitate
haphazard – methodical
harass – soothe
hardy – delicate
harmful – innocuous
harmonious – discordant
harsh – mild
hasty – leisurely
haughty – humble
hazardous – safe
hearten – discourage
heartfelt – insincere
heretical – orthodox
hero – villain
heterogeneous – homogeneous
hoarse – mellow
horizontal – vertical
hostile – friendly
humanize – brutalize
humble – arrogant

I

ignite – douse
ignominious – reputable

ill-timed – timely
illusion – reality
illustrious – undistinguished
imitation – genuine
immaculate – contaminated
immature – ripe
imminent – remote
impair – enhance
impalpable – tangible
impartial – biased
impeach – vindicate
impecunious – affluent
imperious – docile
impertinent – polite
imperturbable – excitable
impetuous – cautious
implicate – absolve
implicit – explicit
impolitic – prudent
important – insignificant
imposing – modest
impoverish – enrich
impracticable – feasible
impregnable – vulnerable
improbable – likely
impromptu – prepared
improvident – thrifty
impudent – respectful
impulsive – cautious
inadvertent – intentional
inaugurate – terminate
inborn – acquired
incentive – deterrent
incessant – intermittent
incidental – essential
incite – deter
include – exclude
incompatible – consistent
increase – decrease

inculpate – exonerate
indecent – seemly
indecision – resolution
indefensible – justifiable
indestructible – fragile
indigenous – foreign
indigent – wealthy
indispensable – unnecessary
indisputable – questionable
indolent – industrious
induce – dissuade
indulgent – stern
inert – active
infamous – reputable
inferior – superior
infinitesimal – huge
inflate – deflate
inflexible – pliable
ingenuous – guileful
inhale – exhale
inhibited – extrovert
initial – final
innocuous – harmful
inordinate – moderate
insert – extract
instinctive – reasoned
insubordinate – obedient
insufferable – bearable
insult – flatter
insuperable – surmountable
intelligible – incomprehensible
intensify – diminish
intentional – inadvertent
interior – exterior
intermittent – continuous
intolerable – endurable

intractable – submissive
intransigent – flexible
intricate – simple
intrinsic – extrinsic
inventive – unimaginative
invincible – defenceless
involuntary – intentional
irresponsible – trustworthy

J

jaundiced – optimistic
jaunty – sedate
jocular – solemn
jovial – morose
jubilant – despondent
judicious – imprudent
junior – senior
juvenile – mature

K

knack – blind spot
knowledgeable – ill-informed
kudos – dishonour

L

laconic – loquacious
lamentable – fortunate
languid – energetic
lassitude – vigour
lasting – ephemeral
latent – obvious
laudable – blameworthy
lavish – meagre
lax – rigorous
legendary – historical
lengthen – curtail
lengthy – concise
lenient – merciless
lethal – harmless
levity – gravity
lewd – decent

liabilities – assets
liberty – captivity
literal – metaphorical
lively – torpid
loathsome – loveable
loquacious – taciturn
loyal – treacherous
lucrative – unprofitable

M

magnify – minimize
major – minor
male – female
malevolent –
  benevolent
malignant – benign
mammoth – minuscule
mandatory – optional
marked – imperceptible
masculine – feminine
massive – minute
matchless –
  commonplace
maximum – minimum
meagre – ample
meek – arrogant
melodious – discordant
memorable –
  commonplace
mendacious – truthful
mercy – inhumanity
methodical – disorderly
meticulous – sloppy
microcosm –
  macrocosm
militant – pacific
military – civil
misanthrope –
  philanthropist
miserly – generous
mitigate – aggravate
mobile – stationary
mollify – exacerbate
momentous –
  insignificant

moron – genius
morose – cheerful
munificent – stingy
muscular – feeble
musical – discordant
mutinous – loyal
mysterious – intelligible
mythical – real

N

nadir – zenith
naive – sophisticated
negate – confirm
negative – positive
negligible – significant
neurotic – stable
niggardly – lavish
nominal – actual
nondescript –
  distinctive
nonentity – celebrity
normal – abnormal
noticeable –
  unobtrusive
nullify – ratify

O

obdurate – compliant
obligatory – voluntary
oblivious – mindful
obscurity – clarity
obsolete – up-to-date
obstinate – tractable
obstructive –
  cooperative
occasional – habitual
official – informal
ominous – auspicious
opaque – transparent
opiate – stimulant
opponent – ally
optional – compulsory
ornate – unadorned
orthodox –
  unconventional

ostensible – actual
ostracize – fraternize
outlandish –
  conventional
outspoken – reticent
overt – covert

P

pacific – aggressive
pacify – provoke
painstaking – negligent
paramount – secondary
parochial –
  cosmopolitan
passionate – apathetic
passive – active
paucity – abundance
peaceable – belligerent
peevish – affable
pejorative – laudatory
perfunctory –
  meticulous
permanent – temporary
pernicious – beneficial
pernickety – equable
perpetual – intermittent
perseverance –
  inconstancy
persuade – dissuade
pertinacious – tentative
pessimistic – optimistic
petty – major
piquant – bland
placid – temperamental
plebeian – patrician
plentiful – sparse
pliable – rigid
poky – roomy
pollute – purify
pompous –
  unpretentious
porous – impervious
postpone – expedite
pragmatic – theoretical

praiseworthy – blameworthy

precocious – backward

predecessor – successor

prelude – conclusion

presence – absence

prestigious – obscure

pretentious – modest

prevalent – rare

previous – subsequent

primary – secondary

principal – subordinate

private – public

prodigal – thrifty

productive – sterile

profane – sacred

proficient – unskilled

profit – loss

profound – superficial

progressive – reactionary

proliferate – dwindle

prolix – laconic

prologue – epilogue

promiscuous – selective

promote – demote

propinquity – remoteness

prosperous – impecunious

protrude – recede

prove – disprove

proximity – remoteness

puerile – mature

punctilious – careless

puny – robust

puritanical – permissive

pusillanimous – plucky

Q

quarrelsome – peaceable

questionable – indisputable

quiescent – agitated

R

rabble – élite

rambling – coherent

rancid – fresh

rapt – inattentive

rash – prudent

raucous – melodious

reassure – alarm

recalcitrant – docile

recumbent – erect

recurrent – unique

reduce – increase

redundant – essential

reflective – thoughtless

refractory – docile

refuse – accept

regardless – mindful

regional – national

regress – progress

regular – erratic

reinforce – weaken

reliable – treacherous

reluctant – willing

remiss – conscientious

remorseful – impenitent

renowned – obscure

repeal – ratify

repel – attract

repine – acquiesce

reprove – praise

repudiate – recognize

rescind – ratify

reserved – communicative

responsive – impassive

retard – accelerate

reticent – communicative

reveal – conceal

revere – despise

revile – praise

revoke – enact

rife – rare

rightful – illegitimate

rigid – flexible

robust – frail

roomy – poky

roundabout – direct

rudimentary – advanced

rural – urban

ruthless – humane

S

sacred – profane

salient – inconspicuous

salubrious – unhealthy

sanction – ban

sang-froid – agitation

sanguine – despondent

satirical – eulogistic

scanty – abundant

scorn – admiration

scraggy – plump

scruffy – spruce

scrutinize – ignore

scurry – dawdle

seasonable – untimely

seasoned – callow

secondary – primary

secrecy – publicity

secular – religious

secure – precarious

sedative – stimulant

seductive – repulsive

segregate – combine

selfish – altruistic

senile – juvenile

senior – junior

sensual – ascetic

seraphic – devilish

serious – frivolous

severe – mild

shallow – profound

shrewd – ingenuous

shy – forward
significant – negligible
simple – complex
sin – virtue
skilful – incompetent
skinny – obese
sloth – energy
slovenly – tidy
snub – compliment
sociable – unfriendly
solemn – frivolous
somnolent – wakeful
soothe – disturb
sorry – unrepentant
spacious – cramped
sparing – lavish
spasmodic – regular
specific – vague
speechless – voluble
spicy – bland
spiteful – benevolent
spontaneous –
    premeditated
sporadic – regular
sprightly – lethargic
spruce – shabby
spurious – genuine
stagnant – fresh
static – mobile
staunch – untrustworthy
steadfast – fickle
steep – gradual
sterile – fertile
stern – lenient
stifle – vivify
stimulant – sedative
stingy – lavish
strength – weakness
striking – commonplace
stringent – lenient
stroll – scurry
stubborn – docile
sturdy – frail

suave –
    unsophisticated
subdue – provoke
subjective – objective
submissive – obdurate
subsequent – prior
subservient –
    overbearing
subtle – obvious
succinct – diffuse
succumb – resist
summit – base
sumptuous – humble
superfluity – deficiency
superior – inferior
supine – erect
surplus – deficit
surreptitious – overt
susceptible – immune
suspicious –
    unsuspecting
sustained – intermittent
swarthy – fair
sybaritic – abstemious
systematic – haphazard

T

tacit – explicit
taciturn –
    communicative
tactical – strategic
tangible – visionary
tardy – premature
tasty – insipid
tawdry – elegant
tedious – exciting
temperate –
    immoderate
temporal – spiritual
temporary – permanent
tenable – indefensible
tenacity – vacillation
tentative – definite
terse – verbose
theoretical – practical

thrifty – improvident
timeless – ephemeral
titanic – diminutive
tongue-tied – garrulous
toothsome – unsavoury
topical – outdated
torpid – active
total – partial
tractable – refractory
traditional –
    unconventional
tragedy – comedy
tranquil – agitated
transient – permanent
transparent – opaque
treacherous – loyal
trifling – considerable
trite – original
trivial – profound
truculent – placid
truncate – extend
truth – falsehood
tuneful – discordant
turbulent – calm

U

ulterior – overt
unanimity –
    disagreement
unassuming –
    pretentious
unbecoming – seemly
unbridled – restrained
uncompromising –
    flexible
uncouth – polished
underhand – above-
    board
undoubted –
    questionable
undying – transient
unequivocal –
    ambiguous
unfeeling – sympathetic
ungainly – graceful

unity – discord
unkempt – tidy
unprecedented – normal
unruly – orderly
unsightly – attractive
unsung – celebrated
unwonted – customary
urbane – uncouth
Utopian – realistic

V

vague – precise
valiant – timorous
variety – uniformity
vast – minute
vehemence – apathy
venial – inexcusable
verbose – taciturn
verify – disprove
vertical – horizontal

veteran – novice
vice – virtue
victorious – defeated
vigilant – inattentive
vigorous – feeble
virile – effeminate
vivid – nondescript
volatile – stable
voluble – uncommunicative
voluntary – compulsory
voluptuous – ascetic
vulnerable – impregnable

W

wan – florid
wane – wax
warlike – pacific
wary – cautious
wasteful – economical
watchful – inattentive

wayward – tractable
wearisome – refreshing
well-built – slight
whole – partial
wholesale – selective
wide – narrow
wilful – accidental
willingly – reluctantly
wily – straightforward
winsome – repulsive
wisdom – folly
withhold – grant
wonted – unaccustomed
worldly – spiritual
worthless – valuable

Y

yield – resist
youthful – elderly

Z

zenith – nadir

Word Elements

One can often work out the meaning of an unknown word by means of its parts. Since the 'combining form' *bio-* means 'life', and *-graphy* means 'writing', it is logical that a *biography* is a written account of somebody's life. These word parts usually appear in dictionaries as prefixes, which occur at the beginning, suffixes which come at the end, and the more 'word-like' combining forms which can occupy either position. They are an important part of that linguistic stock which is available to us for making new English words, as we continually do when they are needed: *tele-* has recently given rise to *tele-shopping*, and *-nik* makes *computernik*. The following list of word parts should be useful both in word-creation and in making intelligent guesses.

A

a- not, without: *amoral, aseptic, asymmetry*.

acro- high: *acrophobia, acropolis*.

-aemia (also **-haemia**, *US* **-emia, -hemia**) shows something is present in the blood: *toxaemia, septicaemia*.

aero- air, aircraft: *aerobatics, aerofoil*.

-agogue (*US* **-agog**) leader, teacher: *pedagogue, demagogue*.

agro- agricultural: *agrochemical, agronomy*.

-algia pain in a specified part: *neuralgia*.

allo- other: *allopathy, allomorph*.

ambi- both sides, both ways: *ambidextrous, ambivalent*.

amphi- both: *amphibious*.

an- without: *anarchy, anaemia*.

-ana things associated with: *Victoriana, Americana*.

Anglo- English, British: *Anglo-Catholic, Anglophobe*.

ante- before: *antenatal, ante-room*.

anthrop- human: *anthropology, philanthropy*.

anti- against, opposite: *anti-aircraft, anti-clockwise*.

ap- away from: *aphelion, apogee.*
aqua- water: *aqualung, aquatic.*
arch- superior, pre-eminent: *archduke, arch-enemy.*
-archy government: *anarchy, matriarchy.*
-arian concerned with or believing in: *Parliamentarian, vegetarian.*
-arium place for a purpose: *aquarium, planetarium.*
arthr- joint: *arthritis, arthropod.*
astro- stars, space: *astronomy, astronaut.*
atto- 10^{-18}
audio- sound, hearing: *audio-visual, audiotape.*
Austro- Austrian: *Austro-Hungarian.*
auto- self, or automatic: *autobiography, automobile.*

B

bi- two, double: *bicycle, bilingual, bifocals.*
biblio- book: *bibliophile, bibliography.*
bio- life: *biography, biology, antibiotic.*
brachi- arm: *brachial, brachiopod.*
brachy- short: *brachycephalic, brachypterous.*
broncho- lungs and windpipe, bronchi: *bronchopneumonia, bronchoscope.*

C

calc- lime or calcium: *calcify.*
carbo- carbon: *carbohydrate, carboniferous.*
carcino- cancer: *carcinogenic.*
cardi- heart: *cardiac, cardiogram.*
carn- flesh: *carnal, carnivorous.*
cent- hundredth, or hundred: *centimetre, centenarian, percentage.*
-centric centre, centred: *heliocentric, egocentric, centrifugal.*
-cephalic, -cephalous headed: *dolichocephalic, hydrocephalic, cephalopod.*
cerebro- brain: *cerebrospinal.*
chiro-, cheiro- hand: *chiropractor, chiromancy.*
chloro- green, or chlorine: *chlorophyll, chlorofluorocarbon.*
chrom- colour: *chromolithograph, monochrome.*
chron- time: *chronology, chronometer, anachronism.*
-cide killing: *suicide, insecticide.*
cine- films: *cine-camera, cinematic.*
circum- round, about: *circumference, circumnavigate, circumcise.*
cis- on this side of: *cisatlantic, cislunar.*
clavi- key: *clavichord, clavicle.*
co- with, jointly: *co-author, co-education.*
contra- against: *contraception, contraflow;* (Music) pitched an octave below: *contrabassoon.*

cosm- cosmos, world, universe: *cosmology, macrocosm, cosmopolitan.*

-cracy form of government or rule: *bureaucracy, meritocracy.*

cranio- cranium, skull: *cranial, craniometry.*

-cratic of a form of government or rule: *democratic.*

crypto- secret: *crypto-Communist, cryptogram.*

cupro- copper: *cupro-nickel.*

cycl- circle or wheel: *cyclorama, tricycle.*

cyno- dog: *cynocephalus, cynophobia.*

cyst- urinary bladder: *cystitis, cystotomy.*

D

-dactyl finger: *pterodactyl.*

deca- ten: *decade, decalitre, decathlon.*

deci- tenth: *decimate, decilitre.*

demi- half: *demigod, demisemiquaver*

demo- the people: *democratic, demography.*

dendr- tree: *dendrology, rhododendron.*

derm- skin: *dermatitis, hypodermic.*

dextr- to the right: *dextral, dextrorotatory.*

di- two: *dioxide, dimorphic.*

dia- through, across: *diameter, diarrhoea.*

didact- teaching, taught: *didactic, autodidact.*

dodeca- twelve: *dodecahedron.*

-dox opinion: *orthodox, heterodox, paradox.*

-drome place for racing or movement: *aerodrome, hippodrome.*

dys- bad, difficult: *dyslexia, dyspepsia.*

E

eco- ecology: *ecosystem, eco-friendly.*

ecto- outside: *ectoderm, ectoplasm.*

-ectomy surgical removal: *vasectomy, appendectomy.*

-eme (*Linguistics*) unit of language: *morpheme, phoneme.*

encephalo- brain: *encephalograph.*

endo- internal: *endogamy.*

enter- intestine: *enterovirus, enteritis.*

entomo- insect: *entomology.*

epi- upon, above: *epicentre, epidermis.*

equi- equal: *equinox, equidistant.*

eroto- erotic: *erotology.*

-esque in the style of: *Schumannesque, Chaplinesque.*

ethno- ethnic: *ethnography.*

-etum collection of trees: *arboretum, pinetum.*

eu- well, good: *eulogy, euphony.*

exo- external: *exogamy.*
extra- outside: *extraterrestrial, extramural.*

F

-facient causing: *abortifacient.*
-faction making, becoming: *petrifaction, liquefaction.*
femto- 10^{-15}
ferri-, ferro- iron: *ferroconcrete.*
fibro- fibre: *fibro-cement, fibrositis.*
fluoro- fluorine, or fluorescence: *fluorocarbon, fluoroscope.*
fluvi- river: *fluviometer.*
Franco- French: *Francophile, Franco-German.*
-fuge expelling or fleeing: *vermifuge, centrifugal.*

G

Gallo- French, Gaul: *Gallo-Roman.*
-gamy marriage: *monogamy, bigamy.*
gastr- stomach: *gastronome, gastritis.*
-gen, -genic, -genous producing: *hydrogen, carcinogenic, sporogenous.*
genito- genital: *genito-urinary.*
geo- earth: *geography, geology.*
geronto- old age: *gerontology, gerontophilia.*
giga- 10^9: *gigavolt.*
-gon shape with a specified number of angles: *hexagon, polygon, octagon.*
Graeco- (also **Greco-**) Greek: *Graeco-Roman.*
-gram, -graph written or drawn in a particular way: *monogram, telegram; autograph, photograph.*
-graphy writing: *biography, calligraphy.*
gynaeco- (*US* **gyneco-**) woman: *gynaecology.*
gyro- rotation: *gyroscope.*

H

haem- (*US* **hem-**) blood: *haemorrhage, haemoglobin, haematite.*
hagio- saints: *hagiography.*
hecto- hundred: *hectogram.*
-hedron solid with a specified number of sides: *dodecahedron.*
helio- sun: *heliocentric.*
hemi- half: *hemisphere, hemidemisemiquaver.*
hendeca- eleven: *hendecagon.*
hepta- seven: *heptahedron.*
hetero- other, different: *heterodox, heterosexual.*
hexa- six: *hexameter, hexagon.*
Hiberno- Irish: *Hiberno-British.*

hiero- sacred: *hierocracy, hierolatry.*
hippo- horse: *hippodrome, hippogriff.*
Hispano- Spanish: *Hispanophile.*
hist- (*Biology*) tissue: *histology, antihistamine.*
holo- whole: *holograph, holocaust.*
homo- same: *homosexual, homogenize.*
hydr- water: *hydrant, hydrofoil;* (*Chem.*) hydrogen: *hydrochloric.*
hygro- moisture: *hygrometer.*
hyper- over, or above normal: *hyperactive, hyperinflation.*
hypno- sleep: *hypnosis, hypnopaedia.*
hypo- under, or below normal: *hypodermic, hypothermia.*

I

-iasis forms names of diseases: *satyriasis.*
Ibero- Iberian, of Spain and Portugal: *Ibero-American.*
ichthyo- fish: *ichthyology, ichthyosaurus.*
icon- image, picture: *iconoclast, iconography.*
immuno- immunity to infection: *immunotherapy.*
infra- below, under: *infrared, infrastructure.*
inter- between: *intercity, intermarry, inter-war.*
intra- inside, within: *intramural, intravenous.*
iso- equal, same: *isotherm, isotope.*
-itis forms names of diseases: *arthritis, appendicitis.*

J

Judaeo- (*US* **Judeo-**) Jewish: *Judaeo-Christian.*

K

kilo- thousand: *kilometre, kilowatt.*
kine- motion: *kinetics, telekinesis.*

L

labi- lips: *labial, labiodental.*
lachrym-, lachrim- tears, weeping: *lachrymose, lachrymation.*
lact- milk: *lactation, lactiferous.*
laevo- (also **levo-**) to the left: *laevorotatory.*
leuco- white: *leucocyte, leucoma.*
lexic- words, vocabulary: *lexicon, lexicology.*
lign- wood: *ligneous, lignite.*
lith- stone: *lithography, megalith.*
loc- place: *local, locomotive.*
-logue (*US* **-log**) word, talk: *dialogue, monologue.*
-logy subject of study: *biology, sociology.*

lun- moon: *translunar, lunatic.*

-lysis shows disintegration: *electrolysis.*

M

-machy war, fighting: *logomachy, tauromachy.*

macro- long, large: *macrocosm, macrobiotic.*

magneto- magnet, magnetic: *magnetometer.*

mal- bad, faulty: *maltreat, malodorous, malfunction.*

-mancy divination by: *necromancy, chiromancy.*

-mania obsession, or enthusiasm: *megalomania, pyromania.*

-maniac affected with mania: *nymphomaniac.*

matri- mother: *matriarch, matricide.*

maxi- very large or long: *maximize, maxi-coat.*

medi- middle: *medieval, mediocre.*

mega- large, or 10^6: *megalith, megalomania, megawatt.*

men- menstruation: *menopause, menarch, menorrhoea.*

meso- middle, intermediate: *mesolithic, mesosphere.*

meta- change of condition, or behind, beyond: *metamorphosis, metaphysics.*

-meter measuring instrument: *barometer, speedometer;* (Poetry) line of verse with a specified number of feet: *pentameter.*

metr-, -metry measuring: *metronome, geometry.*

-metre (US **-meter**) unit of length in the metric system: *centimetre, kilometre.*

micro- small, or a millionth, 10^{-6}: *microcosm, microchip, microgram.*

milli- thousand, or thousandth, 10^{-3}: *millipede, millimetre.*

mini- small, minor: *minibus, minimize, miniskirt.*

mon- one, single: *monarch, monochrome, monogamy, monocle.*

morph- form, shape: *morphology, metamorphosis.*

multi- many: *multinational, multimillionaire.*

myc- fungus: *mycology.*

N

nano- thousand millionth, 10^{-9}: *nanosecond.*

nas- nose: *nasal, naso-frontal.*

nat- birth, born: *native, nativity, neonate.*

naut- naval, or navigation: *nautical, astronaut.*

necro- corpse: *necromancy, necropolis.*

neo- new, modern: *neoclassical, neolithic.*

nephr- kidneys: *nephritis.*

neur- nerves: *neuralgia, neurosis.*

-nik person associated with something: *beatnik, refusenik.*

nom-, -nym name: *nominal, eponym, pseudonym.*
nona- nine: *nonagenarian.*

O

occipito- the back of the head: *occipito-frontal.*
oct- eight: *octagon, octave, octopus.*
ocul- eye: *oculist, oculo-nasal.*
odont- tooth: *odontology, orthodontics.*
-oid almost, resembling: *humanoid, spheroid.*
ole- oil: *oleometer, oleaginous.*
olig- few: *oligarchy.*
-ology see **-logy.**
-oma abnormal growth: *carcinoma.*
omni- all: *omnipresent, omnivore.*
oneiro- dream: *oneiromancy.*
oo- egg, ovum: *oology, oolite.*
ophi- snake: *ophidian, ophicleide.*
ophthalm- eye: *ophthalmic, ophthalmoscope.*
-opia visual disorder: *myopia.*
-orium a place for something: *auditorium, crematorium.*
ornith- bird: *ornithology.*
ortho- straight, correct: *orthography, orthodontics.*
oscillo- oscillation, especially of electric current: *oscillograph.*
-osis process, condition, or disease: *hypnosis, thrombosis.*
osteo- bone: *osteopath.*
-otic affected by, or producing: *neurotic, narcotic.*
ovi- egg, or sheep: *oviparous, ovine.*

P

paed- (also **ped-**) child: *paediatrics, paedophilia, pedagogue.*
palaeo- (*US* **paleo-**) ancient, prehistoric: *palaeolithic.*
pan- all, whole: *pandemic, pan-American, pantheism.*
para- resembling, or beside, beyond: *paramedic, paratyphoid, paranormal.*
-parous (*fem.* **-para**) bearing the specified kind or number of young: *viviparous, multipara.*
path- disease, suffering: *pathology, osteopath, homeopathy.*
ped-, -pod foot: *pedicure, centipede, cephalopod.*
penta- five: *pentagon, pentathlon.*
pep- digestion: *peptic, dyspepsia.*
peri- around: *perimeter;* (*Astron.*) point nearest to: *perihelion, perigee.*
peta- 10^{15}: *petametre.*
petr- rock, or petroleum: *petrifaction, petrochemical.*

phag-, -phagy, -phagous eating the specified thing: *phagocyte, ichthyophagous, anthropophagy.*

pharyng- the pharynx, between mouth and gullet: *pharyngitis.*

phil-, -phile, -philia shows fondness: *philanthropic, Francophile, necrophilia.*

phleb- vein: *phlebitis.*

-phobe, -phobic, -phobia shows fear or hatred: *claustrophobic, xenophobia.*

phon- sound, or language: *phonics, phonetic, saxophone, anglophone.*

phot-, photo- light, or photography: *photoelectric, phototropic, photogenic.*

phyll- leaf: *phyllophagous, chlorophyll.*

physio- physical, natural science: *physiology, physiotherapy.*

pico- 10^{-12}: *picometre.*

pinni- wing or fin: *pinniped.*

plan- flat, plane: *planisphere, planometer.*

plast- moulding, shaping: *plastic surgery, rhinoplasty.*

platy- broad, flat: *platypus.*

pleur- pleura, in the thorax or lungs: *pleurisy.*

pluri- several: *pluricellular.*

pneumat- air, breath: *pneumatic.*

pneumo- lungs: *pneumonia.*

-polis city: *metropolis, Minneapolis.*

poly- many: *polyglot, polygamy, polythene.*

port- carry: *portable, transport.*

post- after: *postgraduate, postscript, post-war.*

pre- before: *preview, pre-adolescent.*

preter- more than: *preternatural.*

pro- favouring, or substituting for: *pro-communist, proconsul.*

proct- anus and rectum: *proctoscope.*

proto- original, primitive, or first: *proto-Germanic, prototype, protomartyr.*

pseud- not genuine: *pseudonym, pseudo-scientific.*

psych- the mind: *psychology, psychic, psychopath.*

pter- wing: *pterodactyl, helicopter.*

pyro- fire: *pyromania, pyrometer.*

Q

quadr- four: *quadrangle, quadraphonic, quadruped.*

quasi- seemingly but not quite: *quasi-scientific, quasi-independence.*

quat- four: *quatrain, quatercentenary.*

quin-, quinqu- five: *quincentenary, quintuplet, quinquereme.*

R

radio- connected with radio or broadcasting; (*Tech.*) connected with radioactivity, radiation, radioisotopes, or the anatomical radius: *radiobiology, radio-carpal.*

-renal kidneys: *adrenal, suprarenal.*

retro- backwards, behind: *retroactive, retrograde.*

rheo- flow, stream: *rheology, diarrhoea.*

rhino- nose: *rhinoceros, rhinoplasty.*

rhizo- root: *rhizome.*

rhod- rose-coloured: *rhodium, rhododendron.*

S

sacchar- sugar: *saccharine, saccharogenic.*

sacro- (*Anat.*) the sacrum bone in the pelvis: *sacro-iliac.*

salping- Fallopian tubes: *salpingitis.*

sapro- (*Biol.*) rotten: *saprophyte.*

-scape view: *seascape, cityscape.*

-scope device for looking through or at: *telescope, gyroscope.*

seism- earthquake: *seismic, seismology.*

selen- moon: *selenium, selenology.*

sem- sign, meaning: *semantics, semaphore.*

semi- partly, or half: *semi-official, semicircle.*

sept- seven: *septet, septuagenarian.*

sesqui- one and a half: *sesquicentenary.*

sex- six: *sextet, sextuplet.*

sider- star: *sidereal.*

Sino- Chinese: *Sino-Soviet, sinology.*

socio- social, society: *sociology, socio-industrial.*

somat- the body: *somatic, somatotype.*

spectro- spectrum: *spectroscope.*

spermo-, spermato- sperm, seed: *spermatocyte.*

-sphere spherical, or a region round the earth: *bathysphere, atmosphere.*

spiro- spiral, or breath: *spirochaete, spirometer.*

splen- (*Anat.*) the spleen: *splenitis, splenetic.*

sporo- (*Biol.*) spore: *sporogenous.*

-stasis (*Physiol.*) slowing, stopping: *haemostasis.*

-stat regulating, fixing: *thermostat, rheostat.*

stereo- three-dimensional, solid: *stereophonic, stereoscopic.*

sub- secondary, or under: *subcommittee, submarine, subnormal.*

super-, sur- above, or beyond normal, or extra large or strong: *superstructure, superpower, supermarket, surcharge.*

supra- higher than, or transcending: *supranational.*

syn-, sym- together: *synchronize, symmetrical.*

T

tacho-, tachy- speed, swift: *tachometer, tachycardia.*

taur- bull: *taurine, tauromachy.*

tauto- same: *tautology.*

techn- skill, craft: *technician, technology.*

tele- far, or using television or the telephone: *telescope, telepathy, teletext.*

ter- three: *tercentenary.*

tera- 10^{12}: *terametre.*

terato- monster: *teratology.*

tetra- four: *tetrahedron.*

the-, theo- God, gods: *theism, theology.*

therm- heat: *thermostat, thermometer, isotherm.*

thromb- blood clot: *thrombosis, antithrombin.*

thyro- thyroid: *thyroxine.*

-tome cutting instrument, or segment: *microtome.*

-tomy surgical cutting: *phlebotomy.*

toxi- poison: *toxicology.*

tracheo- windpipe: *tracheotomy.*

trans- across, through, or into another state: *transatlantic, transplant.*

tri- three: *triangle, tricycle, triathlon.*

tribo- rubbing, friction: *tribology.*

tricho- hair: *trichogenous.*

turbo- turbine: *turboprop.*

U

-ule forms a diminutive: *globule, animalcule.*

uni- one: *uniform, unicorn, unisex.*

urano- the heavens, or uranium: *Uranus.*

uro- urine: *urology.*

V

vas-, vaso- vessel, duct: *vasectomy.*

vermi- worm: *vermicide, vermicelli.*

vini- wine: *viniculture.*

-vore, -vorous feeding on: *insectivorous, carnivore.*

X

xeno- foreign, other: *xenophobia, xenolith.*

xyl- wood: *xylophagous, xylophone.*

Z

zoo- animal: *zoology, zoomorphic.*

Some of these word parts are particularly 'productive', in the sense that they have formed many words and are continually forming more. We deal here with some particularly important ones, in more detail.

-archy and **-cracy** mean government, or form of government. So for different sorts of government:

anarchy means by nobody; no government.
aristocracy by the nobility.
autarchy, autocracy by one person.
democracy by the people.
diarchy by two authorities.
gerontocracy by the old.
matriarchy by mothers; with the mother as head.
ochlocracy by the mob.
oligarchy by a small group.
patriarchy by a man; by descent through males.
theocracy by God, or priests.

-cide means killer or killing. So the following person or thing kills:

bactericide bacteria.
deicide a god.
fratricide a brother or sister.
genocide a people or nation.
germicide germs.
homicide a human being.
infanticide an infant.
insecticide insects.
matricide a mother.
parricide a near relative.
patricide a father.
pesticide pests.
regicide a king.
sororicide a sister.
spermicide spermatozoa.
suicide himself, herself.
tyrannicide a tyrant.
uxoricide a wife.
vermicide worms.

-gamy means marriage, or spouse. So:

autogamy self-fertilization in plants.
bigamy two.
endogamy within one's tribe.
exogamy outside one's tribe.

misogamy hatred of marriage.
monogamy to one person.
polygamy to many people.

-logy or **-ology** means a subject of study. So the following are concerned with studying:

aerology the upper levels of the atmosphere.
aetiology (*US* **etiology**) the causes of disease.
agriology the history and customs of savages.
anthropology 1 human societies and customs. **2** the structure and evolution of man as an animal.
areology rocks on Mars.
Assyriology Assyria.
astrology the movements and positions of heavenly bodies interpreted as an influence on human affairs.
audiology the science of hearing.
bacteriology bacteria.
bryology mosses, liverworts, etc.
campanology bell-ringing.
cardiology diseases and abnormalities of the heart.
carpology fruit and seeds.
cetology aquatic mammals.
chorology the geographical distribution of animals and plants.
conchology shells.
cosmology the theory of the universe.
craniology the shape and size of the human skull.
criminology crime.
cytology cells.
dendrology trees.
dermatology skin disorders.
ecology 1 the relations of organisms to one another and to their physical surroundings. **2** human ecology; the interaction of people with their environment.
Egyptology ancient Egypt.
embryology embryos.
endocrinology the ductless glands.
entomology insects.
epidemiology the incidence and distribution of diseases, and their control and prevention.
epistemology the theory of knowledge.
escapology escaping from confinement, especially as a form of entertainment.

eschatology the part of theology concerned with death and final destiny.

ethology **1** animal behaviour. **2** character-formation in human behaviour.

etymology the sources of the formation of words, and the development of their meanings.

futurology systematic forecasting of the future from present trends.

genealogy lines of descent from ancestors.

gerontology old age, and the process and special problems of ageing.

gynaecology (*US* **gynecology**) the physiological functions and diseases of women, especially those affecting the reproductive system.

haematology (*US* **hematology**) the physiology of the blood.

hagiology the lives of saints.

helminthology parasitic worms.

heortology Church festivals.

herpetology reptiles.

histology the structure of tissues.

histopathology the changes in tissues caused by disease.

horology the measuring of time, and making of clocks and watches.

hydrology the properties of the earth's water, especially of its movement in relation to land.

hypnology the phenomena of sleep.

ichthyology fish.

immunology immunity; resistance to infection.

lexicology the form, history, and meaning of words.

limnology lakes and other fresh waters.

lithology the nature and composition of rocks.

malacology molluscs.

meteorology the phenomena of the atmosphere and forecasting of weather.

metrology measurement.

microbiology bacteria, viruses, and fungi.

morphology the form of things, especially **1** of organisms. **2** of words.

musicology music, apart from learning to perform or compose it.

mycology fungi.

myology muscles.

mythology myths.

neurology nerve systems.

nosology the classification of diseases.

numerology the supposed occult significance of numbers.

odontology the structure and diseases of teeth.

oenology (*US* **enology**) wines.

oncology tumours.

ontology the nature of being.

oology birds' eggs.

ophthalmology the eye.

ornithology birds.

osteology the skeleton and bony structures.

otology the ear.

otorhinolaryngology ENT; diseases of the ear, nose, and throat.

palaeoclimatology (*US* **paleoclimatology**) the climate in geologically past times.

palaeontology (*US* **paleontology**) life in the geological past.

palynology pollen, spores, etc. from the point of view of rock dating and the study of past environments.

parasitology parasites.

pathology bodily diseases.

pedology soil.

penology the punishment of crime, and prison management.

petrology rocks.

pharmacology the action of drugs on the body.

philology language, especially in its historical and comparative aspects.

phonology the sounds of a language.

phrenology the shape and size of the cranium as a supposed indication of character and mental faculties.

phycology algae.

physiology the functions of living organisms and their parts.

phytopathology plant diseases.

pneumatology the Holy Ghost and other spiritual concepts.

pomology fruit-growing.

potamology rivers.

proctology the anus and rectum.

psephology elections, voting, etc.

psychology the human mind and its functions.

psychopathology mental disorders.

pteridology ferns.

radiobiology the effects of radiation on organisms.

radiology the medical use of X-rays and other high-energy radiation.

reflexology 1 a system of massage through points on the feet, hands, and head. **2** reflex actions.

rheumatology rheumatic diseases.

scatology excrement, either for diagnosis or in the form of fossilized dung.

seismology earthquakes.

selenology the moon.

semiology signs and symbols.

sinology Chinese language, history, etc.

speleology caves.

stomatology the mouth and its diseases.

symptomatology medical symptoms.

teleology the explanation of phenomena by the purpose they serve rather than by postulated causes; the doctrine of design and purpose in the material world.

teratology **1** animal or vegetable monstrosities. **2** fantastic monsters in mythology.

thanatology death.

theology religion.

topology geometrical properties and spatial relations unaffected by change of shape or size.

toxicology poisons.

tribology friction.

trichology the hair.

ufology unidentified flying objects; UFOs.

venereology venereal diseases.

vexillology flags.

virology viruses.

vulcanology volcanoes.

zoology animals.

zymology fermentation.

-mancy means divination by something. So the following do their divining:

ailuromancy by the way a cat jumps.

aleuromancy by meal or flour.

arithmancy by numbers.

belomancy by arrows.

bibliomancy by a book, especially the Bible.

cartomancy by playing-cards.

chiromancy by the hand; palmistry.

empyromancy by fire.

gastromancy **1** by stomach sounds. **2** by crystal-gazing.

geomancy by a handful of earth.

graptomancy by handwriting.

gyromancy by walking in a circle till one falls down from giddiness.

lithomancy by stones.

logomancy by the observation of words.

necromancy by communication with the dead.

oneiromancy by dreams.

pyromancy by fire.

rhapsodomancy by verses picked at random.
selenomancy by the moon.
uromancy by urine.
zoomancy by watching animals.

-mania means obsession or enthusiasm. So one may be particularly enthusiastic about:

Anglomania England.
bibliomania books.
dipsomania alcohol.
egomania oneself.
erotomania sex.
hypomania anything, but only mildly.
kleptomania stealing things.
megalomania one's own importance.
monomania one single idea.
mythomania telling lies.
nymphomania sex, in a female.
pyromania setting fire to things.

Except in the context of poetry, anything ending in **-meter** is a measuring instrument. The following appliances measure:

actinometer radiation.
altimeter altitude.
ammeter electric current, in amperes.
anemometer the wind.
bathometer the depth of water.
bolometer radiant energy.
calorimeter heat.
cathetometer small vertical distances.
chronometer time.
clinometer slopes.
colorimeter the density of colour.
cyclometer 1 circular arcs. **2** the distance traversed by a bicycle etc.
densitometer the photographic density of an image on a film or print.
electrometer electrical potential.
eudiometer changes in the volume of gases during chemical reactions.
goniometer angles.
gravimeter differences in the force of gravity.
heliometer the angular distance between two stars.
hydrometer the density of liquids.
hygrometer humidity.
hypsometer height above sea level.

interferometer wavelengths etc.

Machmeter air speed.

magnetometer magnetic forces.

manometer the pressure of gases and liquids.

micrometer small distances, thicknesses etc.

odometer the distance travelled by a wheeled vehicle.

ohmmeter electrical resistance.

optometer the refractive power and visual range of the eye.

pedometer the distance travelled on foot.

photometer light.

piezometer the magnitude or direction of pressure.

planimeter the area of a plane figure.

pluviometer rainfall.

potentiometer small electrical potentials.

psychrometer humidity.

pyrometer high temperatures, in kilns and furnaces.

radiometer radiation.

saccharometer the sugar content of a solution.

sclerometer hardness.

spectrometer spectra.

spherometer the radius of a sphere, and the thickness of small bodies.

tachometer, **tachymeter** the speed of a vehicle.

taximeter the distance travelled, and fare payable, in a taxi.

tensimeter vapour pressure.

thermometer temperature.

variometer an aircraft's rate of change of altitude.

velocimeter velocity.

voltmeter electric potential, in volts.

-phobe and **-phobia** show fear or hatred, and have given rise to an enormous number of somewhat fanciful combinations (it has been suggested for instance that *arachibutyrophobia* means the fear of peanut butter sticking to the roof of one's mouth). If you have the following phobias, you dislike or are afraid of the following things, or so someone at some time has said—we cannot always vouch for the authenticity:

A

acarophobia mites and ticks.

acidophobia (in plants) acid soils.

acousticophobia sound.

acrophobia heights.

agoraphobia open spaces, or public places.

aichmophobia knives and pointed objects.
ailurophobia cats.
albuminophobia albumin in one's urine.
algophobia pain.
amathophobia dust.
amaxophobia travelling in vehicles.
androphobia males.
anemophobia wind, or draughts.
anginophobia sore throat.
Anglophobia England, or the English.
anthophobia flowers.
anthropophobia people.
aphephobia touching, or being touched.
arachnophobia spiders.
asthenophobia weakness.
astrophobia the influence of the stars.
ataxiophobia disorder.
aurophobia gold.
automysophobia being dirty.
autophobia solitude.

B

bacillophobia germs.
ballistophobia bullets.
basiphobia, bathmophobia walking.
basophobia (in plants) alkaline soils.
bathophobia depths.
batrachophobia frogs.
belonephobia needles and pins.
bogyphobia demons and goblins.
botanophobia plants.
bromidrosiphobia having an unpleasant smell.
brontophobia thunderstorms.

C

cacophobia ugliness.
cainophobia novelty.
callophobia beauty.
cardiophobia heart disease.
cathisophobia sitting down.
catoptrophobia mirrors.
Celtophobia Celts.
cherophobia gaiety.

chionophobia snow.
chirophobia hands.
choleraphobia cholera.
chrematophobia wealth.
chromophobia colours.
chronophobia time.
cibophobia food.
claustrophobia confined spaces.
climacophobia stairs.
coitophobia sexual intercourse.
cometophobia comets.
coprophobia faeces, excrement.
cremnophobia precipices.
crystallophobia glass.
cynophobia dogs.
cypridophobia sexual intercourse.

D

deipnophobia dining, dinner conversation.
demonophobia spirits.
demophobia crowds.
dermatosiophobia skin, skin disease.
diabetophobia diabetes.
dinophobia whirlpools.
diplopiaphobia double vision.
dipsophobia thirst.
dromophobia crossing streets.
dysmorphophobia deformity (usually in others).

E

ecophobia home surroundings, or home life.
eisoptrophobia mirrors.
emetophobia vomiting.
entomophobia insects.
eosophobia the dawn.
eremiophobia solitude.
ergophobia, ergasophobia work.
erimiophobia stillness.
erotophobia sexual feelings.
erythrophobia red, or blushing.
eurotophobia the female genitals.

F

Francophobia France, or the French.

G

galeophobia sharks.
Gallophobia France, or the French.
gametophobia marriage.
gatophobia cats.
genophobia sex.
gephyrophobia crossing a bridge.
geraphobia, gerascophobia old age.
Germanophobia Germany, or the Germans.
gerontophobia old people.
geumatophobia taste.
glossophobia speaking.
gnosiophobia knowledge.
graphophobia writing.
gringophobia (in Latin America) white strangers.
gymnophobia nakedness.
gynophobia women.

H

haematophobia (*US* **hematophobia**) blood.
hagiophobia saints.
hamartophobia sin.
hedonophobia pleasure.
heliophobia sunlight.
helminthophobia infestation by worms.
herpetophobia reptiles.
hierophobia sacred objects.
hippophobia horses.
hodophobia travel.
homichlophobia fog.
homilophobia sermons.
homophobia homosexuals.
hydrophobia water (especially as a symptom of rabies in man).
hydrophobophobia rabies.
hygrophobia dampness.
hylephobia wood.
hypeiagphobia responsibility.
hypnophobia sleep.
hypsophobia high places.

I

iatrophobia doctors, or healing.
ichthyophobia fish.
iophobia poisons.
isopterophobia termites.

J

Judaeophobia Jews, or Jewish culture.

K

kakorrhaphiaphobia failure, or defeat.
kenophobia emptiness.
keraunophobia thunder and lightning.
kinetophobia motion.
kleptophobia stealing, or thieves.
kopophobia fatigue.
kynophobia pseudo-rabies.

L

lalophobia talking.
leprophobia leprosy.
levophobia things on one's left.
logophobia words, or study.

M

mastophobia breasts.
megalophobia large things.
meningitophobia meningitis.
merinthophobia being bound.
metallophobia metals.
meteorophobia meteors, or meteorites.
metrophobia motherhood.
microphobia small things.
molysomophobia infection.
monopathophobia sickness in a specified part of the body.
monophobia solitude.
musicophobia music.
musophobia mice.
mycophobia fungus.
mysophobia dirt.

N

necrophobia death, or dead bodies.
negrophobia black people.
neophobia change.
noctiphobia the night.
nosophobia disease.
nudophobia nakedness.
nyctophobia darkness.

O

ochlophobia crowds.
odontophobia teeth.
odynophobia pain.
oenophobia wine.
olfactophobia smells.
ombrophobia rain.
ommetaphobia eyes.
onomatophobia a certain name.
ophidiophobia snakes.
ophthalmophobia eyes.
ornithophobia birds.
osmophobia, osphresiophobia smells.

P

paedophobia (*US* **pedophobia**) children, or dolls.
panophobia, pantophobia everything.
papaphobia the pope, or the papacy.
paralipophobia neglect of a duty.
paraphobia sexual perversion.
parasitophobia parasites.
parthenophobia young girls.
pathophobia disease.
peccatiphobia sinning.
pediculophobia lice.
pellagraphobia pellagra.
peniaphobia poverty.
phagophobia eating.
phantasmophobia ghosts.
pharmacophobia medicine.
phengophobia daylight.
phennophobia voices.
philosophobia philosophy.

phobophobia fear itself.
photophobia light.
phronemophobia thinking.
phthiriophobia lice.
phthisiophobia tuberculosis.
plutophobia wealth.
pnigerophobia smothering.
podophobia feet.
poinephobia punishment.
politicophobia politicians.
polyphobia many things.
ponophobia fatigue.
pornophobia prostitutes.
potamophobia rivers.
proctophobia disease of the rectum.
proteinphobia protein foods.
psychophobia the mind.
psychrophobia cold temperatures.
pyrexiophobia fever.
pyrophobia fire.

R

rhabdophobia being beaten.
rhypophobia filth.
Russophobia Russia, or the Russians.

S

Satanophobia Satan.
scabiophobia scabies.
scatophobia excrement, or obscene language.
scelerophobia burglars.
scoleciphobia worms.
scopophobia, scoptophobia being looked at.
scotophobia the dark.
siderodromophobia railways and train travel.
siderophobia the stars.
sitophobia, sitiophobia food.
spectrophobia mirrors.
stasibasiphobia standing and walking.
sthenophobia strength.
stygiophobia hell.
synophobia togetherness.
syphiliphobia syphilis.

T

tabophobia wasting sickness.
taeniphobia tapeworms.
taphephobia being buried alive.
tapinophobia small things.
technophobia technology.
teleophobia teleology.
telephonophobia using the telephone.
teratrophobia monsters.
Teutophobia, Teutonophobia Germany, or the Germans.
thalassophobia the sea.
thanatophobia death, or dying.
theatrophobia theatres.
theophobia God, or gods.
thermophobia heat.
tomophobia surgical operations.
tonitrophobia thunder.
topophobia certain places.
toxicophobia, toxiphobia poison.
traumatophobia war, or physical injury.
tremophobia trembling.
trichophobia hair.
tridecaphobia the number 13.
tuberculophobia tuberculosis.
tyrannophobia tyrants.

U

uranophobia homosexuality.
urophobia passing urine.

V

vaccinophobia vaccines and vaccination.
vermophobia worms.

X

xenophobia foreigners, or strangers.

Z

zoophobia animals.

Part 3

The Topics

Animals, Birds, Sea Life

CREATURE	MALE	FEMALE	YOUNG	GROUP*	RELATED ADJECTIVE
antelope	buck	doe	kid	herd	
ape, monkey				band, troop, shrewdness	simian, pongid
ass, donkey	jackass	jenny	colt (male), filly (female)	herd, drove, pace	asinine
badger	boar	sow	cub	cete	meline
bear	boar	sow	cub	sloth	ursine
bee				hive, swarm	apian
boar	boar	sow		sounder	
buffalo	bull	cow	calf	herd, obstinacy	
camel	bull	cow	calf	flock	
cat	tom	queen	kitten	clowder	feline
cattle	bull	cow	calf, heifer (female)	herd	bovine, taurine (male)
crab/ lobster/ shrimp					crustacean

*Some group words are merely fanciful and have never been seriously used.

CREATURE	MALE	FEMALE	YOUNG	GROUP*	RELATED ADJECTIVE
crow				murder	corvine
deer	stag, buck	doe	fawn, kid	herd	cervine
dog	dog	bitch	pup, puppy, whelp	kennel, pack	canine
domestic fowl/ pheasant/ partridge, etc.	cock, or *US* rooster	hen	chick, cockerel (male) pullet (female)	brood	gallinaceous
duck	drake	duck	duckling	paddling	
eagle			eaglet	convocation	aquiline
eel			elver	swarm	anguilliform
elephant	bull	cow	calf	herd	elephantine
ferret/ skunk	dog, buck, jack	bitch, gill, jill		business	musteline
fox	dog	vixen	cub	earth, skulk	vulpine
frog/toad			tadpole	army/knot	batrachian
giraffe			calf	herd	
goat	billygoat	nannygoat	kid	herd, flock	caprine, hircine
goose	gander	goose	gosling	gaggle (on ground), skein (flying)	anserine
guinea-pig	boar	sow			
hare	buck	doe	leveret	drove	leporine
horse	stallion	mare	foal, colt (male) filly (female)	herd	equine
kangaroo	buck, boomer	doe	joey	mob, troop	macropine

CREATURE	MALE	FEMALE	YOUNG	GROUP*	RELATED ADJECTIVE
leopard	leopard	leopardess	cub	leap	pardine
lion	lion	lioness	cub	pride	leonine
lizard					saurian
lobster	cock	hen			
mole					talpine
mongoose/ civet					viverrid
mouse/rat	buck	doe			murine
otter	dog	bitch	cub		lutrine
parrot				flock, pandemonium	psittacine
peacock	peacock	peahen		muster	
pig	boar, hog (esp. castrated)	sow, gilt	piglet		porcine, suilline
rabbit	buck	doe			oryctolagine
rhinoceros	bull	cow	calf	crash	rhinocerotic
seal/sea-lion/walrus	bull	cow	pup, cub	pod	otarine, phocoid
sheep	ram, tup	ewe	lamb	flock	ovine
snake					anguine, colubrine, ophidian, serpentine
sparrow					passerine
spider					arachnoid
squirrel				dray	sciurine
swallow				flight	hirundine
swan	cob	pen	cygnet	herd	
thrush				mutation	turdine

CREATURE	MALE	FEMALE	YOUNG	GROUP*	RELATED ADJECTIVE
tiger	tiger	tigress	cub		tigrine
tortoise/ turtle/ terrapin				bale	chelonian
viper					viperine, viperous
whale/ dolphin/ porpoise	bull	cow	calf	school, pod	cetacean
wolf	dog	bitch	pup, cub, whelp	pack	lupine
worm					vermiform
zebra	stallion	mare	foal, colt (male), filly (female)	herd	zebrine

Architectural Terms

A

abacus the flat slab on top of a capital, supporting the architrave.

acanthus a conventionalized representation of the leaf of the herbaceous shrub *Acanthus*, used especially as a decoration for Corinthian column capitals.

adytum the innermost part of an ancient temple.

aisle part of a church, especially one parallel to and divided by pillars from the nave, choir, or transept.

annulet a small fillet or band encircling a column.

anthemion a flower-like ornament.

apse a large semi-circular or polygonal recess, arched or with a domed roof, especially at the eastern end of a church.

arcade a set of arches supporting or set along a wall.

architrave **1** (in classical architecture) a main beam resting across the tops of columns. **2** a moulded frame around a doorway or window. **3** a moulding round the exterior of an arch.

arris a sharp edge formed by the meeting of two flat or curved surfaces.

ashlar a kind of large square-cut stone used in masonry.

astragal a small semi-circular moulding round the top or bottom of a column.

B

baguette a small moulding, semi-circular in section.

bailey **1** the outer wall of a castle. **2** a court enclosed by it.

banderole a stone band shaped like a ribbon-like scroll, bearing an inscription.

baptistery the part of a church, or formerly a separate building next to a church, used for baptism.

barbican the outer defence of a city, castle, etc., especially a double tower above a gate or drawbridge.

bargeboard a board (often ornamental) fixed to the gable-end of a roof to hide the ends of the roof timbers.

barrel vault a vault forming a half cylinder.

bay 1 a space created by a window-line projecting outwards from a wall. **2** a recess; a section of wall between buttresses or columns, especially in the nave of a church etc.

Architecture

A Classical Greek Doric temple

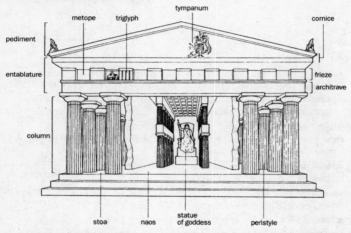

Orders of classical architecture: Greek origin

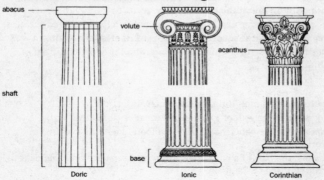

Structure

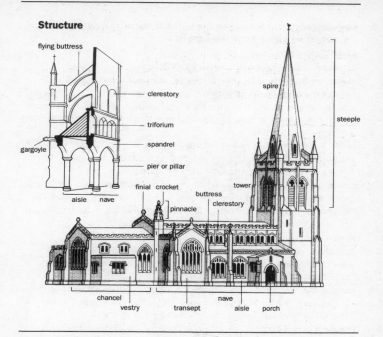

billet each of a series of short rolls inserted at intervals in Norman decorative mouldings.

boss a piece of ornamental carving, etc. covering the point where the ribs in a vault or ceiling cross.

breastsummer a beam across a broad opening, sustaining a superstructure.

broach spire an octagonal church spire rising from a square tower without a parapet.

buttress a projecting support of stone or brick etc. built against a wall.

c

cable a rope-shaped ornament.

cantilever a projecting beam etc. fixed at only one end.

capital the head or cornice of a pillar or column.

cartouche 1 a scroll-like ornament, e.g. the volute of an Ionic capital. **2** a tablet imitating, or a drawing of, a scroll with rolled-up ends, used ornamentally or bearing an inscription.

caryatid a pillar in the form of a draped female figure, supporting an entablature.

chancel the part of a church near the altar, usually enclosed by a screen or separated from the nave by steps.

choir the chancel.

cinquefoil a five-cusped ornament in a circle or arch.

clerestory an upper row of windows in a cathedral or large church, above the level of the aisle roofs.

cloister a covered walk, often with a wall on one side and a colonnade open to a quadrangle on the other, especially in a convent, monastery, college, or cathedral.

coffer a sunken panel in a ceiling etc.

composite of the fifth classical order of architecture, consisting of elements of the Ionic and Corinthian orders.

coping the top (usually sloping) course of masonry in a wall or parapet.

corbel **1** a projection of stone, timber, etc., jutting out from a wall to support a weight. **2** a short timber laid longitudinally under a beam to help support it.

cordon a string-course.

Corinthian of an order of architecture characterized by ornate decoration and flared capitals with rows of acanthus leaves, used especially by the Romans.

cornice **1** an ornamental moulding round the wall of a room just below the ceiling. **2** a horizontal moulded projection crowning a structure, especially the top of an entablature above the frieze.

corona a broad vertical face of a cornice, usually of considerable projection.

cove a concave arch or arched moulding, especially at the junction of a wall with a ceiling.

crenel an indentation or gap in a parapet, originally for shooting through.

crocket a small carved ornament (usually a bud or curled leaf) on the inclined side of a pinnacle etc.

cruck either of a pair of curved timbers extending to the ground in the framework of a type of medieval house-roof.

cupola a rounded dome forming a roof or ceiling, or adorning a roof.

curtain-wall a piece of plain wall not supporting a roof.

cusp a projecting point between small arcs in Gothic tracery.

cyma an ogee moulding of a cornice.

D

dado **1** the lower part of the wall of a room when visually distinct from the upper part. **2** the plinth of a column.

Decorated style the second stage of English Gothic (fourteenth century), with increasing use of decoration and geometrical tracery.

dentil each of a series of small rectangular blocks as a decoration under the moulding of a classical cornice.

dog-tooth a small pointed ornament or moulding, especially in Norman or Early English architecture.

donjon the great tower or innermost keep of a castle.

Doric of the oldest, sturdiest, and simplest of the Greek architectural orders.

dormer window a projecting upright window in a sloping roof.

drip-stone a stone etc. projection that deflects rain etc. from walls.

drum **1** the solid part of a Corinthian or composite capital. **2** a stone block forming a section of a shaft.

duomo an Italian cathedral.

E

echinus a rounded moulding below an abacus on a Doric or Ionic capital.

Early English of the first stage of English Gothic (twelfth–thirteenth centuries), characterized by narrow lancet windows.

engaged (of a column) attached to a wall.

entablature the upper part of a classical building, supported by columns and comprising architrave, frieze, and cornice.

entasis a slight convex curve in a column shaft, to correct the visual illusion that the straight sides are curving inwards.

epistyle an architrave.

F

fan vaulting ornamental tracery in a church roof that spreads out like a series of fans.

fascia **1** a long flat surface between mouldings on a classical architrave. **2** a flat surface covering the ends of rafters.

fenestella a niche in a wall south of an altar, containing the piscina and often the table that holds the Eucharist.

fenestration the arrangement of windows in a building.

fillet a narrow band separating two mouldings, or between the flutes of a column.

finial an ornament finishing off the apex of something; the top of a pinnacle.

flamboyant (of decoration) done in wavy flamelike lines.

flanch (especially of a chimney) to slope inwards towards the top.

flèche a slender spire, often perforated with windows, especially at the intersection of a church nave and transept.

flute an ornamental vertical groove in a column.

flying buttress a buttress slanting from a separate column, usually forming an arch with the wall it supports.

foil a leaf-shaped curve formed by the cusping of an arch or circle.

foliation decoration on an arch or door-head with foils.

fret an ornamental pattern made of continuous combinations of straight lines joined usually at right angles.

frieze the part of an entablature between the architrave and the cornice, often filled with a horizontal band of sculpture.

frontispiece 1 the principal face of a building. **2** a decorated entrance. **3** a pediment over a door etc.

G

gable 1 the triangular upper part of a wall at the end of a ridged roof. **2** a gable-topped wall. **3** a gable-shaped canopy over a window or door.

gambrel a roof like a hipped roof but with gable-like ends.

gargoyle a grotesque carved human or animal face or figure projecting from the gutter of (especially a Gothic) building, usually as a spout to carry water clear of a wall.

gazebo a small building or structure such as a summer-house or turret, designed to give a wide view.

glyph 1 a sculptured character or symbol. **2** a vertical groove, especially that on a Greek frieze.

Gothic in the style of architecture prevalent in Western Europe in the twelfth–fifteenth centuries, characterized by pointed arches.

groin 1 an edge formed by intersecting vaults. **2** an arch supporting a vault.

guilloche an architectural ornament imitating braided ribbons.

H

hammerbeam a wooden beam (often carved) projecting from a wall to support the principal rafter or the end of an arch.

helix a spiral ornament.

hipped-roof a roof with the sides and the ends inclined.

hood-mould a dripstone.

hypostyle a roof supported by pillars.

hypotrachelion the neck of the capital of a column; in the Doric order, the groove between neck and shaft.

I

Ionic of an order of architecture characterized by a column with scroll-shapes on either side of the capital.

J

jamb a side-post or surface of a doorway, window, or fireplace.

K

keystone a central stone at the top of an arch, locking the whole together.

L

lancet a narrow arch or window with a pointed head.

lantern a raised structure on a dome, room, etc., glazed to admit light.

lierne (in vaulting) a short rib connecting the bosses and intersections of the principal ribs.

loggia 1 an open-sided gallery or arcade. 2 an open-sided extension of a house.

louvre 1 each of a set of overlapping slats that admit air and some light and exclude rain. 2 a domed structure on a roof with side openings for ventilation etc.

M

machicolation openings between supporting corbels on a parapet, for dropping things on attackers.

mansard a roof with four sloping sides that become steeper halfway down.

merlon the solid part of a fortified parapet between the openings.

metope a square space between triglyphs in a Doric frieze.

mezzanine a low storey between two others (usually between the ground and first floors).

modillion a projecting bracket under the corona of a cornice in the Corinthian order etc.

motte a mound forming the site of a castle, camp, etc.

moulding an ornamentally shaped outline as an architectural feature, especially in a cornice.

mullion a vertical bar dividing the lights in a window (compare TRANSOM).

mutule a block derived from the ends of wooden beams projecting under a Doric cornice.

N

naos the inner part of an ancient Greek temple.

narthex a railed-off antechamber or porch at the western entrance of a church.

nave the central part of a church, usually from the west door to the chancel and excluding the side aisles.

neck the lower part of a capital.

newel 1 the supporting central post of winding stairs. 2 the top or bottom supporting post of a stair-rail.

Norman the style of Romanesque architecture found in Britain under the Normans.

O

ogee an S-shaped line or moulding.

ogive **1** a pointed or Gothic arch. **2** a diagonal groin or rib of a vault. **3** an S-shaped line.

order any of the five classical styles of architecture (Doric, Ionic, Corinthian, Tuscan, and composite) based on the proportions of columns, amount of decoration, etc.

oriel a large recess, with windows, built out from an upper storey and supported from the ground or on corbels.

ovolo a rounded convex moulding.

P

parpen a stone passing through a wall from side to side with two smooth vertical faces.

parvis **1** an enclosed area in front of a cathedral, church, etc. **2** a church porch.

pediment the triangular front part of a classical building, surmounting especially a portico of columns.

pendentive a curved triangle of vaulting formed by the intersection of a dome with its supporting arches.

Perpendicular of the third stage of English Gothic (fifteenth–sixteenth centuries), with vertical tracery in large windows.

piano nobile the main storey of a large house.

pier **1** a support of an arch or bridge; a pillar. **2** solid masonry between windows etc.

pilaster a rectangular column, especially one projecting from a wall.

piscina a stone basin near the altar in Roman Catholic and pre-Reformation churches for draining water used in the Mass.

plafond an ornately decorated ceiling.

plinth the lower square slab at the base of a column.

podium a continuous projecting base round a room or house etc.

pronaos the space in front of an ancient Greek temple, enclosed by a portico and projecting side walls.

propylaeum the entrance to a temple.

putlog a short horizontal timber projecting from a wall, on which scaffold floorboards rest.

Q

quatrefoil a four-pointed or four-leafed ornament in architectural tracery, like a flower or clover leaf.

quirk a hollow in a moulding.

quoin **1** an external angle in a building. **2** a stone or brick forming an angle; a cornerstone.

R

reeding a small semi-cylindrical moulding or ornamentation.

reglet a narrow strip separating mouldings.

reredos an ornamental screen covering the wall behind an altar.

respond a half-pillar or half-pier attached to a wall to support an arch, especially at the end of an arcade.

Romanesque a style of architecture prevalent in Europe *c*.900–1200, with massive vaulting and round arches (compare NORMAN).

rood-screen a carved screen separating nave and chancel.

rustication masonry with sunk joints or a roughened surface.

S

scantling 1 a timber beam of small cross-section. **2** a set of standard dimensions for parts of a structure, especially in shipbuilding.

scotia a concave moulding, especially at the base of a column.

soffit the under-surface of an architrave, arch, balcony, etc.

spandrel 1 the almost triangular space between one side of an arch, a wall, and the ceiling or framework. **2** the space between the shoulders of adjoining arches and the ceiling or moulding above.

squinch a straight or arched structure across an interior angle of a square tower to carry a superstructure, e.g. a dome.

stoa a portico or roofed colonnade in ancient Greek architecture.

strap-work ornamentation imitating plaited straps.

stria a fillet between the flutes of a column.

string-course a raised horizontal band or course of bricks etc. on a building.

stucco plaster or cement used for coating wall surfaces or moulding into architectural decorations.

stylobate a continuous base supporting a row of columns.

T

taenia a fillet between a Doric architrave and frieze.

talon an ogee moulding.

telamon a male figure used as a pillar to support an entablature.

terminus a figure of a human bust or an animal ending in a square pillar from which it appears to spring, originally as a boundary-mark.

torus a large convex bun-shaped moulding, especially as the lowest part of the base of a column.

trabeation the use of beams instead of arches or vaulting in construction.

tracery ornamental stone openwork, especially in the upper part of a Gothic window.

transept either arm of the part of a cross-shaped church at right angles to the nave.

transom a horizontal stone or wooden bar across a window or the top of a door (compare MULLION).

triforium a gallery or arcade above the arches of the nave, choir, and transepts of a church.

triglyph each of a series of tablets with three vertical grooves, alternating with metopes in a Doric frieze.

Tuscan of the least ornamented of the classical orders of architecture.

tympanum 1 a vertical triangular space forming the centre of a pediment. **2** a similar space over a door between the lintel and the arch.

V

vault 1 an arched roof. **2** a continuous arch. **3** a set or series of arches whose joints radiate from a central point or line.

volute a spiral scroll characteristic of Ionic, Corinthian, and composite capitals.

Art Techniques
and Styles

A

abstract achieving the effect by grouping shapes and colours in satisfying patterns rather than by the recognizable representation of physical reality.

action painting a form of abstract expressionism, with paint applied by the artist's random or spontaneous gestures.

aquarelle painting in thin, usually transparent water-colours.

aquatint the process of producing prints resembling water-colour, from a copper plate etched with nitric acid.

art deco the predominant decorative art style of the period 1910–30, characterized by precise and boldly delineated geometric motifs, shapes, and strong colours.

art nouveau a European art style of the late 19th century, characterized by flowing lines and natural organic forms.

B

baroque a highly ornate and extravagant style of European art of the 17th and 18th centuries.

batik a method (originally Javanese) of producing coloured designs on textiles by applying wax to the parts to be left uncoloured.

bas-relief sculpture or carving in which the figures project slightly from the background.

brass-rubbing impressions produced by rubbing heelball etc. over paper laid on engraved brass.

Byzantine of a highly decorated art style developed in the Eastern Empire.

C

cameo a design carved in relief on hard stone with a background of a different colour (compare INTAGLIO).

cartoon **1** a humorous drawing in a newspaper etc., especially on a topical subject. **2** an artist's full-size drawing on paper as a preliminary design for a painting, tapestry, mosaic, etc.

ceramics the art of making baked clay articles.

champlevé a type of enamelwork in which hollows made on a metal surface are filled with coloured enamels (compare CLOISONNÉ).

chiaroscuro the treatment of light and shade in drawing and painting.

cinquecento the style of Italian art and literature of the sixteenth century, with a reversion to classical forms.

cire perdue a method of bronze-casting using a clay core and a wax coating placed in a mould; the wax is melted in the mould and bronze poured into the space left, producing a hollow bronze figure when the core is discarded.

cloisonné an enamel finish produced by forming areas of different colours separated by strips of wire placed edgeways on a metal backing (compare CHAMPLEVÉ).

collage a form of art in which various unrelated things (e.g. photographs, pieces of paper, matchsticks) are arranged and glued to a backing.

collotype a lithographic print made using a sheet of gelatin exposed to light and treated with reagents.

colour-wash painting using coloured distemper.

constructivism a Russian movement in which assorted (usually mechanical or industrial) objects are combined into non-representational and mobile structural forms.

craquelure a network of fine cracks in a painting or its varnish.

cubism a style and movement in art, especially painting, in which objects are represented as an assemblage of geometrical forms.

D

Dada an early 20th-century movement in art, literature, music, and film, repudiating and mocking artistic and social conventions.

diptych a painting, especially an altarpiece, on two hinged usually wooden panels which may be closed like a book.

dry-point an engraving made with a needle on a bare copper plate without acid.

E

encaustic **1** (in painting, ceramics, etc.) using pigments mixed with hot wax, which are burned in as an inlay. **2** (of bricks and tiles) inlaid with differently coloured clays burnt in.

engraving a print made by cutting a design in lines on a metal plate.

etching a print made by etching a design on a metal plate with acid.

expressionism a style of painting, music, drama, etc. in which the artist or writer seeks to express emotional experience rather than impressions of the external world.

F

fauvism a style of painting associated with the school of Matisse, involving the use of vivid colour.

finger-painting the applying of paint with the fingers.

fresco a painting done in water-colour on a wall or ceiling while the plaster is still wet.

frottage the taking of a rubbing from an uneven surface to form the basis of a work of art.

futurism a movement in art, literature, music, etc. with violent departure from traditional forms so as to express movement and growth.

G

gesso plaster of Paris or gypsum as used in painting or sculpture.

glyptic of carving, especially on precious stones.

gouache a method of painting in opaque pigments ground in water and thickened with a glue-like substance.

grisaille a method of painting in grey monochrome, often to imitate sculpture.

grotesque 1 a decorative form interweaving human and animal features. **2** a comically distorted figure or design.

I

illuminate to decorate (an initial letter, a manuscript, etc.) with gold, silver, or brilliant colours.

impasto the process of laying on paint thickly.

impressionism a style or movement in art concerned with the expression of feeling by visual impression, especially from the effect of light on objects.

intaglio an incised carving on a gem or other hard material (compare CAMEO).

J

Jugendstil the German name for ART NOUVEAU.

K

kinetic art a form of art that depends on movement for its effect.

kitsch garish, pretentious, or sentimental art, usually vulgar and worthless.

L

linocut a print made from a design carved on a block of linoleum.

lithography a process of obtaining prints from a stone or metal surface so treated that what is to be printed can be inked but the remaining area rejects ink.

M

mannerism a style of Italian art preceding the Baroque, characterized by lengthened figures.

marbled (of paper, book edges, etc.) stained to look like variegated marble.

marquetry inlaid work in wood, ivory, etc.

mezzo-rilievo a raised surface in the form of half-relief, in which the figures project half their true proportions.

mezzotint a print produced by roughening the surface of a plate, so that it produces tones and half-tones.

minimalism the use in art of simple or primary forms or structures etc., often geometric or massive.

Minoan of the art of the Bronze Age civilization centred on Crete, *c*.3000–1100 BC.

mobile a decorative structure that may be hung so as to turn freely.

monotype an impression on paper made from an inked design painted on glass or metal.

montage a composition produced from fragments of pictures etc.

morbidezza the delicate painting of flesh tints.

mosaic a picture or pattern made by arranging small variously coloured pieces of glass or stone.

Mughal of the art of the Muslim dynasty in India in the 16th–19th centuries.

mural a painting executed directly on a wall.

N

naturalism the representation of nature realistically and in great detail.

O

op art optical art; a style of painting that gives the illusion of movement by the precise use of pattern and colour.

P

pastel a work of art done in crayons made of powdered pigments bound with gum.

paysage landscape painting.

pentimento the phenomenon of earlier painting showing through paint on a canvas.

photogravure the process of producing images from a photographic negative transferred to a metal plate and etched in.

photomontage the technique of producing a montage with photographs.

pietà a picture or sculpture of the Virgin Mary holding the dead body of Christ on her lap or in her arms.

plein-air representing outdoor scenes.

pointillism a technique of impressionist painting using tiny dots of various pure colours, which become blended in the viewer's eye.

pop art art based on modern popular culture and the mass media, especially as a critical comment on traditional fine art values.

post-impressionism artistic aims and methods developed as a reaction against impressionism, and intending to express the individual artist's conception of the objects represented rather than the ordinary observer's view.

post-modernism a movement reacting against modern tendencies, especially by drawing attention to former conventions.

Pre-Raphaelite of the art of a group of English nineteenth-century artists, including Holman Hunt, Millais, and D. G. Rossetti, emulating the work of Italian artists before the time of Raphael.

primitive 1 a painter of the period before the Renaissance. **2** an untutored painter with a direct naive style.

putto a representation of a naked child, especially a cherub or cupid, in (especially Renaissance) art.

Q

quattrocento the style of Italian art of the 15th century.

R

repoussé ornamental metalwork fashioned by hammering into relief from the reverse side.

Renaissance of the art developed under the revived influence of classical models in the 14th–16th centuries.

rococo of a highly ornamented style of decoration prevalent in eighteenth-century continental Europe, with asymmetrical patterns involving scrollwork, shell motifs, etc.

S

screen printing a process like stencilling, with ink forced through a prepared sheet of fine material, originally silk.

scumble to modify (a painting) by applying a thin opaque coat of paint to give a softer or duller effect.

secco the technique of painting on dry plaster with pigments mixed in water.

sfumato the technique of allowing tones and colours to shade gradually into one another, resulting in indistinct outlines.

sgraffito a form of decoration made by scratching through wet plaster on a wall or through slip on ceramic ware, showing a different-coloured undersurface.

social realism the expression of social or political views in art.

stencil a pattern etc. produced by applying ink, paint, etc. through holes cut in a thin sheet of plastic, metal, card, etc.

still life a painting or drawing of inanimate objects such as fruit or flowers.

surrealism a 20th-century movement in art, aiming at expressing the subconscious mind, e.g. by the irrational juxtaposition of images.

symbolism an artistic movement using symbols and indirect suggestion to express ideas, emotions, etc.

T

tachism a form of action painting with dabs of colour arranged randomly to evoke a subconscious feeling.

tempera a method of painting using an emulsion e.g. of pigment with egg, especially in fine art on canvas.

tondo a circular painting or relief.

trecento the style of Italian art and literature of the 14th century.

triptych a picture or relief carving on three panels, usually hinged vertically together and often used as an altarpiece.

trompe l'œil a still-life painting etc. designed to give an illusion of reality.

V

verism realism in art.

vorticism a school of painting influenced by futurism and using the 'vortices', the engrossing systems and occupations, of modern civilization as a basis.

W

water-colour (US **-color**) a picture painted in pigments diluted with water and not oil.

woodcut a print made, especially as a book illustration, from a relief cut on a block of wood sawn along the grain.

wood-engraving a print made from a relief cut on a block of wood sawn across the grain.

Z

zincograph a print made from a zinc plate with a design etched in relief.

Astronomy Terms

A

aberration the apparent displacement of a celestial body, meteor, etc. caused by the observer's velocity.

absolute magnitude the magnitude, i.e. brightness, of a celestial body as seen at a standard distance of 10 parsecs (opp. APPARENT MAGNITUDE).

alidade an instrument for determining directions or measuring angles.

almucantar a line of constant altitude above the horizon.

aphelion the point in a body's orbit where it is furthest from the sun (opp. PERIHELION).

apogee the point in a body's orbit where it is furthest from the earth (opp. PERIGEE).

apparent magnitude the magnitude, i.e. brightness, of a celestial body as seen from the earth (opp. ABSOLUTE MAGNITUDE).

armillary sphere a representation of the celestial globe constructed from metal rings and showing the equator, the tropics, etc.

asterism a cluster of stars.

asteroid any of the minor planets revolving round the sun, mainly between the orbits of Mars and Jupiter.

astrolabe an instrument, usually consisting of a disc and pointer, formerly used to make astronomical measurements, especially of the altitudes of celestial bodies, and as an aid in navigation.

astronomical unit a unit of measurement in astronomy equal to the mean distance from the centre of the earth to the centre of the sun, 1.495×10^{11} metres or 92.9 million miles.

astronomical year the time occupied by the earth in one revolution round the sun, 365 days, 5 hours, 48 minutes, and 46 seconds (compare SIDEREAL YEAR).

azimuth the angular distance from a north or south point of the horizon to the intersection with the horizon of a vertical circle passing through a given celestial body.

B

big bang theory the theory that the universe began with the explosion of dense matter.

binary star a system of two stars orbiting each other.

black hole a region of space possessing a strong gravitational field from which matter and radiation cannot escape.

C

celestial equator the great circle of the sky in the plane perpendicular to the earth's axis.

celestial globe a spherical representation of the constellations.

celestial horizon a great circle of the celestial sphere, the plane of which passes through the centre of the earth and is parallel to that of the apparent horizon of a place.

celestial sphere an imaginary sphere round the earth on which celestial bodies appear to lie, from the point of view of finding or identifying them.

coelostat an instrument with a rotating mirror that continuously reflects the light from the same area of sky allowing the path of a celestial body to be monitored.

collapsar a black hole.

comet a hazy object usually with a nucleus of ice and dust surrounded by gas and with a tail pointing away from the sun, moving about the sun in an eccentric orbit.

conjunction the alignment of two bodies in the solar system so that they have the same longitude on the celestial sphere as seen from the earth.

constellation a group of fixed stars whose outline is traditionally regarded as forming a particular figure.

continuous creation the creation of the universe or the matter in it regarded as a continuous process.

Copernican system, Copernican theory the theory that the planets (including the earth) move round the sun.

corona 1 a small circle of light round the sun or moon. **2** the rarefied gaseous envelope of the sun, seen as an irregularly shaped area of light around the moon's disc during a total solar eclipse.

cosmogony 1 the origin of the universe. **2** a theory about this.

cosmography a description or mapping of general features of the universe.

cosmology the science or theory of the universe, especially its origin and evolution.

D

declination the angular distance of a star etc. north or south of the celestial equator.

double star two stars actually or apparently very close together.

E

ecliptic the sun's apparent path among the stars during the year.

epact the number of days by which the solar year exceeds the lunar year.

equinox the time or date (twice each year) at which the sun crosses the celestial equator, when day and night are of equal length (compare SOLSTICE).

F

Fraunhofer lines the dark lines in the spectra of the sun and other stars.

G

galaxy 1 any of many independent systems of stars, gas, dust, etc. held together by gravitational attraction. **2 (the Galaxy)** the galaxy of which the solar system is a part.

gibbous (of a moon or planet) having the bright part greater than a semicircle and less than a circle.

L

light year the distance light travels in a year, nearly 6 million million miles.

M

magnitude 1 the absolute or apparent brightness of a star. **2** a class of stars arranged according to this (*of the third magnitude*).

meteor a small body of matter from outer space that becomes incandescent as a result of friction with the earth's atmosphere.

meteorite a fallen meteor, or fragment of natural rock or metal, that reaches the earth's surface from outer space.

Milky Way a faintly luminous band of light emitted by countless stars encircling the heavens; the Galaxy.

moon 1 the natural satellite of the earth. **2** a satellite of any planet.

N

nadir the part of the celestial sphere directly below an observer (opp. ZENITH).

nebula 1 a cloud of gas or dust, sometimes glowing and sometimes appearing as a dark silhouette against other glowing matter. **2** a bright area caused by a galaxy, or a large cloud of distant stars.

neutron star a very dense star composed mainly of neutrons.

nova a star showing a sudden large increase of brightness and then subsiding.

nutation a periodic oscillation of the earth's poles.

O

octant 1 a point in a body's apparent course 45° distant from a given point, especially a point at which the moon is 45° from conjunction or opposition with the sun. **2** an instrument in the form of a graduated eighth of a circle, used in astronomy and navigation.

orrery a model of the solar system.

P

parallax the apparent difference in the position or direction of an object caused when the observer's position is changed.

parhelion a bright spot on the solar halo.

parsec a unit of stellar distance, equal to about 3.25 light years (3.08 × 10¹⁶ metres), the distance at which the mean radius of the earth's orbit subtends an angle or one second of arc.

perigee the point in a celestial body's orbit where it is nearest the earth (opp. APOGEE).

perihelion the point of a planet's or comet's orbit nearest to the sun's centre (opp. APHELION).

precession of the equinoxes 1 the slow retrograde motion of equinoctial points along the ecliptic. **2** the resulting earlier occurrence of equinoxes in each successive sidereal year.

Ptolemaic system, Ptolemaic theory the theory that the earth is the stationary centre of the universe (compare COPERNICAN SYSTEM).

pulsar a cosmic source of regular and rapid pulses of radiation usually at radio frequencies, e.g. a rotating neutron star.

Q

quadrature 1 each of two points at which the moon is 90° from the sun as viewed from earth. **2** the position of a heavenly body in relation to another 90° away.

quasar any of a class of starlike celestial objects having a spectrum with a large red shift.

R

rational horizon celestial horizon.

red shift the displacement of the spectrum to longer wavelengths in the light coming from distant galaxies etc. that are receding.

rille a cleft or narrow valley on the moon's surface.

S

sidereal day the time between successive meridional transits of a star or especially of the first point of the constellation Aries, about four minutes shorter than the solar day.

sidereal time time measured by the apparent motion of the stars in a day.

sidereal year a year 20 minutes 23 seconds longer than the solar year because of precession.

siderostat an instrument for keeping the image of a celestial body in a fixed position.

singularity a point in space-time when matter is infinitely dense.

solar constant the quantity of heat reaching the earth from the sun.

solar system the sun and the celestial bodies whose motion it governs.

solar wind the continuous flow of charged particles from the sun.

solstice the time or date (twice each year) at which the sun is furthest from the equator, about 21 June (summer solstice in the northern hemisphere) and 22 December (winter solstice in the northern hemisphere).

steady state an unvarying condition, e.g. of the universe, with no beginning and no end.

supernova a star that suddenly increases very greatly in brightness because of an explosion ejecting most of its mass.

syzygy conjunction or opposition, especially of the moon with the sun.

T

true horizon celestial horizon.

U

umbra 1 a total shadow usually cast on the earth by the moon during a solar eclipse. **2** the dark centre of a sunspot.

V

vespertine setting near the time of sunset.

W

window an interval during which atmospheric and astronomical circumstances are suitable for the launch of a spacecraft.

Z

zenith the part of the celestial sphere directly above an observer (opp. NADIR).

Botanical Terms

A

abscission the natural detachment of leaves, branches, flowers, etc.

achene a small dry one-seeded fruit that does not open to liberate the seed (e.g. a strawberry pip).

acinus 1 any of the small elements that make up the fruit of the blackberry, raspberry, etc. **2** the seed of a grape or berry.

alga a non-flowering stemless water-plant, especially seaweed and vegetable plankton.

alternation of generations reproduction by alternate processes, e.g. sexual and asexual.

androecium the stamens taken collectively.

anemophilous wind-pollinated.

angiosperm any plant producing flowers and reproducing by seeds enclosed within a carpel, including herbaceous plants, herbs, shrubs, grasses, and most trees (opp. GYMNOSPERM).

annual a plant that lives only for a year or less.

annual ring a ring in the cross-section of a plant, especially a tree, produced by one year's growth.

anther the tip of a stamen containing pollen.

antheridium the male sex organ of algae, mosses, ferns, etc.

axil the upper angle between a leaf and the stem it springs from, or between a branch and a bud.

auxin a plant hormone that regulates growth.

B

bark the tough protective outer sheath of the trunks, branches, and twigs of trees or woody shrubs.

benthos the flora and fauna found at the bottom of a sea or lake.

biennial a plant that takes two years to grow from seed to fruition and die.

bract a modified and often brightly coloured leaf, with a flower or an inflorescence in its axil.

bryophyte a plant of the class that includes mosses and liverworts.

C

calyx the sepals collectively, forming the protective layer of a flower in bud.

cambium a cellular plant tissue responsible for the increase in girth of stems and roots.

capitulum an inflorescence with flowers clustered together like a head, as in the daisy family.

carpel the female reproductive organ of a flower, consisting of a stigma, style, and ovary.

catkin a spike of usually downy or silky male or female flowers hanging from a willow, hazel, etc.

cladode a flattened leaflike stem.

cleistogamic (of a flower) permanently closed and self-fertilizing.

clubmoss any of an order of low often trailing and branching flowerless plants with upright stems of spore-cases.

collenchyma a tissue of cells with thick cellulose cell walls, strengthening young stems, etc.

conifer any tree of a mostly evergreen group usually bearing cones, including pines, yews, cedars, and redwoods.

cordate heart-shaped.

corm an underground swollen stem base of some plants, e.g. crocus.

corolla a whorl or whorls of petals forming the inner envelope of a flower.

corymb a flat-topped cluster of flowers with the flower-stalks proportionately longer lower down the stem.

cotyledon 1 an embryonic leaf in seed-bearing plants. **2** any succulent plant of the genus *Umbilicus*, e.g. pennywort.

cruciferous having flowers with four petals arranged in a cross.

cryptogam a plant with no true flowers or seeds, e.g. ferns, mosses, fungi.

cycad any palmlike plant of the order *Cycadales* (including fossil forms) inhabiting tropical and subtropical regions and often very tall.

cyme a flower cluster in which one flower at the tip develops first and those on lower spikes come later (compare RACEME).

D

deciduous (of a tree) shedding its leaves annually.

dehiscent (of a pod or seed vessel) gaping or bursting open.

dentate toothed; serrated.

dicotyledon any flowering plant with two cotyledons.

dioecious having male and female organs on separate plants.

drupe any fleshy or pulpy fruit whose stone contains one or a few seeds, e.g. an olive, plum, or peach.

drupel a small drupe usually in an aggregate fruit, e.g. a blackberry or raspberry.

E

epigeal **1** having one or more cotyledons above the ground. **2** growing above the ground.

epiphyte a plant growing but not parasitic on another, e.g. a moss.

evergreen (of a plant) retaining green leaves throughout the year.

F

filament the part of the stamen that supports the anther.

flagellum a runner; a creeping shoot.

floret **1** each of the small flowers making up a composite flower head. **2** each of the flowering stems making up a head of cauliflower, broccoli, etc. **3** a small flower.

G

gametophyte the sexually productive form of a plant that has alternation of generations between that and the asexual form.

glume a bract surrounding the spikelet of grasses or the florets of sedges.

graft a shoot or scion inserted into a slit of stock, from which it receives sap.

guard cell either of a pair of cells surrounding the stomata in plants.

gymnosperm any plant with seeds unprotected by an ovary, including conifers, cycads, and gingkos.

gynandrous with stamens and pistils united in one column as in orchids.

gynoecium the carpels of a flower taken collectively.

H

hastate triangular like the head of a spear.

haulm a stalk or stem, especially those of peas, beans, potatoes, etc.

heartwood the dense inner part of a tree-trunk yielding the hardest timber.

heliotropism the directional growth of a plant in response to sunlight.

herbaceous perennial a plant whose growth dies down annually but whose roots etc. survive.

hesperidium a fruit with sectioned pulp inside a separable rind, e.g. an orange or grapefruit.

heterogamy **1** the alternation of generations, especially between sexual and asexual. **2** a state in which a plant has two types of flower.

heterophyllous bearing leaves of different forms on the same plant.

homogamy 1 a state in which the flowers of a plant are hermaphrodite or of the same sex. **2** the simultaneous ripening of the stamens and pistils of a flower.

hydrophyte an aquatic plant, or one which needs much moisture.

hydroponics the growing of plants in sand, gravel, or liquid, without soil and with added nutrients.

I

indehiscent (of fruit) not splitting open when ripe.

inflorescence the complete flower-head of a plant including stems, stalks, bracts, and flowers.

involucre a whorl of bracts round an inflorescence.

L

lanceolate shaped like a lance-head, tapering to each end.

legume the seed pod of a plant of the family *Leguminosae*, including peas and beans.

lichen a usually green, grey, or yellow plant organism composed of a fungus and an alga in association and growing on rocks, tree trunks, walls, etc.

linear long and narrow and of uniform breadth.

liverwort any small leafy or thalloid plant of the class Hepaticae, of which some have liver-shaped parts.

M

monadelphous (of a plant) having the filaments of the stamens joined into one bundle.

monocotyledon any flowering plant with a single cotyledon.

monoecious with male and female organs on the same plant.

moss any small cryptogam of the class Musci, growing in dense clusters on the ground, in bogs, on trees, etc.

mycelium the growing part of a fungus, consisting of microscopic threadlike filaments.

N

nectary the nectar-secreting organ of a flower or plant.

O

ovary the hollow base of the carpel of a flower, containing one or more ovules.

ovate egg-shaped as a solid or in outline.

ovule the part of the ovary of seed plants that contains the germ cell; an unfertilized seed.

P

palea a chaff-like bract, especially in a flower of grasses.

panicle a loose branching cluster of flowers, as in oats.

pappus a group of hairs on the fruit of thistles, dandelions, etc.

parenchyma the usually soft and succulent cell material found especially in the softer parts of leaves, pulp of fruits, bark and pith of stems, etc.

pedicel a small especially subordinate stalklike structure in a plant (compare PEDUNCLE).

peduncle a stalk, especially a main stalk bearing a solitary flower or subordinate stalks (compare PEDICEL).

peltate shield-like.

pepo any fleshy fruit of the melon or pumpkin type, with many seeds and a hard skin.

perennial a plant lasting several years.

perianth the outer part of a flower.

pericarp the part of a fruit formed from the wall of the ripened ovary.

perigynous (of stamens) surrounding the pistil or ovary.

petal each of the parts of the corolla of a flower.

petiole the slender stalk joining a leaf to a stem.

phanerogam a plant that has stamens and pistils, a flowering plant (compare CRYPTOGAM).

phloem the tissue conducting food material in plants.

photosynthesis the process in which organisms, especially green plants, use the energy of sunlight to synthesize carbohydrates from carbon dioxide and water.

phyllode a flattened leaf-stalk resembling a leaf.

pileus the caplike top of a mushroom or other fungus.

pinnate (of a compound leaf) having leaflets arranged on either side of the stem, usually in pairs opposite each other.

pistil the female organs of a flower, comprising the stigma, style, and ovary.

placenta (in flowers) part of the ovary wall carrying the ovules.

pollen the fine dustlike grains discharged from the male part of a flower to fertilize the female ovule.

pome a firm-fleshed fruit in which the central carpels enclose the seeds, e.g. the apple, pear, and quince.

procumbent growing along the ground.

pseudocarp a fruit formed from parts other than the ovary, e.g. the strawberry or fig.

pyrene the stone of a plum, peach, etc.

R

raceme a flower cluster with the separate flowers attached by short equal stalks at equal distances along a central stem (compare CYME).

radicle the part of a plant embryo that develops into the primary root; a rootlet.

receptacle 1 the common base of floral organs. **2** the thalloid or leafy part of some algae where the reproductive organs are.

rhizome an underground rootlike system bearing both roots and shoots.

rootstock 1 a rhizome. **2** a plant into which a graft is inserted. **3** a primary form from which offshoots have arisen.

ruderal (of a plant) growing on or in rubbish or rubble.

runner 1 a creeping plant that can take root. **2** a twining plant.

S

saprophyte any plant or organism living on dead or decayed organic matter.

sapwood the soft outer layers of recently formed wood, between the heartwood and the bark.

schizocarp any of a group of dry fruits that split into single-seeded parts when ripe.

scion a shoot of a plant etc., especially one cut for grafting or planting.

sclerenchyma the woody tissue in a plant, usually providing support.

sepal each of the divisions of the calyx of a flower.

siliqua the long narrow seed-pod of a cruciferous plant.

spadix a spike of flowers closely arranged round a fleshy central column and usually enclosed in a spathe.

spathe a large bract or pair of bracts enveloping a spadix or flower-cluster.

spike a flower-cluster formed of many flower-heads attached closely on a long stem.

spore a specialized reproductive cell of many plants and micro-organisms.

spur a slender hollow projection from part of a flower.

stamen the male fertilizing organ of a flowering plant, including the anther containing pollen.

stele the central cylinder of conducting tissue in the stem and roots of most plants.

stigma the part of a pistil that receives the pollen in pollination.

stock a plant into which a graft is inserted.

stolon a horizontal stem or branch that takes root at points along its length, forming new plants.

stoma a minute pore in the outer cell layer of a leaf.

style the narrow extension of the ovary supporting the stigma.

succulent a plant with thick fleshy leaves, especially a cactus.

sucker a shoot springing from the rooted part of a stem, from the root some way from the main stem, from an axil, or sometimes from a branch.

sympetalous having the petals united.

sympodium the apparent main stem of a vine, etc. made up of successive secondary stems.

syncarp a compound fruit from a flower with several carpels, e.g. a blackberry.

T

tap root a tapering root growing vertically downwards.

testa the outer skin of a seed.

thalamus the receptacle of a flower.

thalloid (of a plant) without conducting tissue and not differentiated into root, stem, and leaves.

torus the receptacle of a flower.

trifoliate (of a compound leaf) having three leaflets.

tuber **1** the short thick rounded part of a stem or rhizome, usually growing underground and covered with modified buds, e.g. in a potato. **2** the similar root of a dahlia etc.

turgor the rigidity of cells due to the absorption of water.

U

umbel a flower-cluster in which stalks nearly equal in length spring from a common centre and form a flat or curved surface, as in parsley.

umbilicus a navel-like formation.

V

vascular plant a plant with conducting tissue.

vernalization the cooling of seed before planting, in order to accelerate flowering.

vernation the arrangement of leaves in a leaf-bud.

X

xylem woody tissue.

Computers and Information Theory

A

access to reach (an area of information); gain access to.

accumulator a register in a computer used to contain the results of an operation.

ALGOL a high-level computer programming language.

analog computer a former kind using physical variables, e.g. voltage, weight, or length, to represent numbers.

ASCII American Standard Code for Information Interchange.

ATM Automated Teller Machine; a machine which carries out banking transactions automatically; a cash dispenser.

B

backup a security copy of data.

bar code a machine-readable code consisting of a series of lines and spaces of varying width, used for stock control on goods for sale, library books, etc.

BASIC a computer programming language using familiar English words, designed for beginners and widely used on microcomputers.

BCD a code representing decimal numbers as a string of binary units.

binary code a coding system using 0 and 1 to represent a letter, digit, or other character in a computer.

binary system a system in which information can be expressed by combinations of the digits 0 and 1 (corresponding to 'off' and 'on' in computing).

bit a unit of information expressed as a choice between two possibilities: 0 or 1 in binary notation.

block a set of data or instructions; a group of locations in a memory, or of words treated as a single unit.

browse to use the appropriate command to see what Internet options are available on a particular topic.

buffer a temporary memory area or queue for data, to aid its transfer between devices or programs operating at different speeds etc.

bug *slang* an error in a computer program or system etc.

byte a group of eight binary digits, often used to represent one character.

C

CD-ROM compact disk read-only memory (for retrieval of text or data on a VDU screen).

character any of a group of symbols, representing a letter etc.

chip a microchip; a small piece of semi-conductor (usually silicon) used to carry electronic circuits.

COBOL a programming language designed for use in commerce.

code a piece of program text.

command an instruction causing a computer to perform one of its basic operations.

computer graphics a mode of processing and output giving visual information on a VDU.

computer virus a hidden code within a computer program, intended to corrupt a system or destroy data stored in it.

cps characters per second.

CPU central processing unit; the principal operating part of a computer; MAINFRAME 1.

cursor a movable indicator on a VDU screen, identifying a particular position in the display, especially the position that the program will operate on with the next keystroke.

D

daisy wheel a disc of spokes extending radially from a central hub, each terminating in a printing character, used as a printer in word processors and typewriters.

database a structured set of data held in a computer, especially one that is accessible in various ways.

data processing a series of operations on data to retrieve or classify etc. information.

debug *colloq.* to identify and remove errors from (a computer program etc.).

dedicated (of a computer) designed for a specific purpose.

default a preselected option adopted by a computer program when no alternative is specified by the user or programmer.

desktop publishing the production of printed matter with a microcomputer and printer.

digital computer one operating on data represented as a series of usually binary digits or in similar discrete form.

disk 1 magnetic disk; a computer storage device consisting of several flat circular magnetically coated plates formed into a rotatable disc. **2** optical disk; a smooth non-magnetic disc with large storage capacity for data recorded and read by laser.

disk drive a mechanism for rotating a disk and reading or writing data from or to it.

DOS disk operating system; a program for manipulating information on a disk.

dot matrix printer one with characters formed from dots.

down (of a computer) unavailable for use, especially temporarily.

E

e-mail messages distributed from one computer system through the Internet to one or more recipients.

F

fax facsimile transmission; the production of an exact copy of a document etc. by electronic scanning and transmission of the resulting data.

file a collection of (usually related) data stored under one name.

floppy disk a flexible removable magnetic disk for the storage of data.

format to prepare (a storage medium) to receive data.

FORTRAN a high-level programming language used especially for scientific calculations.

G

GIGO 'garbage in, garbage out'; the principle that a computer system is only as good as the input it receives.

H

hacker a person who uses computers to gain unauthorized access to data.

hard copy printed material produced by computer, usually on paper, suitable for ordinary reading.

hard disk a large-capacity rigid usually magnetic storage disk.

hardware the mechanical and electrical components of a computer etc. (opp. SOFTWARE).

heuristic proceeding to a solution by trial and error.

high-level language one that is not machine-dependent and is usually at a level of abstraction close to natural language.

hypermedia a method of structuring and presenting text, graphics, sound, etc. so that related items of information occur together.

hypertext machine-readable text so structured that related pieces of text are displayed together.

I

ink-jet printer one that forms characters by squirting ink on to the medium.

input to supply (data, programs, etc. to a computer, program, etc.).

integrated circuit a small chip etc. of material replacing several separate components in a conventional electrical circuit.

interface an apparatus for connecting two pieces of equipment so that they can be operated jointly.

Internet an international network pooling the information held on computer systems in institutions, government agencies, and industry, accessible by modem links, and enabling its users to communicate by e-mail.

intranet a private in-house system corresponding to the Internet.

J

joystick a lever that can be moved to control the movement of an image on a VDU.

K

K a kilobyte; 1,024 (i.e. 2^{10}) bytes as a measure of memory size.

L

light-pen a penlike device held to a VDU screen for passing information on to it.

logic a system or set of principles underlying the arrangement of elements in a computer or electronic device so as to perform a specified task.

low-level language one close in form to machine language.

M

machine-code or **language** a computer language that a particular computer can respond to directly.

machine-readable in a form that a computer can process.

magnetic tape tape coated with magnetic material for recording sound or pictures or for the storing of information.

mainframe 1 the central processing unit and primary memory of a computer. **2** a large computer system.

megabyte 1,048,576 (i.e. 2^{20}) bytes as a measure of data capacity.

memory the storage capacity of a computer.

menu a list of options showing the commands or facilities available.

microcircuit an integrated circuit on a microchip.

microcomputer a small computer with a microprocessor as its central processor.

microfloppy disk one with a diameter of less than $5^1/_4$ inches (usually $3^1/_2$ inches).

microinstruction a machine-code instruction that effects a basic operation in a computer system.

microprocessor an integrated circuit that contains all the functions of a central processing unit.

microprogram a microinstruction program that controls the functions of a central processing unit.

modem a device (a box or card) for transmitting data between computers over a telephone line.

monitor a VDU.

mouse a small hand-held device which controls the cursor on a VDU screen.

N

node a component in a computer network.

O

OCR optical character recognition; the identification of printed characters using photoelectric devices.

on-line (of equipment or a process) directly controlled by or connected to a central processor.

open loop a programmed system of instruction without feedback, each operation or activity being affected only by those earlier in the sequence.

output (of a computer) to supply (results etc.).

P

PASCAL a programming language especially used in education.

PC personal computer; one designed for use by a single individual, especially in an office or business environment.

peripheral (of equipment, e.g. a modem) used with a computer etc. but not an integral part of it.

pixel any of the minute illuminated areas that make up a computer graphics display on a VDU.

preprocessor a program that modifies data to conform with the input requirements of another program.

printout computer output in printed form.

program a series of coded instructions to control the operation of a computer etc.

R

RAM random access memory; a memory having all parts directly accessible, so that it need not be read sequentially.

read-in the entry of data in an electronic storage device.

read-out information retrieved from a computer.

read-write capable of reading existing data and accepting alterations or further input.

real-time (of a system) in which the response time is of the order of milliseconds.

record a number of related items of information which are handled as a unit.

ROM read-only memory; a memory read at high speed but holding permanent instructions, so not capable of being changed by program instructions.

S

save to keep a permanent copy of (a file) in its current state.

scroll to move (a display on a VDU) up or down.

software the programs and other operating information used by a computer (opp. HARDWARE).

subroutine a routine designed to perform a frequently used operation without a program.

surf to scan (the Internet) at random for whatever may seem interesting.

system a group of related hardware units or programs or both, especially when dedicated to a single application.

systems analysis the analysis of operations in data processing, and designing of directions to improve their efficiency.

T

time-sharing the operation of a computer system by several users for different operations at one time.

translator a program that translates from one (especially programming) language into another.

U

up (of a computer) running and available for use.

V

VDU visual display unit; a device displaying data as characters on a screen and usually incorporating a keyboard.

virtual reality the use of computer animation to create the experience of moving about within an environment.

W

web site the point at which any particular item of knowledge in the WWW is located.

window a part of a VDU display selected to show a particular category or part of the data.

word processor a computer system for electronically storing text entered from a keyboard, incorporating corrections, and providing a printout.

WWW World Wide Web; an information system on the Internet which allows the user to move from one document to another, via hypertext links.

WYSIWYG 'what you see is what you get'; the appearance of the text on-screen exactly corresponds to how it will look on a printout.

Currencies

MONEY	COUNTRY
afghani	Afghanistan
baht	Thailand
balboa	Panama
Belorussian rouble	Belarus
birr	Ethiopia
bolivar	Venezuela
cedi	Ghana
colón	Costa Rica, El Salvador
cordoba	Nicaragua
dalasi	Gambia
dinar	Algeria, Bahrain, Croatia, Iraq, Jordan, Kuwait, Libya, Macedonia, Sudan, Tunisia, former Yugoslavia (=Serbia and Montenegro)
dirham	Morocco, United Arab Emirates
dobra	São Tomé and Principe
dollar	Antigua and Barbuda, Australia, Bahamas, Barbados, Belize, Bermuda, Brunei, Canada, Cayman Islands, Dominica, Fiji, Grenada, Guyana, Hong Kong, Jamaica, Liberia, New Zealand, St Kitts and Nevis, St Lucia, St Vincent and the Grenadines, Singapore, Solomon Islands, Taiwan, Trinidad and Tobago, USA, Virgin Islands, Zimbabwe
dong	Vietnam
drachma	Greece
dram	Armenia
escudo	Cape Verde, Portugal
forint	Hungary

MONEY	COUNTRY
franc	Belgium, Benin, Burkina Faso, Burundi, Cameroon, Central African Republic, Chad, Comoros, Congo, Djibouti, Equatorial Guinea, France, Gabon, Guinea, Ivory Coast, Luxembourg, Madagascar, Mali, Niger, Rwanda, Senegal, St Pierre and Miquelon, French Polynesia, New Caledonia, the Wallis and Fortuna Islands, Switzerland, Togo
gourde	Haiti
guarani	Paraguay
guilder	Netherlands, Suriname
hryvnia	Ukraine
kina	Papua New Guinea
kip	Laos
koruna	Czech Republic, Slovakia
krona	Iceland, Sweden
krone	Denmark, Norway
kroon	Estonia
kwacha	Malawi, Zambia
kwanza	Angola
kyat	Myanmar
lary	Georgia
lat	Latvia
lek	Albania
lempira	Honduras
leone	Sierra Leone
leu	Romania
lev	Bulgaria
lilangeni	Swaziland
lira	Italy, Malta, Turkey
litas	Lithuania
loti	Lesotho
mark	Germany
markka	Finland
metical	Mozambique
naira	Nigeria
ngultrum	Bhutan
ouguiya	Mauritania
pa'anga	Tonga
pataca	Macao

MONEY	COUNTRY
peseta	Spain
peso	Argentina, Chile, Colombia, Cuba, Dominican Republic, Guinea-Bissau, Mexico, Philippines, Uruguay
pound	Cyprus, Egypt, Lebanon, Syria, UK
pula	Botswana
punt	Ireland
quetzal	Guatemala
rand	South Africa
real	Brazil
rial	Iran, Oman
riel	Cambodia
ringgit	Malaysia
riyal	Qatar, Saudi Arabia, Yemen
rouble	Russia
rufiyaa	Maldives
rupee	India, Mauritius, Nepal, Pakistan, Seychelles, Sri Lanka
rupiah	Indonesia
schilling	Austria
shekel	Israel
shilling	Kenya, Somalia, Tanzania, Uganda
sol	Peru
som	Uzbekistan
sucre	Ecuador
taka	Bangladesh
tala	Western Samoa
tolar	Slovenia
tugrik	Mongolia
vatu	Vanuatu
won	North Korea, South Korea
yen	Japan
yuan	China
zaire	Zaire
zloty	Poland

Diseases and Physical Disorders

A

acne red pimples, usually on the face.

acromegaly abnormal growth of the hands, feet, and face, caused by excessive activity of the pituitary gland.

Addison's disease a disease with progressive anaemia and debility and brown discoloration of the skin.

AIDS acquired immune deficiency syndrome; caused by a virus transmitted in the blood, marked by severe loss of resistance to infection and often fatal.

allergy the condition of reacting adversely to particular foods, pollen, fur, dust, etc.

Alzheimer's disease a serious disorder of the brain manifesting itself in premature senility.

amenorrhoea an abnormal absence of menstruation.

anaemia (US **anemia**) a deficiency in the blood, usually of red cells or their haemoglobin, resulting in pallor and weariness.

aneurysm an excessive local enlargement of an artery.

angina 1 an attack of intense constricting pain often causing suffocation. **2** angina pectoris; chest pain brought on by exertion, owing to an inadequate blood supply to the heart.

ankylosis abnormal stiffening and immobility of a joint by fusion of the bones.

anosmia loss of the sense of smell.

anthrax a disease of sheep and cattle transmissible to humans.

aphasia loss of ability to speak or understand speech, owing to brain damage.

The Body

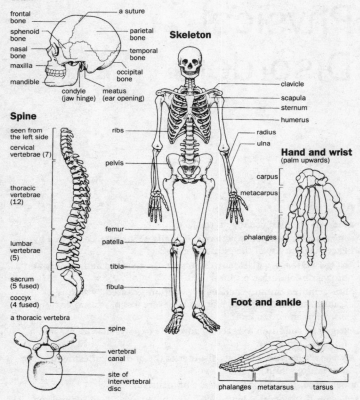

Skull

frontal bone
sphenoid bone
nasal bone
maxilla
mandible
a suture
parietal bone
temporal bone
occipital bone
condyle (jaw hinge)
meatus (ear opening)

Skeleton

clavicle
scapula
sternum
humerus
radius
ulna
ribs
pelvis
femur
patella
tibia
fibula

Spine

seen from the left side
cervical vertebrae (7)
thoracic vertebrae (12)
lumbar vertebrae (5)
sacrum (5 fused)
coccyx (4 fused)

a thoracic vertebra
spine
vertebral canal
site of intervertebral disc

Hand and wrist
(palm upwards)

carpus
metacarpus
phalanges

Foot and ankle

phalanges   metatarsus   tarsus

aphonia loss of the voice through a disease of the larynx or mouth.

appendicitis inflammation of the appendix.

arteriosclerosis hardening of the arteries, especially in old age.

arthritis inflammation of the joints.

asbestosis lung disease caused by inhaling asbestos particles.

asthma a usually allergic respiratory disease, often with paroxysms of difficult breathing.

atherosclerosis narrowing of the arteries by the gradual deposition of cholesterol.

athlete's foot a fungal foot condition affecting especially the skin between the toes.

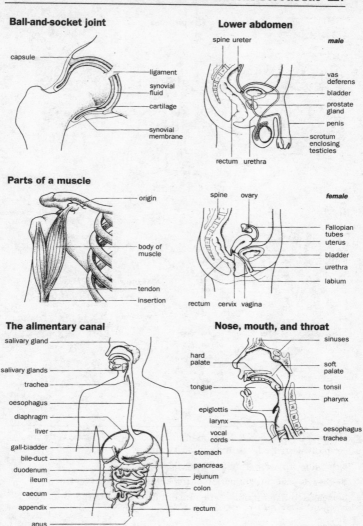

Ball-and-socket joint

capsule
ligament
synovial fluid
cartilage
synovial membrane

Lower abdomen

spine   ureter   *male*
vas deferens
bladder
prostate gland
penis
scrotum enclosing testicles
rectum   urethra

Parts of a muscle

origin
body of muscle
tendon
insertion

spine   ovary   *female*
Fallopian tubes
uterus
bladder
urethra
labium
rectum   cervix   vagina

The alimentary canal

salivary gland
salivary glands
trachea
oesophagus
diaphragm
liver
gall-bladder
bile-duct
duodenum
ileum
caecum
appendix
anus
stomach
pancreas
jejunum
colon
rectum

Nose, mouth, and throat

sinuses
hard palate
soft palate
tongue
tonsil
pharynx
epiglottis
larynx
vocal cords
oesophagus
trachea

B

beriberi inflammation of the nerves due to a deficiency of vitamin B1.

bilharzia a chronic tropical disease, caused by a parasitic flatworm in blood vessels in the human pelvic region.

Respiration

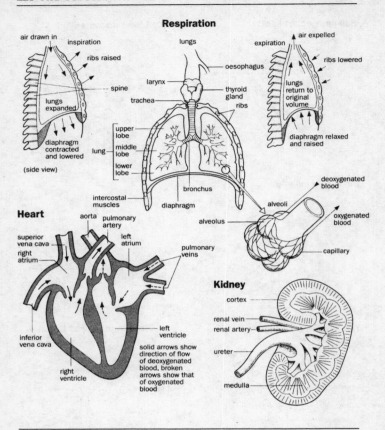

Heart

Kidney

---

blackwater fever a complication of malaria, in which blood cells are rapidly destroyed, resulting in dark urine.

blepharitis inflammation of the eyelids.

Bright's disease inflammation of the kidney; nephritis.

bronchitis inflammation of the mucous membrane in the bronchial tubes.

brucellosis a bacterial disease of cattle, causing undulant fever in humans.

c

cancer disease caused by a malignant growth or tumour from an abnormal and uncontrolled division of body cells; carcinoma.

Brain

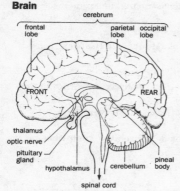

Ear

Eye

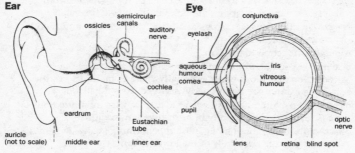

catalepsy a state of trance or seizure with loss of sensation and consciousness, and rigidity of the body.

cataract progressive opacity of the eye-lens, resulting in blurred vision.

cerebral palsy paralysis from brain damage before or at birth, with jerky or uncontrolled movements.

Chagas's disease a kind of sleeping-sickness transmitted by blood-sucking bugs.

chickenpox an infectious disease, especially of children, with a rash of small blisters.

cholera an infectious and often fatal bacterial disease of the small intestine, with severe vomiting and diarrhoea.

cirrhosis a chronic liver disease caused by alcoholism, hepatitis, etc. and marked by degeneration of cells and thickening of surrounding tissue.

coeliac disease a digestive disease of the small intestine brought on by contact with proteins in cereals.

colitis inflammation of the lining of the colon.

conjunctivitis inflammation of the mucous membrane inside the eyelids.

consumption an old word for pulmonary tuberculosis.

coronary thrombosis a blockage of the blood supply to the heart, caused by a blood clot.

cramp painful involuntary contraction of a muscle.

cyanosis a bluish skin discoloration caused by oxygen-deficiency in the blood.

cystic fibrosis a hereditary glandular disease usually resulting in respiratory infections.

cystitis inflammation of the urinary bladder, usually accompanied by frequent painful urination.

D

decompression sickness a condition caused by the sudden lowering of air pressure and formation of bubbles in the blood; the bends.

dengue an infectious viral tropical disease, causing fever and acute pains in the joints.

dermatitis infection of the skin.

diabetes any metabolic disorder with excessive thirst and the production of copious urine; especially diabetes mellitus, in which sugar and starch are not properly absorbed from the blood.

diphtheria an acute infectious bacterial disease with inflammation of the throat, causing difficulty in breathing and swallowing.

diverticulitis inflammation of a blind tube forming at a weak point in a cavity or passage, especially of the lower colon.

Down's syndrome a congenital disorder due to a chromosome defect, characterized by mental retardation and physical abnormalities; Mongolism.

DVT deep-vein thrombosis: blood clots in the legs.

dysentery inflammation of the intestines, causing severe diarrhoea with blood and mucus.

dysmenorrhoea painful or difficult menstruation.

dyspnoea difficult breathing.

E

eclampsia a condition involving convulsions leading to coma, occurring especially in pregnant women.

eczema inflammation of the skin, with itching and discharge from blisters.

elephantiasis gross enlargement of the body, especially of the limbs, due to obstruction of the lymph glands by a parasitic worm.

embolism obstruction of an artery by a blood-clot, air-bubble, etc.

emphysema enlargement of the air sacs of the lungs, causing breathlessness.

encephalitis inflammation of the brain.

enteritis inflammation of the intestines.

epilepsy a nervous disorder with convulsions and often loss of consciousness.

erysipelas a bacterial infection producing red inflammation of the skin, especially of the face and scalp.

F

fibrosing alveolitis inflammation and scarring in the lungs.

fibrositis a usually painful rheumatic inflammation of fibrous tissue.

G

gallstone a small hard mass forming in the gall-bladder.

gangrene death and decomposition of a body part, usually from obstructed circulation.

gastritis inflammation of the stomach lining.

gastro-enteritis inflammation of the stomach and intestines.

German measles an infectious virus disease like mild measles, with a red rash; rubella.

gingivitis inflammation of the gums.

glandular fever an infectious virus disease characterized by swelling of the lymph glands and prolonged lassitude.

glaucoma increased pressure within the eyeball, causing gradual loss of sight.

goitre swelling of the neck, caused by enlargement of the thyroid gland.

gonorrhoea a venereal disease with discharge from the bladder or vagina.

gout inflammation of the smaller joints, especially the toe, caused by an excess of uric acid in the blood.

Graves' disease protrusion of the eyes and swelling of the neck, caused by an overactive thyroid gland.

H

haemophilia (*US* **hemo-**) a usually hereditary failure of the blood to clot normally.

haemorrhoids (*US* **hemo-**) swollen veins round the anus; piles.

hay fever a catarrhal and asthmatic allergy caused by pollen or dust.

hemiplegia paralysis of one side of the body.

hepatitis inflammation of the liver.

hernia protrusion of part of an organ through its containing cavity, especially the abdominal wall.

herpes 1 herpes simplex: a viral infection which may produce blisters or conjunctivitis. **2** herpes zoster: shingles.

Hodgkins' disease a very virulent cancer of lymphatic tissue.

Huntington's chorea a disorder involving jerky involuntary movements and progressive dementia.

hydrocephalus fluid in the brain, especially of children, making the head enlarge and sometimes causing mental deficiency.

hydrophobia rabies, especially in man.

hyperlipidaemia too much fat in the blood.

hypertension too high blood pressure.

hyperthermia abnormally high body temperature.

hyperthyroidism overactivity of the thyroid, causing rapid heartbeat and faster metabolism.

hypoglycaemia deficiency of glucose in the blood.

hypotension too low blood pressure.

hypothermia abnormally low body temperature.

hypothyroidism subnormal activity of the thyroid, causing cretinism and mental and physical slowing.

I

ichthyosis a disease in which the skin becomes dry and horny like fish scales.

impetigo a contagious bacterial skin infection forming pustules and yellow crusty sores.

infarct a small area of dead tissue caused by an inadequate blood supply.

ischaemia reduction of the blood supply to part of the body.

J

jaundice a condition with yellowing of the skin or whites of the eyes, caused by obstruction of the bile duct or by liver disease.

K

kala-azar a tropical parasitic disease transmitted by sandflies.

Kreutzfeld-Jacob disease a brain disease involving the central nervous system.

kwashiorkor malnutrition, especially among children in the tropics, caused by protein deficiency.

kyphosis excessive outward curvature of the spine, causing hunching of the back (opp. LORDOSIS).

L

Lassa fever an acute and often fatal viral fever of tropical Africa.

legionnaires' disease a form of bacterial pneumonia.

leprosy a contagious bacterial disease causing disfigurement.

leptospirosis an infectious bacterial disease of mammals that can be transmitted to man.

leukaemia a form of cancer involving the production of too many white blood cells.

lordosis inward curvature of the spine (opp. KYPHOSIS).

lupus any of various ulcerous skin diseases, especially tuberculosis of the skin.

M

malaria an intermittent fever caused by a parasite and transmitted by the bite of a mosquito.

mastitis inflammation of the breast.

mastoiditis inflammation of the mastoid, a conical projection behind the ear.

ME myalgic encephalomyelitis; a disease involving tiredness, depression, and symptoms like those of influenza.

measles an acute infectious virus disease marked with red spots; rubeola.

meningitis inflammation of the membranes round the brain and spinal cord, due to viral or bacterial infection.

migraine a recurrent throbbing headache, usually on one side, often with nausea and visual disturbance.

Mongolism Down's syndrome.

mountain sickness a sickness caused by the thinness of air at great heights.

multiple sclerosis a chronic and progressive disease of the nervous system, entailing paralysis, speech defects, etc.

mumps a contagious and infectious viral disease with swelling of the glands in front of the ear.

muscular dystrophy hereditary progressive wasting of the muscles.

myasthenia progressive weakening of certain muscles.

myoclonus convulsive action of the muscles.

myxoedema a consequence of hypothyroidism, which results in weight gain, fatigue, mental dullness, and sensitivity to cold.

N

narcolepsy a disease with fits of uncontrollable sleepiness.

nephritis inflammation of the kidneys; Bright's disease.

neuralgia intense intermittent pain along a nerve, especially in the head or face.

O

oedema (*US* **edema**) excess of watery fluid in the body tissues; dropsy.

orchitis inflammation of the testicles.

osteitis inflammation of the substance of a bone.

osteoarthritis a degenerative disease of joint cartilege, especially in the elderly.

osteoporosis a condition of brittle bones caused by hormonal changes or calcium deficiency.

otitis inflammation of the ear.

P

paraplegia paralysis of the legs and part or all of the trunk.

paresis partial paralysis.

Parkinson's disease a progressive disease of the nervous system with tremor, muscular rigidity, and emaciation.

pellagra a disease caused by lack of one of the B vitamins, with cracking of the skin, often resulting in insanity.

peptic ulcer an ulcer in the stomach or duodenum.

pericarditis inflammation of the membrane round the heart.

peritonitis inflammation of the membrane lining the abdomen.

pernicious anaemia defective formation of red blood cells through lack of certain B vitamins.

phenylketonuria an inherited inability to process the aminoacid phenylalaline, ultimately leading to mental deficiency if untreated.

phlebitis inflammation of the walls of a vein.

plague a deadly contagious disease spreading rapidly over a wide area; especially bubonic plague, a bacterial disease with fever, delirium, and swollen glands.

pleurisy inflammation of the membranes round the lungs, with chest pain, fever, etc.

pneumoconiosis a lung disease caused by inhaling dust or small particles.

pneumonia a bacterial infection of one or both lungs.

poliomyelitis an infectious viral disease that affects the central nervous system and can cause paralysis; infantile paralysis.

porphyria a genetic disorder associated with abnormal processing of various pigments.

prickly heat itchy inflammation of the skin, common in hot countries.

psittacosis a contagious viral disease of birds, transmissible to man as a form of pneumonia.

psoriasis a skin disease involving red scaly patches.

puerperal fever fever caused by infection of the womb after childbirth.

pulmonary tuberculosis tuberculosis caused by inhaling the tubercular bacillus into the lungs.

pyorrhoea a disease causing shrinking of the gums and loosening of the teeth.

Q

Q fever a mild fever caused by the parasite that also causes typhus.

quinsy inflammation of the throat, especially an abscess near the tonsils.

R

rabies a contagious fatal viral disease, especially of dogs, transmissible through the saliva to man and causing madness and convulsions; hydrophobia.

rachitis rickets.

rheumatic fever a non-infectious fever with inflammation and pain in the joints.

rheumatism any disease with inflammation and pain in the joints, muscles, or fibrous tissue, especially rheumatoid arthritis.

rheumatoid arthritis a chronic progressive disease causing inflammation and stiffness of the joints.

rickets a disease of children, with softening, especially of the spine and bow legs, caused by lack of vitamin D; rachitis.

ringworm a fungus skin infection causing round inflamed patches; tinea.

rubella German measles.

rubeola measles.

S

St Vitus's dance Sydenham's chorea.

salmonella food poisoning caused by bacteria of that name.

salpingitis inflammation of the Fallopian tubes.

scabies a contagious itchy skin disease.

scarlet fever an infectious bacterial fever, especially of children, with a scarlet rash.

sciatica neuralgia of the hip and thigh; a pain in the sciatic nerve.

scoliosis abnormal sideways spinal curvature.

scrofula a disease with glandular swellings, probably a form of tuberculosis.

scurvy a disease caused by lack of vitamin C, with swollen bleeding gums and the opening of previously healed wounds.

seborrhoea excessive oily secretion from the glands that lubricate skin and hair.

septicaemia blood-poisoning.

shingles acute painful viral inflammation of nerve-cells, with a skin eruption often round the waist.

sickle-cell anaemia a type of severe hereditary anaemia with sickle-shaped blood cells.

silicosis damage to the lungs from breathing dust containing silica.

sinusitis inflammation of a nasal cavity.

sleeping sickness any parasitic tropical disease with extreme lethargy, transmitted by a tsetse-fly bite.

sleepy sickness a viral infection with headache and drowsiness, sometimes leading to coma.

smallpox a former acute contagious viral disease with fever and pustules, usually leaving permanent scars.

spastic *adj.* suffering from cerebral palsy.

spina bifida a congenital spinal defect, in which part of the spinal cord and its enclosing membrane are exposed through a gap in the backbone.

spondylitis inflammation of the vertebrae.

sprue a tropical disease with ulceration of the mucous membrane of the mouth and chronic enteritis.

strangury painful and inadequate passing of urine.

stroke a sudden disabling attack or loss of consciousness, caused by blockage or rupture of a brain artery; apoplexy.

Sydenham's chorea a disorder, especially of children, involving jerky involuntary movements as a form of rheumatic fever; St Vitus's dance.

synovitis inflammation of the membrane whose fluid lubricates joints and tendons.

syphilis a contagious venereal disease progressing from the genitals to other body parts and to the brain.

T

tabes **1** emaciation. **2** locometer ataxia; a form of syphilis.

tachycardia an abnormally rapid heartbeat.

tetanus a bacterial disease of the nervous system, with involuntary muscular spasm.

thrombosis blockage of a blood vessel by clotting.

thrush **1** a disease, especially of children, with whitish blisters in the mouth and throat. **2** a similar disease of the vagina.

tinea ringworm.

tinnitus a ringing in the ears.

tonsillitis inflammation of the tonsils.

toxaemia **1** blood-poisoning. **2** increased blood pressure in pregnancy.

trachoma a contagious eye disease with inflamed roughening inside the eyelids.

trichinosis a disease caused by parasitic worms in meat, with indigestion, fever, and muscular rigidity.

tuberculosis an infectious viral disease characterized by rounded swelling, especially in the lungs.

typhoid an infectious bacterial fever with red spots and severe intestinal discomfort.

typhus an infectious fever caused by a parasitic micro-organism, involving a purple rash, headaches, fever, and usually delirium.

U

undulant fever brucellosis in humans.
urticaria nettle-rash.

V

venereal disease any disease transmitted chiefly by sexual intercourse.

W

whooping cough an infectious bacterial disease, especially of children, with a series of short violent coughs followed by a whoop.

Y

yaws a contagious tropical skin disease with large red swellings.
yellow fever a tropical virus disease with fever and jaundice.

Financial Terms

A

acceptance agreement to meet a bill of exchange.

actuary an expert in statistics, especially one who calculates insurance risks and premiums.

agio 1 the percentage charged on the exchange of one currency into another more valuable. **2** the excess value of one currency over another.

agiotage share dealing, or financial speculation.

amortize 1 gradually to extinguish (a debt) by money regularly put aside. **2** gradually to write off the initial cost of (assets).

arbitrage the buying and selling of stocks or bills of exchange to take advantage of varying prices in different markets.

asset-stripping the practice of taking over a company and selling off its assets to make a profit.

B

backwardation the percentage paid by a person selling stock on the British Stock Exchange for the right of delaying the delivery of it (compare CONTANGO).

balance of payments the difference in value between payments into and out of a country.

balance of trade the difference in value between imports and exports.

bank-rate, base rate the rate of interest per cent per annum fixed from time to time by the Bank of England.

bear a person who sells shares on the Stock Exchange, hoping to buy them back later at a lower price (compare BULL).

bed-and-breakfast to sell and immediately buy (or buy and immediately sell) a share for tax advantage.

bill of exchange a written order to pay a sum of money on a given date to the drawer or to a named payee.

bimetallism a system of allowing the unrestricted currency of two metals (e.g. gold and silver) at a fixed ratio to each other as coined money.

blue-chip of shares of reliable investment, though less secure than gilt-edged stock.

bond a certificate issued by a government or a public company promising to repay borrowed money at a fixed rate of interest at a specified time; a debenture.

bridging loan a loan from a bank etc. to cover the short interval between buying a house etc. and selling another.

broker a member of the Stock Exchange dealing in stocks and shares.

building society a public finance company which accepts investments at interest and lends capital for mortgages on houses etc.

bull a person who buys shares on the Stock Exchange, hoping to sell them at a higher price later (compare BEAR).

C

capital gain a profit from the sale of investments or property.

capital goods goods, especially machinery, plant, etc., used or to be used in producing commodities (opp. CONSUMER GOODS).

capital levy 1 the appropriation by the State of a fixed proportion of the wealth in the country. **2** a wealth tax.

capitalism 1 an economic system in which the production and distribution of goods depend on invested private capital and profit-making. **2** a political system involving the dominance of private owners of capital and production for profit.

cartel an informal association of manufacturers or suppliers to maintain prices at a high level, and control production, marketing arrangements, etc.

cash flow the movement of money into and out of a business, as a measure of profitability, or as affecting liquidity.

c.i.f. cost, insurance, freight (as being included in a price).

consols British government securities without redemption date and with fixed annual interest.

consumer goods goods used by consumers, not used in producing other goods (opp. CAPITAL GOODS).

contango 1 the postponement of the transfer of stock on the British Stock Exchange from one account day to the next. **2** a percentage paid by the buyer for such a postponement (compare BACKWARDATION).

cost-benefit assessing the relation between the cost of an operation and the value of the resulting benefits (*cost-benefit analysis*).

cost push factors other than demand that cause inflation.

cumulative (of shares) entitling holders to arrears of interest before any other distribution is made.

D

debenture an acknowledgement of indebtedness, especially a bond of a British company or corporation acknowledging a debt and providing for payment of interest at fixed intervals.

deflation reduction of the amount of money in circulation to increase its value as a measure against inflation.

demand pull available money as a factor causing inflation.

demurrage 1 a rate or amount paid to a shipowner by a charterer for failure to load or discharge a ship within the time agreed. **2** a similar charge on railway trucks or goods.

depreciation 1 the amount of wear and tear (of a property etc.) for which a reduction may be made in a valuation, an estimate, or a balance sheet. **2** a decrease in the value of a currency.

devaluation reduction in the value of a currency in relation to other currencies or to gold (opp. REVALUATION).

direct tax a tax levied on the person who ultimately bears the burden of it, especially on income.

discounted cash flow the assessment of the present worth of the money in a business, to determine viability.

disinflation a policy designed to counteract inflation without causing deflation.

dividend a sum of money to be divided among a number of persons, especially that paid by a company to shareholders.

dividend stripping the evasion of tax on dividends, by arrangement between a company liable to pay tax and another able to claim repayment of tax.

Dow-Jones index a figure based on the average price of selected stocks, indicating the relative price of shares on the New York Stock Exchange.

E

ECU European Currency Unit.

elastic (of demand) variable according to price.

entrepreneur 1 a person who undertakes an enterprise or business, with the chance of profit or loss. **2** a contractor acting as an intermediary.

equities stocks and shares not bearing fixed interest.

exchange rate the value of one currency in terms of another.

F

fiduciary (of a paper currency) depending for its value on public confidence or securities.

finance company/house a company concerned mainly with providing money for hire-purchase transactions.

financial year a year as reckoned for taxing or accounting (e.g. the British tax year, reckoned from 6 April).

fiscal of public revenue (*fiscal policy*).

float 1 to bring (a company etc.) into being; launch. 2 to offer (stock etc.) on the stock market. 3 (of currency) to be allowed to have a fluctuating exchange rate.

floating debt a debt repayable on demand, or at a stated time.

foreign exchange market the banks etc. that deal in foreign currencies.

free trade international trade left to its natural course without restriction on imports or exports.

FTSE Financial Times Stock Exchange; the index of British Stock Exchange prices; especially the 'footsie', which lists the 100 largest companies.

fund to convert (a floating debt) into a more or less permanent debt at fixed interest.

futures goods and stocks sold for future delivery.

G

GATT General Agreement on Tariffs and Trade; established in 1947 to negotiate the reduction of tariffs etc.

GDP gross domestic product; the total value of goods produced and services provided in a country in one year.

gilt-edged (of securities, stock, etc.) highly reliable as an investment.

GNP gross national product; the gross domestic product and the total net income from abroad.

gold reserve a reserve of gold coins or bullion held by a central bank etc.

gold standard a system by which the value of a currency is defined in terms of gold, for which the currency may be exchanged.

Gresham's law the tendency for money of lower intrinsic value to circulate more freely than money of higher intrinsic and equal nominal value.

H

hard (of currency, prices, etc.) high; not likely to fall in value.

hyper-inflation so rapid a fall in the purchasing power of money as to lead to total economic collapse.

I

index-linked related to the value of a retail price index.

indirect tax a tax levied on goods and services and not on income or profits.

inflation 1 a general increase in prices and fall in the purchasing value of money. 2 an increase in available currency, regarded as causing this.

interest money paid for the use of money lent, or for not requiring the repayment of a debt.

investment trust a trust that buys and sells shares in selected companies to make a profit for its members.

invisible exports (or **imports** etc.) items, especially services, involving payment between countries but not constituting tangible commodities.

L

laissez-faire, laisser-faire the theory or practice of governmental abstention from interference in the workings of the market etc.

liquid (of assets) easily converted into cash.

M

marginal cost the cost added by making one extra copy etc.

market maker a member of the British Stock Exchange granted certain privileges and trading to prescribed regulations.

mercantilism an old economic theory that money is the only form of wealth.

merchant bank a British bank dealing in commercial loans and finance.

monetarism the doctrine that the economy is best stabilized by controlling the supply of money, through interest rates etc.

money market trade on the Stock Market in short-term stocks, loans, etc.

multiplier a factor by which an increment of income exceeds the resulting increment of saving or investment.

N

national income the total money earned within a nation.

negative income tax an amount credited as allowance to a taxed income, and paid as benefit when it exceeds debited tax.

O

OEIC open-ended investment company; a hybrid of a unit trust and an investment trust.

open market an unrestricted market with free competition of buyers and sellers.

ordinary shares shares entitling holders to a dividend from net profits (compare PREFERENCE SHARES).

P

par the face value of stocks and shares.

parity equivalence of one currency with another; being at par.

PAYE pay-as-you-earn; the deduction of British income tax from wages at source.

PEP Personal Equity Plan; a scheme for limited personal investment in shares, unit trusts, etc.

portfolio a range of investments held by a person, a company, etc.

post-obit a bond given to a lender by a borrower, securing a sum for payment on the death of another person from whom the borrower expects to inherit.

preference shares shares or stock whose entitlement to dividend takes priority over that of ordinary shares.

prime cost the direct cost of a commodity in terms of materials, labour, etc.

profit margin the profit remaining in a business after costs have been deducted.

R

rally (of share prices etc.) to increase after a fall.

reflation the inflation of a financial system to restore its previous condition after deflation.

retail price index an index of the variation in the prices of retail goods.

revaluation giving a higher value to a currency in relation to other currencies or gold (opp. DEVALUATION).

revolving credit credit that is automatically renewed as debts are paid off.

risk capital money put up for speculative business investment.

S

scrip 1 a provisional certificate of money subscribed to a bank or company etc., entitling the holder to a formal certificate and dividends. **2** an extra share or shares instead of a dividend.

self-assessment the calculation of income tax by each individual payer rather than by the tax inspector.

shares the equal parts into which a company's capital is divided, entitling their owners to a proportion of the profits.

sinking fund money set aside for the gradual repayment of a debt.

snake a system of interconnected exchange rates for the EC currencies.

stag a person who applies for shares of a new issue on the British Stock Exchange, with a view to selling at once for a profit.

stagflation a state of inflation without a corresponding increase of demand and employment.

stocks 1 shares. **2** money lent to a government at fixed interest.

strong (of a market) having steadily high or rising prices.

supply-side denoting a policy of low taxation and other incentives to produce goods and invest.

T

top slicing the treatment by the tax authorities of income accrued over several years but taken in one year, as having been earned equally over the whole period.

trade cycle recurring periods of boom and recession.

treasury bill a bill of exchange issued by a government to raise money for temporary needs.

U

unit trust a British investment company investing combined contributions from many persons in various securities and paying them dividends in proportion to their holdings.

V

valorize to raise or fix the price of (a commodity etc.) by artificial means, especially by government action.

valuta the value of one currency with respect to another.

VAT value added tax; a British tax on the amount by which the value of an article has been increased at each stage of its production.

visible exports exports consisting of actual goods.

W

wage the part of total production that rewards labour rather than remunerating capital.

write off to cancel the record of (a bad debt etc.); acknowledge the loss of (an asset).

Geological Terms

A

ablation the wasting or erosion of a glacier, iceberg, or rock by melting or the action of water.

agglomerate a mass of large volcanic fragments bonded under heat (compare CONGLOMERATE).

aggregate a mass of minerals formed into solid rock.

anticline a ridge or fold of stratified rock in which the strata slope down from the crest (compare SYNCLINE).

aquifer a layer of rock or soil able to hold or transmit much water.

arenaceous (of rocks) containing sand; having a sandy texture.

asbestos a fibrous incombustible silicate mineral, used for heat-resistance or insulation.

azoic (of an age etc.) having left no organic remains.

B

basalt a dark volcanic rock whose strata sometimes form columns.

batholith a dome of igneous rock extending inwards to an unknown depth.

bauxite a claylike mineral which is the chief source of aluminium.

boss a large mass of igneous rock.

boulder clay a mixture of boulders etc. formed by deposition from massive bodies of melting ice, to give distinctive glacial formations.

breccia a rock of angular stones etc. cemented by finer material.

C

caldera a large volcanic depression.

Cambrian of the first period in the Palaeozoic era, marked by the occurrence of many forms of invertebrate life.

carboniferous 1 producing coal. 2 (**Carboniferous**) of the fifth period in the Palaeozoic era, with evidence of the first reptiles and extensive coal-forming swamp forests.

cataclasis the natural process of fracture, shearing, or breaking up of rocks.

Cenozoic of the most recent era of geological time, marked by the evolution and development of mammals, birds, and flowers (compare MESOZOIC, PALAEOZOIC).

chalk a white soft earthy limestone formed from the skeletal remains of sea creatures.

clastic composed of broken pieces of older rocks.

cleavage the splitting of rocks, crystals, etc. in a preferred direction.

concretion a small round mass of rock particles embedded in limestone or clay.

conglomerate a rock made up of small stones held together (compare AGGLOMERATE).

corrasion erosion of the earth's surface by rock material being carried over it by water, ice etc.

creep the gradual downward movement of disintegrated rock due to gravitational forces, etc.

cretaceous 1 of the nature of chalk. **2 (Cretaceous)** of the last period of the Mesozoic era, with evidence of the first flowering plants, the extinction of dinosaurs, and extensive deposits of chalk.

culm strata under coal measures, especially in SW England.

D

deflation the removal of particles of rock etc. by the wind.

denude to lay (rock or a formation etc.) bare by removing what lies above.

detritus matter produced by erosion, such as gravel, sand, silt, rock-debris, etc.

Devonian of the fourth period of the Palaeozoic era, with evidence of the first amphibians and tree forests.

dogger a large round mass of particles embedded in sedimentary rock.

drum, drumlin a large oval mound of boulder clay moulded by glacial action.

dyke an intrusion of igneous rock across sedimentary strata.

E

Eocene of the second epoch of the Tertiary period, with evidence of an abundance of mammals including horses, bats, and whales.

epicentre the point at which an earthquake reaches the earth's surface.

erratic block a large rock carried from a distance by glacial action.

F

fault an extended break in the continuity of strata or a vein.

flint a hard grey stone of nearly pure silica, occurring naturally as nodules or bands in chalk.

fool's gold iron pyrites.

fossil the remains or impression of a (usually prehistoric) plant or animal hardened in rock.

fumarole an opening in or near a volcano, through which hot vapours emerge.

G

geode a small cavity lined with crystals or other mineral matter.

glacial produced by the presence or agency of ice.

granite a granular crystalline igneous rock of quartz, mica, etc., used for building.

grit coarse sandstone.

H

hade an incline from the vertical.

haematite (*US* **hem-**) a form of iron ore.

hardpan a hardened layer of clay occurring in or below the soil.

Holocene of the most recent epoch of the Quaternary period, with evidence of human development and intervention, and the extinction of large mammals.

horst a raised elongated block of land bounded by faults on both sides.

I

ice age a glacial period, especially in the Pleistocene epoch.

igneous (especially of rock) produced by volcanic or magmatic action.

inlier a structure or area of older rocks completely surrounded by newer rocks.

intrusion an influx of molten rock between or through strata etc. but not reaching the surface.

J

joint a fissure in a mass of rock.

Jurassic of the second period of the Mesozoic era, with evidence of many large dinosaurs, the first birds, and mammals.

K

karst a limestone region with underground drainage and many cavities and passages caused by the dissolution of the rock.

L

lapis lazuli a blue mineral containing sodium and sulphur, used as a gemstone and formerly to make a bright blue pigment.

lava the molten matter which flows from a volcano, forming a solid substance on cooling.

lignite a soft brown coal, between coal and peat.

limestone a whitish sedimentary rock used as building material and in making cement.

lode a vein of metal ore.

lodestone magnetic oxide of iron, which can be used as a magnet.

M

magma the fluid or semifluid material from which igneous rocks are formed.

mantle the region between the crust and the core of the earth.

marble limestone in a metamorphic state capable of taking a polish, used in sculpture and architecture.

Mesozoic of an era of geological time marked by the development of dinosaurs, and evidence of the first mammals, birds, and flowering plants (compare CENOZOIC, PALAEOZOIC).

metamorphic (of rock) having undergone transformation by natural agencies such as heat and pressure.

Miocene of the fourth epoch of the Tertiary period, with evidence for the diversification of primates, including early apes.

moho a boundary of discontinuity separating the earth's crust and mantle.

moulin a nearly vertical shaft in a glacier, formed by surface water percolating through a crack in the ice.

N

neck solidified lava or igneous rock in an old volcano crater or pipe.

O

oil-shale a fine-grained rock from which oil can be extracted.

Oligocene of the third epoch of the Tertiary period, with evidence of the first primates.

Ordovician of the second period of the Palaeozoic era, with evidence of the first vertebrates and an abundance of marine invertebrates.

orogeny the process of the formation of mountains.

outcrop a stratum, vein, or rock, emerging at the surface.

outlier a younger rock formation isolated in older rocks.

P

Palaeocene (*US* **Paleo-**) of the earliest epoch of the Tertiary period, with evidence of the emergence and development of mammals.

Palaeozoic (also **Paleo-**) of an era of geological time marked by the appearance of marine and terrestrial plants and animals, especially invertebrates (compare CENOZOIC, MESOZOIC).

peneplain a fairly flat area of land produced by erosion.

Permian of the last period of the Palaeozoic era, with evidence of the development of reptiles and amphibians, and deposits of sandstone.

pitchblende a mineral occurring in pitchlike masses and yielding radium.

plate tectonics the study of the earth's surface based on the concept of moving 'plates', the rigid sheets of rock thought to form the earth's outer crust.

Pleistocene of the first epoch of the Quaternary period, marked by great fluctuations in temperature, with glacial periods followed by interglacial periods; the Ice Age.

Pliocene of the last epoch of the Tertiary period, with evidence of the extinction of many mammals and the development of that primate family which includes humans.

plug a mass of solidified lava filling the neck of a volcano.

plutonic (of rock) formed as igneous rock by solidification below the earth's surface.

Precambrian of the earliest era of geological time, from the formation of the earth to the first forms of life.

Proterozoic of the later part of the Precambrian era, characterized by the oldest forms of life.

pumice a light porous volcanic rock often used as an abrasive for cleaning or polishing.

pyrites a shiny yellow form of iron.

pyroclastic (of rocks etc.) formed as the result of a volcanic eruption.

Q

quartz a mineral form of silica that crystallizes as hexagonal prisms.

Quaternary of the most recent period of the Cenozoic era, with evidence of many species of present-day plants and animals.

R

reliquiae fossil remains of animals or plants.

reverse strata a fault in which the overlying side of a mass of rock is displaced upward in relation to the underlying side.

rock any natural material, hard or soft (e.g. clay) consisting of one or more minerals.

rudaceous (of rock) composed of fairly large fragments.

S

sandstone 1 any rock composed of particles visible to the naked eye. **2** a sedimentary rock of consolidated sand, usually red, yellow, brown, grey, or white.

sarsen a sandstone boulder carried by ice during a glacial period.

schist a stratified metamorphic rock composed of layers of different minerals and splitting into thin irregular plates.

scree a mountain slope covered with small loose stones.

sedimentary (of rock) composed of matter that was carried by water or wind and deposited on the surface of the land to become consolidated.

selvage an alteration zone at the edge of a rock mass.

series 1 a set of strata with a common characteristic. 2 the rocks deposited during a specific epoch.

shale soft finely stratified rock that splits easily, consisting of consolidated mud or clay.

shear a strain produced by pressure in the structure of a substance, when its layers are laterally shifted in relation to each other.

silica a form of the element silicon occurring as quartz etc. and as a principal constituent of sandstone and other rocks.

sill a flat sheet of igneous rock intruded between other rocks and parallel with their plane.

Silurian of the third period of the Palaeozoic era, with evidence of the first fish and land plants, and the formation of mountains and new land areas.

slate a fine-grained grey, green, or bluish-purple metamorphic rock easily split into flat, smooth plates.

stalactite a deposit of calcium in the form of an icicle hanging from the roof of a cave etc. and formed by the trickling of water.

stalagmite a corresponding deposit of calcium in the form of an inverted icicle rising from the floor of a cave etc. and formed by the dripping of water.

syncline a rock-bed forming a trough (opp. ANTICLINE).

T

talus a sloping mass of fragments at the foot of a cliff.

tephra fragmented rock etc. ejected by a volcanic eruption.

Tertiary of the first period in the Cenozoic era, with evidence of the development of mammals and flowering plants.

transgress (of the sea) to spread over (the land).

Triassic of the earliest period of the Mesozoic era, with evidence of an abundance of reptiles (including the earliest dinosaurs) and the emergence of mammals.

tuff rock formed by the consolidation of volcanic ash.

vesicle a cavity in volcanic rock produced by gas bubbles.

X

xenolith an inclusion within an igneous rock mass.

Heraldry

A

achievement an escutcheon with devices in memory of a distinguished feat.

argent silver; silvery white.

arms heraldic devices.

azure blue.

B

bar a narrow horizontal stripe across a shield.

base the lowest part of a shield.

baton a narrow truncated bend.

bearing a device or charge.

bend a diagonal stripe from top right to bottom left of a shield.

bezant a gold disc.

blazon a shield, bearings, or banner.

bordure a border round the edge of a shield.

C

canting arms arms containing an allusion to the name of the bearer.

canton a square division, less than a quarter, in the upper (usually dexter) corner of a shield.

charge a device; a bearing.

chevron a bent bar of an inverted V shape.

chief the upper third of a shield.

coat of arms the heraldic bearings or shield of a person, family, or corporation.

cockatrice a fabulous animal, a cock with a serpent's tail.

cognizance a distinctive device or mark.

couchant (of an animal) lying with the body resting on the legs and the head raised.

crest a device above the shield and helmet of a coat of arms.

D

dexter on the right-hand side (the observer's left) of a shield etc.

difference an alteration in a coat of arms distinguishing members of a family.

dormant (of a beast) lying with its head on its paws.

E

embattled like battlements in form.

ermine a white fur marked with black spots.

escutcheon a shield or emblem bearing a coat of arms.

F

fess a horizontal stripe across the middle of a shield.

field the surface of an escutcheon or one of its divisions.

fimbriate having a narrow border.

fleur-de-lys a lily composed of three petals bound together near the base.

fleury decorated with fleurs-de-lys.

fret a device of narrow bands and a diamond interlaced.

fur a representation of tufts on a plain ground.

G

guardant depicted with the body sideways and the face towards the viewer.

gules red.

H

hatchment a large usually diamond-shaped tablet with a deceased person's armorial bearings, affixed to that person's house, tomb, etc.

I

impale to combine (two coats of arms) by placing them side by side on one shield, separated by a vertical line down the middle.

issuant (especially of a beast with only the upper part shown) rising from the bottom or top of a bearing.

L

label the mark of an eldest son, consisting of a superimposed horizontal bar with usually three downward projections.

lambrequin a mantling.

lozenge a diamond-shaped device.

M

mantling ornamental drapery etc. behind and round a shield.

martlet an imaginary footless bird borne as a charge.

moline (of a cross) having each extremity broadened and curved back.

mound a ball of gold etc. representing the earth and usually surmounting a crown.

O

or gold or yellow.

ordinary a charge of the earliest, simplest, and commonest kind; a bar, cross, etc.

orle a narrow band or border of charges near the edge of a shield.

P

pale a vertical stripe in the middle of a shield.

pall a Y-shaped bearing with crosses, representing the front of an ecclesiastical vestment.

paly divided into equal vertical shapes.

passant (of a beast) walking and looking to the dexter side, with three paws on the ground and the right forepaw raised.

pile a wedge-shaped device.

potent with a crutch-head shape.

proper in the natural, not conventional, colours.

purpure purple.

Q

quarter each of four divisions on a shield.

quarterings the coats of arms marshalled on a shield to denote the alliances of a family with the heiresses of others.

quarterly in the four, or in two diagonally opposite, quarters of a shield.

R

rampant (of a beast) standing on its left hind foot with its forepaws in the air.

regardant looking backwards.

rustre a lozenge with a round hole.

S

sable black.

salient (of a lion etc.) standing on its hind legs with the forepaws raised.

saltire two diagonal stripes forming a St Andrew's cross.

sanguine blood red.

sejant (of a beast) sitting upright on its haunches.

seme sprinkled with small stars, fleurs-de-lys, etc.

shield a stylized representation of a shield used for displaying a coat of arms etc.

sinister on the left-hand side (the observer's right) of a shield etc.

supporter an animal etc., usually one of a pair, holding up or standing beside an escutcheon.

T

tierced divided into three parts with different tinctures.

tincture any metal, colour, or fur used in coats of arms.

V

vair fur represented by small shield-shaped or bell-shaped figures usually alternately azure and argent.

vert green.

voided (of a bearing) having the middle cut away to show the field.

W

wyvern a winged two-headed dragon with a barbed tail.

Language

A

ablative the case (especially in Latin) of nouns and pronouns, and words in agreement with them, indicating an agent, instrument, or location.

ablaut a change of vowels in related words or forms, especially in Indo-European languages, e.g. in *sing, sang, sung*.

absolute **1** (of a construction) syntactically independent of the rest of the sentence, as in *dinner being over, we left*. **2** (of an adjective or verb) used without its noun or object, e.g. *the deaf, guns kill*.

accidence the part of grammar that deals with the variable parts or inflections of words (compare SYNTAX).

accusative the case of nouns, pronouns, and adjectives, expressing the object of an action or the goal of motion.

acronym a word, usually pronounced as such, formed from the initial letters of other words, e.g. *laser, Nato*.

active the form of a verb that attributes the action to the person or thing that performs it, e.g. the verbs in *guns kill; we saw him*.

adjunct a word or phrase used to explain or amplify the predicate, subject, etc.

affix an addition placed at the beginning or end or in the middle of a word to modify its meaning; a prefix, suffix, or infix.

affricate a sound combining a plosive with an immediately following fricative, e.g. the *ch* of *chin*.

agentive indicating the one that performs the action, e.g. the *-er* of *farmer*.

agglutinative (of language) combining simple words without change of form to express compound ideas.

agree to have the same number, gender case, or person as.

alliteration the recurrence of the same sound at the beginning of adjacent or nearby words, e.g. in *cool, calm, and collected*.

allomorph any of two or more alternative forms of a morpheme.

allophone any of the variant sounds forming a single phoneme.

alveolar (of a consonant) pronounced with the tip of the tongue touching the ridge behind the front teeth.

anacoluthon a sentence or construction which lacks grammatical sequence, e.g. *where can I oh thank you.*

anacrusis an unstressed syllable at the beginning of a verse of poetry.

analytical (of a language) using separate words instead of inflections (compare SYNTHETIC).

anaphora 1 the repetition of a word or phrase at the beginning of successive clauses. **2** the use of a word referring to or replacing one earlier in a sentence, e.g. *do* in *I like it and so do they.*

anastrophe the reversion of the usual order of words or clauses.

antecedent a word, phrase, clause, or sentence to which another word (especially a relative pronoun, usually following) refers.

antinomy a contradiction between two beliefs or conclusions that are themselves reasonable; a paradox.

antithesis 1 (usually followed by *of, between*) contrast or opposition between two things. **2** a contrast of ideas, expressed by parallelism of strongly contrasted words.

antonomasia 1 the substitution of an epithet or title etc. for a name, e.g. *his Grace* for an archbishop. **2** the use of a name for a general idea, e.g. *a Scrooge* for a miser.

antonym a word opposite in meaning to another, e.g. *bad* and *good.*

aorist an unqualified past tense of a verb (especially in Greek), without reference to duration or completion.

aphesis the gradual loss of an unstressed vowel at the beginning of a word, e.g. of *e* from *esquire* to form *squire.*

apocope the omission of part of the end of a word, as in the formation of *curio* from *curiosity.*

apodosis the main clause of a conditional sentence, e.g. *I would agree* in *if you asked me I would agree.*

apostrophe an exclamatory passage in a speech or poem, addressed to a person (often dead or absent) or thing (often personified).

appellative (of a noun) designating a class; common.

apposition the placing of a word, especially a noun, next to another, to qualify or explain the first, e.g. *William the Conqueror, my friend Sue.*

aspect a verbal category or form expressing beginning, duration, or completion.

assimilation the making of a sound more like another in the same or next word.

assonance the resemblance of sounds between two nearby words, as to either the vowels or the consonants, without making a true rhyme, e.g. *sonnet, porridge,* and *killed, cold.*

asyndeton the omission of a conjunction.

attributive (of an adjective or noun) preceding and describing a word, e.g. *old* in the *old dog* (but not in *the dog is old*) and *expiry* in *expiry date.*

auxiliary verb one used in forming tenses, moods, and voices of other verbs.

B

back-formation a word formed from its seeming derivative, e.g. *laze* from *lazy.*

back slang slang using words spelt backwards, e.g. *yob.*

base a root or stem as the origin of a word or a derivative.

bilabial (of a sound) made with closed or nearly closed lips.

blend a portmanteau word.

boustrophedron (of written words) from right to left and left to right in alternate lines.

C

calque a loan-translation.

cant language peculiar to a class, profession, etc.; jargon.

cardinal numbers those denoting quantity: *one, two, three,* etc.

case 1 the relation of a word to other words in the sentence. **2** a form of a noun, adjective, or pronoun expressing this.

causative expressing cause.

cedilla 1 a mark written under the letter *c*, especially in French, to show that it is sibilant (as in façade). **2** a similar mark under *s*, in Turkish and other oriental languages.

chiasmus inversion in the second of two parallel phrases of the order followed in the first, e.g. *to stop, too fearful, and too faint to go.*

clause a distinct part of a sentence, including a subject and predicate.

cliché a hackneyed phrase.

closed syllable one ending in a consonant.

cognate (of a word) belonging to the same linguistic family as another, e.g. English *father*, German *Vater*, Latin *pater.*

cognate object an object related in origin and sense to its verb, e.g. in *live a good life.*

collective noun one that is grammatically singular but denotes a group, e.g. *assembly, troop.*

collocation the juxtaposition of one word with another.

common (of gender) referring to individuals of either sex, e.g. *teacher*.

common noun a name denoting a class or concept as opposed to an individual, e.g. *boy, chocolate, beauty*.

comparative (of an adjective or adverb) expressing a higher but not the highest degree of a quality, e.g. *braver, more fiercely* (compare POSITIVE, SUPERLATIVE).

comparison the positive, comparative, and superlative degrees of adjectives and adverbs.

complement a word or phrase added to a verb to complete the predicate of a sentence.

complex sentence one containing a subordinate clause or clauses.

compound sentence a sentence with more than one subject or predicate.

concessive 1 (of a preposition or conjunction) introducing a phrase or clause which might be expected to preclude the action of the main clause, but does not, e.g. *in spite of, although*. **2** (of a phrase or clause) introduced in this way.

concord agreement between words in gender, number, etc.

conditional (of a clause, mood, etc.) expressing a condition.

conjugation a system of verbal inflection.

coordinate (of parts of a compound sentence) equal in status (compare SUBORDINATE).

copula a word, in English especially a part of the verb *be*, connecting a subject and predicate.

copulative 1 (of a word) connecting words or clauses linked in sense (compare DISJUNCTIVE). **2** connecting a subject and predicate.

correlative (of words) corresponding to each other and regularly used together, e.g. *neither* and *nor*.

countable (of a noun) that can form a plural or be used with the indefinite article, e.g. *book, kindness*.

Creole a language formed from the contact of a European language, especially English, French, or Portuguese, with another (especially African) language.

D

dative the case of nouns and pronouns, and words grammatically agreeing with them, indicating an indirect object or recipient.

declension 1 the variation in the form of a noun, pronoun, or adjective, which identifies its case, number, and gender. **2** the class in which a noun etc. is put according to the exact form of this variation.

defective not having all the usual inflections.

deictic a pointing, demonstrative word.

demonstrative (of an adjective or pronoun) indicating the person or thing referred to, e.g. *this*, *that*, *those*.

dependent (of a clause, phrase, or word) subordinate to a sentence or word.

deponent (of a verb, especially in Latin or Greek) passive or middle in form but active in meaning.

derivation 1 the formation of a word from another word or from a root. **2** a word derived from another, e.g. *quickly* from *quick*.

determiner any of a class of words, e.g. *a*, *the*, *every*, that determine the kind of reference a noun or noun-substitute has.

diachronic concerned with the historical development of a language (opp. SYNCHRONIC).

diacritic a sign (e.g. an accent, diaeresis, cedilla) used to indicate different sounds or values of a letter.

diaeresis 1 a mark (as in naïve) over a vowel to indicate that it is sounded separately. **2** a break where a metric foot ends at the end of a word.

dialect 1 a form of speech peculiar to a region. **2** a subordinate variety of a language, with non-standard vocabulary, pronunciation, or grammar.

digraph a group of two letters representing one sound, as in *ph* and *ey*.

diminutive (of a word or suffix) implying smallness, e.g. *-let*, *-kin*.

diphthong 1 a speech sound in one syllable in which the articulation moves from one vowel to another, as in *coin*, *loud*, *side*. **2** two letters representing the sound of a diphthong or single vowel, as in *feat*.

direct object the primary object of the action of a transitive verb.

direct speech words actually spoken, not reported in the third person (compare REPORTED SPEECH).

disjunctive (especially of a conjunction) expressing a choice between two words etc., e.g. *or* in *asked if he was going or staying*.

distributive (of a pronoun etc.) referring to each individual of a class, not to the class collectively, e.g. *each*, *either*.

double negative a negative statement containing two negations, e.g. *didn't say nothing*.

dual (in some languages) denoting two people or things (additional to singular and plural).

E

elision the omission of a vowel or syllable in pronouncing, as in *I'm*, *let's*.

ellipsis 1 the omission from a sentence of words needed to complete the construction or sense. **2** a set of three dots indicating an omission.

enclitic (of a word) pronounced with so little emphasis that it forms part of the preceding word.

epicene denoting either sex without change of gender.

epistrophe the repetition of a word at the end of successive clauses.

euphemism a mild or vague expression substituted for one thought to be too harsh or direct, e.g. *pass over* for *die*.

F

feminine of or denoting the gender proper to women's names.

final clause a clause expressing purpose, introduced by *in order that, lest,* etc.

finite (of part of a verb) having a specific number and person.

folk etymology a popular modification of a word or phrase to make it seem more familiar, e.g. *sparrow-grass* for *asparagus*.

franglais a corrupt version of French, using many words and idioms borrowed from English.

frequentative a verbal form expressing frequent repetition or intensity, e.g. *chatter, twinkle*.

fricative a consonant made by the friction of breath through a narrow opening, e.g. *f* and *h*.

future (of a tense or participle) expressing an event yet to happen.

future perfect a tense giving the sense *will have done*.

G

gender the grammatical classification of nouns and related words, roughly corresponding to the two sexes and to sexlessness.

generative grammar a set of rules whereby permissible sentences may be generated from the elements of a language.

genitive the case of nouns, pronouns, etc. corresponding to *of, from,* and such other prepositions as indicate possession or close association.

gerund a form of a verb functioning as a noun, ending in *-ndum* (declinable) in Latin, and in *-ing* in English, as in *do you mind my asking you?*

gerundive a form of a Latin verb ending in *-ndus* (declinable) and functioning as an adjective meaning 'that should or must be done'.

glottal stop a sound produced by the sudden opening or shutting of the glottis, between the top of the windpipe and the vocal cords, as in a common non-standard pronunciation of the *ttl* of *bottle*.

govern (especially of a verb or preposition) to have (a noun or pronoun or its case) depending on it.

grammar **1** the rules of the way a language shows the relation between words, including its sound system. **2** a person's application of the rules of grammar.

H

hard (of a consonant) guttural, as with *c* in *cat*, *g* in *go*.

hendiadys the expression of an idea by two words joined by 'and' instead of by modification, e.g. *nice and warm* for *nicely warm*.

hiatus a break between two vowels coming together but not in the same syllable, as in *go on*.

hieroglyphics writing consisting of pictures representing a word, syllable, or sound, as in ancient Egyptian.

homograph a word spelt like another but of different meaning or origin, e.g. *light* (=not dark) and *light* (=not heavy).

homonym a homograph or homophone.

homophone a word with the same sound as another but of different meaning or origin, e.g. *pair* and *pear*.

hyperbaton the inversion of normal word order, especially for emphasis, e.g. *this I must see*.

hyperbole an exaggerated statement not meant to be taken literally.

hysteron proteron a figure of speech involving inversion of the natural order, e.g. *I die! I faint! I fail!*

I

imperative (of a mood) expressing a command, e.g. *come here!*

imperfect (of a tense) denoting a usually past action in progress but not completed at the time in question, e.g. *they were singing*.

impersonal (of a verb) used only with a formal subject and expressing an event with no real subject, e.g. *it is snowing*.

indicative (of a mood) denoting simple statement of a fact.

indirect object a person or thing affected by a verbal action but not primarily acted on, e.g. *him* in *give him the book*.

indirect speech reported speech.

Indo-European the family of languages spoken over most of Europe and Asia as far as Northern India.

infinitive a form of a verb without reference to a subject, tense, etc., e.g. *see* in *we came to see*, *let him see*.

infix an affix inserted into the body of a word.

inflection the process of changing the form of a word to express tense, gender, number, mood, etc.

instrumental the case of nouns and pronouns, and of words in grammatical agreement with them, indicating a means or instrument.

intensive (of an adjective, adverb, etc.) expressing intensity; giving force, e.g. *really* in *my feet are really cold.*

interrogative a word asking a question, e.g. *who? what? why?*

intransitive (of a verb or sense of a verb) that does not take or require a direct object, whether expressed or implied, e.g. *look* in *look at the sky* (opp. TRANSITIVE).

irregular (of a verb, noun, etc.) not inflected according to the usual rules.

iterative frequentative.

J

jussive expressing a command.

L

langue d'oc the form of medieval French spoken south of the Loire, the basis of modern Provençal.

langue d'oïl medieval French as spoken north of the Loire, the basis of modern French.

lexeme a basic lexical unit of a language, comprising one or several words, the elements of which do not separately convey the meaning of the whole.

lexical of the words of a language.

liaison the sounding of an ordinarily silent final consonant before a word beginning with a vowel (or a mute *h* in French).

litotes ironical understatement, especially the expressing of an affirmative by the negative of its contrary, e.g. *I shan't be sorry* for *I shall be glad.*

loan-translation an expression adopted by one language from another in a more or less literally translated form.

loanword a word adopted, usually with little modification, from a foreign language.

locative the case of nouns, pronouns, and adjectives, expressing location.

M

malapropism the use of a word in mistake for one sounding similar, to comic effect, e.g. *allegory* for *alligator.*

masculine of or denoting the gender proper to men's names.

mass noun a noun that is not countable and cannot be used with the indefinite article or in the plural, e.g. *bread.*

metaphor a name or descriptive term or phrase applied to an object or action to which it is imaginatively but not literally applicable, as in *a glaring error.*

metathesis the transposition of sounds or letters in a word.

metonymy the substitution of the name of an attribute or adjunct for that of the thing meant, e.g. *Crown* for *king*; *the turf* for *horse-racing.*

middle voice the voice of (especially Greek) verbs that express reciprocal or reflexive action.

modal verb an auxiliary verb (e.g. *would*) used to express the mood of another verb.

modifier a word, especially an adjective or noun used attributively, that qualifies the sense of another word, e.g. *good* and *family* in *a good family house.*

mood a form or set of forms of a verb indicating whether it expresses fact, command, wish, etc., e.g. *the subjunctive mood.*

morpheme a meaningful unit of a language that cannot be further divided, e.g. *in*, *come*, *-ing*, forming *incoming.*

N

neologism a new word or expression.

neuter neither masculine nor feminine.

nominal used like a noun.

nominative the case of nouns, pronouns, and adjectives, expressing the subject of a verb.

nonce-word a word coined for one occasion.

number the classification of words by their singular or plural forms.

O

object a noun or its equivalent governed by an active transitive verb or by a preposition.

objective (of a case or word) constructed as or appropriate to the object of a transitive verb or preposition.

onomastics the study of the origin and formation of (especially personal) proper names.

onomatopeia the formation of a word whose sound echoes its meaning, e.g. *cuckoo*, *sizzle.*

optative a mood expressing a wish.

ordinal numbers those denoting order: *first*, *second*, *third*, etc.

oxymoron the combining of apparently contradictory terms, e.g. *faith unfaithful kept him falsely true.*

P

palindrome a word or phrase that reads the same backwards as forwards, e.g. *sex at noon taxes*.

paradigm a representative set of the inflections of a noun, verb, etc.

paralipsis the device of giving emphasis by professing to say little or nothing of a subject, as in *not to mention their unpaid debts of several millions*.

parataxis the placing of clauses etc. one after another, without words to indicate coordination or subordination, e.g. *Tell me, how are you?*

paronomasia a play on words; a pun.

participle a word formed from a verb (e.g. *going, gone, being, been*) and used in compound verb forms (e.g. *is going, has been*) or as an adjective (e.g. *working woman, burnt toast*).

particle 1 a minor part of speech, especially a short undeclinable one. **2** a common prefix or suffix such as *-in, -ness*.

partitive a word (e.g. *some, any*) or form denoting part of a collective group or quantity.

passive the form of a verb in which the subject undergoes the action of the verb, e.g. in *they were killed* (compare ACTIVE).

past expressing a past action or state.

past perfect pluperfect.

perfect (of a tense) denoting a completed action or event in the past, formed in English with *have* or *has* and the past participle, as in *they have eaten*.

performative denoting an utterance that effects an action by being spoken or written, e.g. *I bet, I apologize*.

periphrastic 1 of or involving circumlocution. **2** (of a case, tense, etc.) formed by combination of words rather than by inflection, e.g. *did go, of the people* rather than *went, the people's*.

person any of three classes of personal pronouns, verb forms, etc.: the person speaking (**first person**); the person spoken to (**second person**); the person spoken of (**third person**).

personal pronoun a pronoun replacing the subject, object, etc. of a clause etc., e.g. *I, we, you, them, us*.

phoneme any of the units of sound that distinguish one word from another in a language, e.g. *p,b,d,t* as in *pad, pat, bad, bat*.

phrasal verb a phrase consisting of a verb and an adverb or preposition, e.g. *break down, see to*.

pidgin a simplified language containing vocabulary from two or more languages, used for communication between people with no common language.

plosive pronounced with a sudden release of breath.

pluperfect (of a tense) denoting an action completed before some past time, formed in English with *had* and the past participle, as in *he had gone by then*.

plural (of a word or form) denoting more than one or (in languages with dual number) more than two.

polysyllabic (of a word) having many syllables.

portmanteau word one that blends the sounds and combines the meanings of two others, e.g. *motel*, *Oxbridge*.

positive (of an adjective or adverb) expressing a simple quality without comparison (compare COMPARATIVE, SUPERLATIVE).

possessive case the case of nouns and pronouns expressing possession.

possessive pronoun one indicating possession, e.g. *my*, *your*, *his*, *their*, or one of the corresponding absolute forms, e.g. *mine*, *yours*, *his*, *theirs*.

postposition a word or particle placed after the word it modifies, e.g. *-ward* in *homeward* and *at* in *the books we looked at*.

pragmatics the branch of linguistics dealing with language in use.

predicate what is said about the subject of a sentence etc., e.g. *went home* in *John went home*.

predicative (of an adjective or noun) forming or contained in the predicate, e.g. *old* in *the dog is old* (but not in *the old dog*) and *house* in *there is a large house* (opp. ATTRIBUTIVE).

prefix an addition placed at the beginning of a word to modify its meaning, e.g. *ex-*, *non-*, *re-*.

prepositional phrase one introduced by a preposition and relating a noun or pronoun to the rest of the sentence, as in the man *on the platform*, came *after dinner*, what did you do it *for*?

present expressing an action etc. now going on or habitually performed.

preterite expressing a past action or state.

proclitic a monosyllable closely attached to a following word and having itself no accent, e.g. *at* in *at home*.

proper noun/name a name used for an individual person, place, etc. and spelt with a capital letter, e.g. *Jane*, *London*, *Everest*.

prosopopeia the rhetorical introduction of a pretended speaker or the personification of an abstract thing.

prosthesis the addition of a letter or syllable at the beginning of a word, e.g. *be-* in *beloved*.

R

reciprocal (of a pronoun) expressing mutual action or relation, as in *each other*.

reflexive 1 (of a word or form) referring back to the subject of a sentence (especially of a pronoun, e.g. *myself*). **2** (of a verb) having a reflexive pronoun as its object, as in *to wash oneself*.

register each of several forms of a language (colloquial, literary, etc.) usually used in particular circumstances.

relative 1 (of a word, especially a pronoun) attaching a subordinate clause to its antecedent, e.g. *which, who*. **2** (of a clause) attached to an antecedent in this way.

reported speech the speaker's words with the changes of person, tense, etc. usual in reports, e.g. *he said that he would go* (compare DIRECT SPEECH).

restrictive clause a relative clause usually without surrounding commas.

root any ultimate unanalysable unit of language; a basis on which words are made by the addition of prefixes, suffixes, etc.

S

schwa 1 the indistinct unstressed vowel sound as in *a* mom*e*nt *a*go. **2** the symbol /ə/ representing this in the International Alphabet.

semantics the branch of linguistics concerned with meaning.

semiotics the study of signs and symbols, especially in language.

semi-vowel a sound intermediate between a vowel and a consonant, e.g. *w, y*.

sentence a set of words expressing a complete thought, containing or implying a subject and predicate, conveying a statement, question, exclamation, or command, and represented in writing between two full stops or equivalent pauses.

simile the comparison of one thing with another of a different kind, as an illustration or ornament, as in *as bold as a lion*.

singular (of a word or form) denoting one person or thing.

soft (of a consonant) sounded as with *c* in *ice*, *g* in *age*.

split infinitive a phrase in which an adverb etc. is inserted between *to* and an infinitive verb, as in *seems to really like it*.

spoonerism the usually accidental transposition of the initial letters etc. of two or more words, as in *town drain* for *down train*.

stem the root or main part of a word to which inflections are added; the part that remains unchanged throughout cases, derivatives, persons, etc.

Strine 1 a comic transliteration of Australian speech, e.g. *Emma Chissitt* = 'How much is it?' **2** (especially uneducated) Australian speech.

strong (of verbs in Germanic languages) forming inflections by vowel changes within the stem rather than by adding a suffix, e.g. *swim, swam* (opp. WEAK).

structuralism structural linguistics; the study of language as a system of interrelated elements.

subject a noun or its equivalent about which a subject is predicated and with which the verb agrees.

subjective of or being the subject.

subjunctive (of a mood) denoting what is imagined or possible or wished, e.g. *if I were you, God help you, be that as it may.*

subordinate (of clauses in a compound sentence) serving as an adjective, adverb, or noun because of either position or a preceding conjunction (compare COORDINATE).

suffix an addition placed at the end of a word to form a derivative, e.g. *-ation, -fy, -ing, -itis.*

superlative (of an adjective or adverb) expressing the highest or a very high degree of a quality, e.g. *bravest, most fiercely* (compare POSITIVE, COMPARATIVE).

syllable a unit of uninterrupted pronunciation forming all or part of a word and usually having one vowel sound often with a consonant or consonants before or after; there are two syllables in *water* and three in *inferno.*

synchronic describing a language as it exists at one point in time (opp. DIACHRONIC).

syncope the omission of interior sounds or letters in a word.

syncretism the merging of different inflectional varieties in the development of a language.

synonym a word or phrase that means exactly or nearly the same as another in the same language, e.g. *shut* and *close.*

syntax the part of grammar that deals with the connection and relation of words (compare ACCIDENCE).

synthetic (of a language) using complex or inflected words (compare ANALYTICAL).

T

tautology the saying of the same thing twice, especially as a fault of style, e.g. *arrived one after the other in succession.*

tmesis the separation of parts of a word by something intervening, e.g. in *any-blooming-where.*

toponymy the study of place names.

transformational grammar a grammar that describes a language by rules for converting one grammatical pattern into another, or for expressing underlying meaning as a statement of syntax.

transitive (of a verb or sense of a verb) taking a direct object, e.g. *saw* in *saw the donkey, saw that she was ill* (opp. INTRANSITIVE).

trope a figurative (i.e. metaphorical or ironical) use of a word.

U

uncountable noun mass noun.

V

vocative the case of nouns, pronouns, and adjectives used in addressing or invoking a person or thing.

voice a verb form or set of forms showing the relation of the subject to the action (*active voice, passive voice*).

W

weak (of verbs in Germanic languages) forming inflections by adding a suffix (opp. STRONG).

Legal Terms

A

affidavit a written statement confirmed by oath, for use in court.

amerce to punish by fine.

ancient lights a window that a neighbour may not deprive of light by building.

appellate a person who appeals to a higher court.

attainder the forfeiture of land and civil rights, formerly suffered as a consequence of a sentence of death for treason or felony.

B

barratry 1 fraud or gross negligence of a ship's master or crew at the expense of its owners or users. **2** formerly, vexatious litigation. **3** the former trade in the sale of Church or State appointments.

bind over to order (a person) to do something, especially to keep the peace.

bona vacantia goods without an apparent owner.

C

case-law the law as established by the outcome of former cases.

chance-medley a fight, especially homicidal, beginning unintentionally.

codicil an addition explaining, modifying, or revoking a will or part of one.

common (of a crime) of lesser importance (compare GRAND).

common law law derived from custom and judicial precedent rather than statutes.

contributory negligence negligence on the part of the injured party through failure to take precautions against an accident.

corpus delicti the facts and circumstances constituting a breach of a law.

D

decree 1 an official legal order. 2 a judgment or decision of certain lawcourts, especially in matrimonial cases.

decree nisi a provisional order for divorce, made absolute unless cause to the contrary is shown within a fixed period.

defendant a person etc. sued or accused in a court of law.

demurrer an objection raised or exception taken.

deponent 1 a person making a deposition under oath. 2 a witness giving written testimony for use in court etc.

deposition (the process of giving) sworn evidence; a testimony.

diriment nullifying.

disclaimer a renunciation or disavowal, especially of responsibility.

distrain to impose seizure of chattels so as to make a person pay rent etc. or meet an obligation.

E

easement a right of way or a similar right over another's land.

emblements crops normally harvested annually, regarded as personal property.

entail to bequeath (property etc.) so that it remains inalienably within a family.

equity the application of the principles of justice to correct or supplement the law.

escrow money, property, or a written bond, kept in the custody of a third party until a specified condition has been fulfilled.

estoppel the principle which precludes a person from asserting something contrary to what is implied by a previous action or statement of that person or by a previous pertinent judicial determination.

estreat 1 a copy of a court record of a fine etc. for use in prosecution. 2 the enforcement of a fine or forfeiture of a recognizance.

executor (fem. **executrix**) a person employed by a testator to carry out the terms of his or her will.

ex-parte in the interests of one side only or of an interested outside party.

F

felony a crime regarded by the law as grave, and usually involving violence.

forensic of or used in connection with courts of law.

fungible (of goods etc. contracted for, when an individual specimen is not meant) that can serve for, or be replaced by, another answering to the same definition.

G

garnish 1 to serve notice on (a person) in order to seize legally money belonging to a debtor or defendant. **2** to summon (a person) as a party to litigation started between others.

grand serious, important (*grand larceny*).

H

habeas corpus a writ requiring a person to be brought before a judge or into court, especially to investigate the lawfulness of his or her detention.

I

in camera in a judge's private room.

indemnity legal exemption from penalties etc. incurred.

indictment a formal accusation.

in flagrante delicto in the very act of committing an offence.

injunction a judicial order restraining a person from an act or compelling redress to an injured party.

instrument a formal legal document.

L

laches delay in performing a legal duty, asserting a right, claiming a privilege, etc.

lex domicilii the law of the country in which a person is domiciled.

lex fori the law of the country in which an action is brought.

lien a right over another's property to protect a debt charged on that property.

M

malice aforethought/prepense the intention to commit a crime.

mandamus a judicial writ issued as a command to an inferior court, or ordering a person to perform a public or statutory duty.

mens rea criminal intent; the knowledge of wrongdoing.

misdemeanour an indictable offence.

mitigating circumstances circumstances permitting greater leniency.

mittimus a warrant committing a person to prison.

N

nolle prosequi the relinquishment by a plaintiff or prosecutor of all or part of a suit.

nuncupate to declare (a will) orally, not in writing.

P

parole the release of a prisoner temporarily for a special purpose, or completely before the expiry of a sentence, on the promise of good behaviour.

pendente lite during the progress of a suit.

petty (of a crime) of lesser importance (*petty sessions*).

plaintiff a person who brings a case against another in court.

postliminy (in international law) the restoration to their former status of persons and things taken in war.

praecipe 1 a writ demanding action or an explanation of non-action. 2 an order requesting a writ.

probate the official proving of a will.

procurator fiscal (in Scotland) a local coroner and public prosecutor.

prove to establish the genuineness and validity of (a will).

puisne denoting a judge of a superior court inferior in rank to chief justices.

R

rebutter a defendant's reply to the plaintiff's surrejoinder.

recognizance a bond by which a person undertakes before a court or magistrate to observe some condition, e.g. to appear when summoned.

rejoinder a reply to a charge or pleading in court.

remise to surrender or make over (a right or property).

S

scire facias a writ to enforce or annul a judgment.

seize, seise (usually followed by *of*) to put in possession of.

sequestrate to take temporary possession of (a debtor's estate etc.)

statute a written law passed by a legislative body, e.g. an Act of Parliament.

stirps 1 a branch of a family. 2 its progenitor.

sub judice under judicial consideration and therefore prohibited from public discussion elsewhere.

subpoena a writ ordering someone to attend a lawcourt.

sui juris of age; independent.

surrebutter the plaintiff's reply to the defendant's rebutter.

surrejoinder the plaintiff's reply to the defendant's rejoinder.

T

tales **1** a writ for summoning jurors to supply a deficiency. **2** a list of persons who may be so summoned.

testator one who has made a will.

testimony an oral or written statement under oath or affirmation.

tort a breach of duty (other than under contract) leading to liability for damages.

traverse to deny (an allegation) by pleading.

U

ultra vires beyond one's legal power or authority.

usufruct (in Roman and Scots law) the right of enjoying the use and advantages of another's property short of its destruction or waste.

V

vindictive damages damages exceeding simple compensation and awarded to punish the defendant.

W

waive to refrain from insisting on (a right, legitimate plea, etc.)

writ a form of written command in the name of a sovereign, court, State, etc. to act or refrain from acting in some way.

Mathematical Terms

abscissa the shortest distance from a point on a graph to the vertical axis (compare ORDINATE).

acute angle an angle less than 90°.

algorithm 1 a process or set of rules for calculation or problem-solving, especially with a computer. **2** the Arabic or decimal notation of numbers.

aliquot part a quantity that divides exactly into a whole (*4 is an aliquot part of 12*).

annulus a ring-shaped area, especially the region between two concentric circles.

Arabic numerals the numerals 0, 1, 2, 3, 4, 5, 6, 7, 8, and 9 (compare ROMAN NUMERALS).

arc part of the circumference of a circle or any other curve.

arithmetic mean 1 the result of adding numbers and then dividing the result by the number of terms. **2** the number halfway between two others (*10 is the arithmetic mean of 8 and 12*).

arithmetic progression a sequence of numbers increasing or decreasing by the same quantity (*e.g. 1, 2, 3, 4, etc., 9, 7, 5, 3, etc.*).

array a rectangular arrangement of quantities and symbols in rows and columns; a matrix.

associative (of quantities connected by operators) giving the same result whatever their grouping as long as their order remains constant (*e.g. $(a \times b) \times c = a \times (b \times c)$*; compare COMMUTATIVE).

asymptote a line that continually approaches a given curve but does not meet it at a finite distance.

average an amount obtained by dividing the total of given amounts in a set by the number of amounts in the set (compare MEAN, MODE, MEDIAN).

axiom a self-evident truth.

axis a fixed reference line used to fix the position of points by distances along it.

B

bar chart a chart using bars to represent quantities.

base **1** a number in terms of which other numbers are expressed, e.g. 10 in the decimal system. **2** a number in terms of which a logarithm is expressed (*e.g.* $1,000 = 10^3$, so 3 is the logarithm of 1,000 to base 10).

binomial an expression containing two terms added or subtracted (*e.g.* $3 + 8, x - y$).

binomial distribution a measurement of the possible number of successful outcomes in a given number of trials, each having an equal chance of success.

Boolean algebra a system of notation to represent logical propositions.

C

calculus **1** any particular method of calculating or reasoning. **2** the infinitesimal calculus.

Cartesian coordinates a system for locating a point by reference to its distance from two or three axes intersecting at right angles.

chord a straight line joining two points on a circle or the ends of an arc.

circumference (the distance round) the enclosing boundary of a circle or other figure enclosed by a curve.

coefficient a quantity placed before and multiplying an algebraic expression (*e.g. 4 in* $4x^2$).

common denominator a common multiple of the denominators of several fractions (*e.g. 12 is the common denominator of* $^1/_3$ *and* $^1/_4$).

commutative unchanged in result by changing the order of quantities (*e.g.* $5 + 9 = 9 + 5$; compare ASSOCIATIVE).

complementary angles two angles that together make up 90°.

complex number a number containing both real and imaginary parts (*e.g.* $4 + 7i$; see i, page 179).

concave curved like the interior of a circle or sphere (compare CONVEX).

concentric (especially of circles) having a common centre (compare ECCENTRIC).

cone a solid figure with a circular (or other curved) base, tapering to a point.

congruent (of two geometrical figures) coinciding exactly when superimposed.

conic section a curve formed by the intersection of a cone and a plane.

constant a quantity in a relationship between variables that does not change its value (*e.g. 4 and 9 are constants in* $x + 4y + 9$, *but x and y are not*; compare VARIABLE).

convex curved like the exterior of a circle or sphere (compare CONCAVE).

coordinates each of a system of measurements used to fix the position of a point, line, or plane.

cosecant the ratio of the hypotenuse of a right-angled triangle to the side opposite an acute angle; the reciprocal of sine.

cosine the ratio of the side adjacent to an acute angle in a right-angled triangle to the hypotenuse.

cotangent the ratio of the side adjacent to an acute angle in a right-angled triangle to the opposite side.

cube 1 a solid contained by six equal squares. **2** the product of a number multiplied by its square.

cube root the number which produces a given number when cubed.

cuboid a solid body of which each face is a rectangle.

cylinder a uniform solid or hollow body with straight sides and a circular cross-section.

D

decimal fraction a fraction in which the number of tenths, hundredths, thousandths, etc. is shown by the positions of units to the right of a decimal point.

decimal point a full stop or dot placed before the beginning of a decimal fraction.

decimal system/scale a number system based on ten, using the digits 0123456789 whose value as units, tens, hundreds, etc. depends on their position.

degree 1 a unit of measurement of angles, one ninetieth of a right angle or one three hundred and sixtieth of a complete rotation. **2** the highest power of unknowns in an equation etc. ($4x^3$ *is a term of the third degree*).

denominator the number below the line in a fraction; a divisor.

derivative a quantity measuring the rate of change of another.

diameter a straight line passing from side to side through the centre of a body or figure, especially a circle or sphere.

diamond a rhombus.

Shapes and Forms in Mathematics

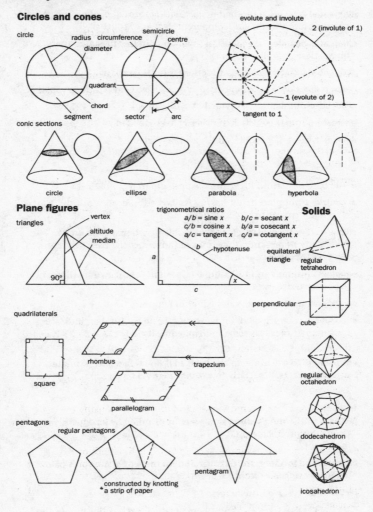

Circles and cones

circle

radius circumference

diameter

semicircle

centre

quadrant

chord

segment

sector arc

evolute and involute

2 (involute of 1)

1 (evolute of 2)

tangent to 1

conic sections

circle ellipse parabola hyperbola

Plane figures

triangles

vertex

altitude

median

90°

trigonometrical ratios

a/b = sine x b/c = secant x
c/b = cosine x b/a = cosecant x
a/c = tangent x c/a = cotangent x

b hypotenuse

a

c

x

Solids

equilateral
triangle regular
tetrahedron

perpendicular

cube

quadrilaterals

rhombus trapezium

square

parallelogram

regular
octahedron

pentagons

regular pentagons

constructed by knotting
a strip of paper

pentagram

dodecahedron

icosahedron

differential an infinitesimal difference between successive values of a variable.

differential calculus a method of calculating rates of change, maximum or minimum values, etc. (compare INTEGRAL CALCULUS).

differential equation an equation involving differentials among its quantities.

differentiate to transform (a function) into its derivative.

direct proportion a relation between quantities whose ratio is constant.

dividend a number to be divided by a divisor.

divisor a number by which another is to be divided.

domain the set of possible values for one variable.

E

e the base of natural logarithms, approximately 2.71828.

eccentric 1 not placed, not having its axis etc. placed centrally. **2** (of a circle) not concentric (to another).

ellipse a regular oval, such as that resulting when a cone is cut diagonally by a plane which does not intersect the base (compare HYPERBOLA, PARABOLA).

equation a statement indicating by the sign $=$ that two mathematical expressions are equal.

equilateral having all its sides equal in length.

exponent a raised symbol or expression beside a number, indicating how many times it is to be multiplied by itself (e.g. $2^3 = 2 \times 2 \times 2$, and has an exponent of 3).

extrapolate to calculate on the basis of (known facts) to estimate unknown facts, especially to extend (a curve) on a graph.

F

factor a whole number etc. that when multiplied by another gives a particular product (e.g. $12 = 3 \times 4$, 2×6, or 1×12, so 1, 2, 3, 4, 6, and 12 are factors of 12).

factorial the product of a number and all the whole numbers below it (e.g. factorial four $= 4 \times 3 \times 2 \times 1$, written 4!).

factorize to resolve into factors.

Fibonacci series a series of numbers in which each is the sum of the two preceding numbers, especially 1, 1, 2, 3, 5, 8, etc.

fluxion the rate at which a variable quantity changes; a derivative.

formula an equation stating the relation between two or more quantities.

fractal a complex geometric figure made of patterns that repeat themselves indefinitely at smaller and smaller scales, resulting in a line of infinite length within a finite area.

fraction a numerical quantity that is not a whole number (*e.g.* $^1/_2$, *0.5*).

frequency distribution a measurement of how often an event or quantity occurs.

frustum the remainder of a cone or pyramid whose top has been cut off.

function a variable connected with another variable in such a way that a change in one produces a change in the other (*x is a function of y and z*).

G

game theory the mathematical analysis of strategy in war, economics, games of skill, etc.

geodesy the branch of mathematics dealing with the figures and areas of the earth or large portions of it.

geometric mean the central number in a geometric progression.

geometric progression a sequence of numbers in which each is obtained by multiplying the previous one by the same amount (*as in 1, 3, 9, 27, 81*).

gnomon the part of a parallelogram left when a similar one has been taken from its corner.

gradient a measure of the steepness of slope, or of the rate of rise or fall of temperature, pressure, etc.

group a set of elements operated on by a binary operation (e.g. addition).

H

harmonic progression a sequence of numbers whose reciprocals are in arithmetic progression.

highest common factor HCF; the highest number that can be divided exactly into each of two or more numbers (*e.g. 4 is the HCF of 16, 36, and 40*).

hyperbola the curve produced when a cone is cut diagonally by a plane that makes a larger angle with the base than the side of the cone makes (compare ELLIPSE, PARABOLA).

hypotenuse the side opposite the right angle of a right-angled triangle.

I

i imaginary number; the square root of -1.

identity an equation that is true for all values of the quantities involved (*e.g.* $(x+1)^2 = x^2 + 2x + 1$).

identity element an element in a set, left unchanged by any specified operation on it (*e.g. 1 is the identity element for multiplication, so a x 1 = 1 × a = a*).

image a set formed by mapping each element from one set to another.

imaginary number the square root of a negative quantity, usually represented on a graph in a direction perpendicular to the axis of real numbers.

improper fraction a fraction whose numerator is greater than or equal to the denominator (*e.g. $^8/_5$*).

index the power to which a number is raised; an exponent.

inequality a formula stating that two expressions are not equal, usually represented by > (is greater than) or < (is less than).

infinitesimal calculus the differential and integral calculuses regarded as one subject.

inflection a change of curvature from convex to concave at a particular point on a curve.

integer any positive or negative whole number, or zero.

integral calculus mathematics concerned with finding the properties and application etc. of quantities subjected to particular rates of change (compare DIFFERENTIAL CALCULUS).

intercept to mark off (a space) between two points etc.

interpolate to estimate (a value) between two others.

inverse an element in a set which, combined with a given element, produces the identity element (*e.g. 0 is the identity element for addition, so 2 + (−2) = 0, so the inverse of 2 is here −2*).

inverse proportion a relation between two quantities such that one increases in proportion as the other decreases.

irrational number (a root etc.) not commensurate with the natural numbers, e.g. a non-terminating decimal such as pi.

isogon a figure having equal angles.

isometric (of a transformation) without change in shape or size.

isosceles triangle a triangle with two sides equal.

K

kite a quadrilateral figure symmetrical about one diagonal, as formed by two isosceles triangles with a common base.

Klein bottle a closed surface with only one side, formed by passing the neck of a tube through the side of the tube to join the hole in the base.

L

least common denominator lowest common multiple.

limit a quantity towards which a series approaches as closely as desired.

linear equation an equation between two variable terms that gives a straight line when plotted on a graph.

locus a curve etc. formed by all the points that satisfy certain conditions, or by a point, line, or surface moving according to stated conditions.

logarithm the number of times a number such as 10 (the base) must be multiplied by itself to produce a given number; making it possible to calculate by using addition and subtraction instead of multiplication and division (*the logarithm of 1,000 to base 10 is 3, and the logarithm of 2 to base 10 is 0.3010*).

long division division of numbers with details of each step written down.

lowest common multiple the least number which is a multiple of two or more given numbers (*e.g. for 6 and 8, the shared multiple is 24*).

lune a crescent-shaped figure formed by two arcs intersecting at two points.

M

magic square a square divided into smaller squares containing numbers such that the total for each row, column, or diagonal is the same.

map to associate each element of (a set) with one element of another set.

matrix a rectangular array of elements in rows and columns that is treated as a single element.

mean the average; the amount obtained by dividing the sum of several quantities by their number.

median the middle value of a series of values arranged in order of size (*in 1, 6, 8, 17, 23, 8 is the median*).

meniscus a crescent-shaped figure.

mixed number an integer and a proper fraction, e.g. $8\frac{1}{2}$.

Möbius strip a one-sided surface formed by joining the ends of a rectangle after twisting one end through 180°.

mode the value that occurs most frequently in a set of quantities.

modulus a number used as a divisor for identifying numbers which when divided by it give the same remainder (*17 and 66 both give 3 with modulus 7*).

Monte Carlo method a way of using the random sampling of numbers in order to estimate the solution to a numerical problem.

multiple a number that can be divided exactly by another (*56 is a multiple of 7*).

multiplicand a quantity to be multiplied.

N

Napierian logarithm, natural logarithm a logarithm to the base e.

natural number any positive integer, 1, 2, 3, etc.

negative (of a quantity) less than zero.

node a point at which lines or curves intersect.

null hypothesis a hypothesis suggesting that the difference between statistical samples does not imply a difference between populations.

null set a set with no members; an empty set.

numerator the number above the line in a fraction.

O

oblate (of a spheroid) flattened at the poles (compare PROLATE).

obtuse angle an angle greater than 90° and less than 180°.

octant **1** an arc of a circle equal to one-eighth of the circumference. **2** such an arc with two radii, forming an area equal to one-eighth of the circle. **3** each of eight parts into which three planes intersecting (especially at right angles) at a point divide the space or the solid body round it.

operator a symbol denoting an operation (*e.g.* ×, +).

order the degree of complexity of the highest power in an equation ($x^3 + 3x^2 + x = 7$ *is of the third order*).

ordinate the shortest distance from a point on a graph to the horizontal axis (compare ABSCISSA).

origin a fixed point from which coordinates are measured.

P

parabola the curve produced when a cone is cut by a plane parallel to its side, resembling the path of a projectile under the action of gravity.

parallelogram a plane figure with four straight sides and opposite sides parallel.

parameter a quantity constant in the case considered but varying in different cases.

percentile one of 99 values of a variable dividing a population into 100 equal groups as regards the value of that variable.

perfect number a number equal to the sum of its factors, including 1 (*the factors of 6 are 1, 2, 3, and 6 = 1 + 2 + 3, so it is a perfect number*).

permutation an ordered grouping of a set of items.

perpendicular at right angles (to a given line, plane, or surface).

pi the Greek letter π, the symbol of the ratio of the circumference of a circle to its diameter (approx. 3.14159).

pie chart a circle divided into sectors to represent relative quantities.

Poisson distribution a frequency distribution which gives the probability of events occurring in a fixed time.

polar coordinates a system by which a point can be located with reference to two angles.

polygon a plane closed figure with many straight sides and angles.

polynomial an expression of more than two algebraic terms, especially the sum of several terms that contain different powers of the same variable.

power the product obtained when a number is multiplied by itself a certain number of times (*2 to the power of 3* $= 2 \times 2 \times 2 = 8$).

prime number a number divisible only by itself and 1 (*e.g. 2, 3, 5, 7, 11*).

prism a solid geometric figure with two ends that are similar, equal, and parallel figures and whose sides are parallelograms.

probability the extent to which an event is likely to happen, measured by the ratio of the favourable cases to the whole number of cases possible.

product a result obtained by multiplying quantities together.

prolate (of a spheroid) lengthened in the direction of the poles (compare OBLATE).

proper fraction a fraction that is less than 1, with the numerator less than the denominator (*e.g.* $^5/_8$).

proportion an equality of ratios between two pairs of quantities (*e.g. 3:5 and 9:15*).

pyramid a solid with a base of three or more sides, the other faces being triangles sloping towards a central apex.

Pythagoras's theorem the theorem stating that the square on the hypotenuse of a right-angled triangle is equal in area to the sum of the squares on the other two sides.

Q

quadrant a quarter of a circle, bounded by two radii at right angles and the arc cut off by them.

quadratic equation an equation involving the second but no higher power of an unknown variable.

quadrature the process of constructing a square with an area equal to that of a curved figure, e.g. a circle.

quaternion a complex number of the form $w + xi + yj + zk$, where w, x, y, z are real numbers and i, j, k are imaginary units that satisfy certain conditions.

quotient a result obtained by dividing one quantity by another.

R

radial symmetry symmetry occurring about any number of lines or planes passing through the centre of an organism etc.

radian an angle equal to an angle at the centre of a circle whose arc equals the radius.

radius a straight line from the centre of a circle or sphere to the circumference.

ratio a comparison of two qualities by expressing one as a fraction of the other (*in the ratio of 3 to 2; the ratios 1:5 and 20:100 are the same*).

rational number a number that can be expressed as a fraction or ratio of the natural numbers (*e.g.* $^3/_4$, *0.4*; compare IRRATIONAL NUMBER).

real number any rational or irrational number (compare IMAGINARY NUMBER).

reciprocal a number so related to another that their product is 1 (*$^1/_2$ is the reciprocal of 2*).

rectangle a plane figure with four straight sides and four right angles, especially one with the adjacent sides unequal.

rectilinear bounded by straight lines.

recurring decimal a decimal fraction in which the same figures are repeated indefinitely.

recursion the repeated application of a procedure or definition to a previous result to obtain a series of values.

reflex angle an angle exceeding 180°.

regular 1 (of a figure) having all sides and all angles equal. **2** (of a solid) bounded by a number of equal figures.

remainder the number left after division or subtraction.

repeating decimal a recurring decimal.

rhombus a parallelogram with oblique angles and equal sides.

right angle an angle of 90°, one quarter of a complete revolution.

roman numerals the Roman letters representing numbers: $I = 1$, $V = 5$, $X = 10$, $L = 50$, $C = 100$, $D = 500$, $M = 1000$.

root 1 a number that when multiplied by itself a specified number of times gives a specified number (*the cube root of 8 is 2*). **2** a value of an unknown quantity that satisfies an equation (*if $2x + 5 = 11$, 3 is the root*).

rotation the turning of a figure about a fixed point.

S

scalar a quantity with only magnitude, not direction (compare VECTOR).

scalene (especially of a triangle) having all sides unequal in length.

secant a line cutting a curve at one or more points.

sector a region enclosed by two radii of a circle, ellipse, etc., and the arc between them.

series a set of numbers whose values are determined by a common relation, e.g. an arithmetic or geometric progression.

set a collection of items that may be classed together to form a unit.

set theory the branch of mathematics concerned with the manipulation of sets.

sign the positiveness or negativeness of a quantity.

significant figure a digit conveying information about a number containing it, and not a zero used simply to fill vacant space at the beginning or end.

similar shaped alike, though not necessarily the same size.

simultaneous equations equations involving two or more unknowns that are to have the same values in each equation.

sine the ratio of the side opposite a given angle (in a right-angled triangle) to the hypotenuse.

skew 1 lying in three dimensions. **2** not lying in the same plane. **3** (of a statistical distribution) not symmetrical.

solid a body or magnitude having three dimensions.

solid angle an angle formed by planes etc. meeting at a point.

solution set the set of all the solutions of an equation or condition.

sphere a solid figure, or its surface, with every point on its surface equidistant from its centre; a ball or globe.

square to multiply (a number) by itself (*3 squared is 9*).

square number a number that is the square of an integer ($3 \times 3 = 9$, *a square number*).

square root the number that multiplied by itself gives a specified number (*3 is the square root of 9*).

standard deviation a quantity calculated to show the extent of deviation for a group.

stationary point a point on a curve where the gradient is zero.

subgroup, subset a set all the elements of which are contained in a larger set.

sum the result of adding.

surd an irrational number.

T

tangent 1 a straight line, curve, or surface that meets another curve or curved surface at one point only. **2** the ratio of the sides opposite and adjacent to an angle in a right-angled triangle.

tesselation an arrangement of polygons without gaps or overlapping, especially in a repeated pattern.

transfinite number a number exceeding all finite numbers.

transformation a change from one geometrical figure, expression, or function to another of the same value, magnitude, etc.

translation the movement of a shape without rotation.

trapezium a quadrilateral with only one pair of sides parallel.

trigonometry the study of the relations of the sides and angles of triangles, used especially in surveying and navigation.

U

unity the number 'one'; the factor that leaves unchanged the quantity on which it operates.

V

variable a quantity able to assume different numerical values (compare CONSTANT).

variance a quantity equal to the square of the standard deviation; a measure of the spread of a group.

vector a quantity having direction as well as magnitude, as with the speed and direction of an aircraft (compare SCALAR).

Venn diagram a diagram of usually circular areas representing sets, the areas intersecting where they have elements in common.

vertex a point where lines or edges meet to form an angle.

vulgar fraction a fraction expressed by numerator and denominator, not in decimals.

W

whole number a number without fractions; an integer.

Z

zero 0; the point from which positive or negative quantities are reckoned.

Music

Musical Directions

A

a battuta return to strict time.

a cappella unaccompanied, in a church style.

accelerando accelerating.

adagietto fairly slow.

adagio slow.

ad libitum at will.

affettuoso tenderly.

affrettando hurrying.

agitato agitated.

al fine to the end.

alla marcia in the style of a march.

allargando getting slower.

allegretto fairly brisk.

allegro brisk.

al segno as far as the sign.

amoroso tender.

andante at walking speed.

andantino faster than andante.

animato spirited.

a piacere at will.

appassionato with passion.

assai very.

a tempo in the original time.

attacca without stopping.

B

ben well.

bis repeat.

bravura boldness and spirit.
brillante brilliantly.

C

calando quieter and slower.
cantando in a singing manner.
capriccioso free and lively.
col legno with the stick of the bow.
con amore tender.
con anima with deep feeling.
con brio vigorous.
con forza with force.
con fuoco fiery.
con grazia graceful.
con moto with movement.
con sordino with a mute.
con spirito with spirit.
crescendo (cresc.) becoming louder.

D

da capo from the beginning.
dal segno from the sign.
deciso decisively.
decrescendo (decresc.) becoming quieter.
delicato delicately.
diminuendo (dim.) becoming quieter.
dolce sweetly.
dolente sorrowfully.
dolore sorrow.
doloroso with sorrow.
doppio double.
doppio movimento at double speed.

E

energetico with energy.
espressione expression.
espressivo with expression.

F

facile easy.
fine the end.
forte (f) loud.
forte piano (fp) loud, then soft.

fortissimo (ff) very loud.
furioso furiously.

G

giocoso playful.
giusto in exact time.
glissando sliding.
grave solemnly.
grazioso gracefully.

I

impetuoso impetuously.
in modo di in the manner of.

L

lacrimoso sadly.
largamente broadly.
larghetto fairly slow.
largo slow.
legato smoothly.
leggiero lightly.
lento slow.
l'istesso tempo at the same speed though the notation changes.
lontano as from a distance.
lusingando soothingly.

M

ma but.
maestoso majestical.
marziale martial.
meno less.
meno mosso slower pace.
mesto sadly.
mezza voce at half strength.
mezzo half.
mezzo forte (mf) fairly loud.
mezzo piano (mp) fairly soft.
misterioso mysteriously.
moderato moderate.
molto very.
morendo dying away.
mosso with animation.
moto motion.

N

nobilmente nobly.
non troppo not too much.

O

obbligato obligatory, essential.
ostinato repeated phrase.

P

parlando in a speaking style.
pastorale in a pastoral style.
pausa pause.
ped pedal.
perdendosi dying away and gradually slower.
pesante heavily.
piacevole agreeably.
piangevole plaintively.
pianissimo (pp) very soft.
piano (p) soft.
più more.
pizzicato plucked (in string music).
poco a little.
poco a poco little by little.
pomposo pompously.
portamento gliding between notes.
precipitoso impetuously.
prestissimo as fast as possible.
presto very fast.

R

rallentando (rall.) slowing down.
ravvivando quickening.
rigoroso resolute, bold.
rinforzando (rfz) accentuated.
ritardando (Ritard.) slowing down.
ritenuto (Rit.) more slowly.
rubato with varying tempo.

S

scherzando playfully.
segno sign.
segue go on without pause.
semplice simply.

sempre throughout.

senza without.

serioso in a serious style.

sforzando (sfz) strongly accented.

simile like.

slentando gradually slower.

smorzando dying away.

soave sweet.

sonore sonorous.

sordino mute.

sostenuto sustained.

sotto voce in an undertone.

spiccato bouncing the bow.

spiritoso spirited.

staccato crisply.

strepitoso noisy, boisterous.

stretto in quicker time.

stringendo gradually faster.

subito immediately.

T

tacet instrument remains silent.

tempo speed, beat.

tempo commodo at a convenient speed.

tempo primo at the original speed.

tenuto held.

tranquillo calm.

troppo too much.

tutti whole orchestra.

U

un poco a little.

V

vif, vivement lively.

vigoroso vigorous.

vivace, vivo lively.

volante flying; swift and light.

Z

zoppa syncopated.

Musical Forms

A

air a tune or melody.

anthem **1** a choral composition usually based on a passage of Scripture. **2** a national anthem.

arabesque a florid melodic section or composition.

aria a long unaccompanied song for solo voice in an opera, oratorio, etc.

aubade a piece of music appropriate to the dawn or early morning.

B

bagatelle a short piece of music, especially for the piano.

ballad a slow sentimental or romantic song.

ballade a short lyrical piece, especially for piano.

barcarole **1** a song sung by Venetian gondoliers. **2** music imitating this.

berceuse **1** a lullaby. **2** an instrumental piece in this style.

blues melancholic music of Black American folk origin, often in a twelve-bar sequence.

C

canon a piece with different parts taking up the same theme successively, either at the same or at a different pitch.

cantata a short narrative or descriptive composition with vocal solos and usually chorus and orchestral accompaniment.

canticle a song or chant with a biblical text.

canzonetta **1** a short light song. **2** a kind of madrigal.

capriccio a lively and usually short musical composition.

cavatina **1** a short simple song. **2** a similar piece of instrumental music, usually slow and emotional.

chaconne a musical form consisting of variations on a ground bass.

chamber music music for a small group of instruments.

chanson a song.

chorale a stately and simple hymn tune, or a harmonized version of this.

concertino **1** a simple or short concerto. **2** a solo instrument, or solo instruments, playing in a concerto.

concerto a composition for a solo instrument, or instruments, accompanied by an orchestra.

concerto grosso a composition for a group of solo instruments accompanied by an orchestra.

concrete music music constructed by mixing recorded sounds.

D

divertimento a light entertaining composition, often in the form of a suite for chamber orchestra.

duet a composition for two voices or instruments.

E

entr'acte a piece of music performed between two acts of a play.

étude a short musical composition or exercise, usually for one player, designed to improve technique.

extravaganza a fanciful musical composition.

F

fantasia a musical composition free in form and often improvisatory in style, or based on several familiar tunes.

farandole a lively Provençal dance, or the music for it.

finale 1 the last movement of an instrumental composition. **2** a piece of music closing an act in an opera.

fugue a composition in counterpoint, in which a short subject is introduced by one part, successively taken up by others, and developed by interweaving the parts.

H

heavy metal a type of highly amplified rock music with a strong beat.

humoresque a short lively piece of music.

I

impromptu a short often songlike piece of usually solo instrumental music.

interlude a piece of music played between other pieces, the verses of a hymn, etc.

intermezzo 1 a short connecting instrumental movement in an opera etc. **2** a similar piece performed independently; a short piece, especially for a solo instrument.

J

jazz music of US Negro origin characterized by improvisation, syncopation, and usually a regular or forceful rhythm.

L

libretto the text of an opera or other long musical vocal work.

lieder German songs, especially of the Romantic period, usually for solo voice with piano accompaniment.

M

madrigal a usually 16th- or 17th-century part-song for several voices, usually arranged in elaborate counterpoint and without instrumental accompaniment.

mass a musical setting of parts of the liturgy of the Eucharist.

minuet music for a slow, stately dance in triple time; or written in that rhythm and style, often as a movement in a suite, sonata, or symphony.

motet a short sacred choral composition.

movement a principal division of a longer musical work, self-sufficient in terms of key, tempo, structure, etc.

musique concrète concrete music.

N

nocturne a short romantic composition, often for piano.

O

obbligato an accompaniment, usually special and unusual in effect, forming an integral part of a composition.

octet a composition for eight voices or instruments.

opera a dramatic work in one or more acts, set to music for singers (usually acting in costume) and instrumentalists.

operetta a short or light opera.

oratorio a semi-dramatic work for orchestra and voices especially on a sacred theme, performed without costumes, scenery, or action.

overture **1** an orchestral piece opening an opera etc. **2** a one-movement composition in this style.

P

partita **1** a suite. **2** an air with variations.

part-song a song with three or more voice-parts, usually singing simultaneously and often without accompaniment.

passacaglia an instrumental piece usually with a ground bass.

pastorale a slow instrumental composition in compound time, usually with continuous fixed bass notes.

polonaise a Polish dance tune in triple time.

prelude **1** an introductory piece of music, often preceding a fugue, forming the first piece of a suite, or beginning an act of an opera. **2** a short piece of music of this kind, especially for piano.

Q

quartet a composition for four voices or instruments.

quintet a composition for five voices or instruments.

R

recitative musical declamation of the kind usual in the narrative and dialogue parts of opera and oratorio.

refrain a recurring group of notes, especially at the end of stanzas of a song.

reggae a West Indian style of music with a strongly accented subsidiary beat.

reprise 1 a repeated musical passage. **2** a repeated item in a musical programme.

requiem the musical setting for a mass for the repose of the dead.

rhapsody a piece of usually emotional music in one extended movement.

ricercar an elaborated instrumental composition, especially of the 16th–18th centuries, in fugal or canonic counterpoint.

rock rock and roll; a type of popular dance-music originating in the 1950s, characterized by a heavy beat and simple melodies, often with a blues element.

rondo a form with a recurring leading theme, often found in the final movement of a sonata or concerto etc.

round a canon for three or more unaccompanied voices singing at the same pitch or in octaves.

S

salsa a kind of dance music of Latin American origin, incorporating jazz and rock elements.

scena **1** a scene or part of an opera. **2** an elaborate dramatic solo usually including recitative.

scherzo a vigorous, light, or playful composition, usually as a movement in a symphony, sonata, etc.

septet a composition for seven voices or instruments.

serenade a piece of music to be played at night, especially by a lover under his lady's window.

sextet a composition for six voices or instruments.

sinfonia 1 a symphony. **2** an orchestral piece of the 17th or 18th centuries introducing an opera, cantata, or suite.

solo a vocal or orchestral piece or passage performed by one person.

sonata a composition for one or two instruments (one usually a piano) in several movements, of which one or more each explore and develop the relationships of two themes.

Sprechgesang a style of dramatic vocalization between speech and song.

suite 1 a set of instrumental compositions, originally in dance style, to be played in succession. **2** a set of pieces from an opera, musical comedy, etc. to be played as one work.

symphonic poem an extended orchestral piece, usually in one movement, on a descriptive or rhapsodic theme.

symphony 1 an elaborate composition usually for full orchestra, in several movements with one or more in sonata form. **2** an interlude for orchestra alone in a large-scale vocal work.

T

toccata a musical composition for a keyboard instrument, designed to exhibit touch and technique.

trio 1 a composition for three voices or instruments. **2** the central, usually contrastive, section of a minuet, scherzo, or march.

V

variation a repetition (usually one of several) of a theme in a changed or elaborated form.

voluntary an organ solo played before, during, or after a church service.

Musical Terms

A

acciaccatura a grace-note performed as quickly as possible before an essential note.

accidental a sign indicating a momentary departure from the key signature by raising or lowering a note.

appogiatura a grace-note performed before an essential note and normally taking half its time-value.

arpeggio the notes of a chord played in succession, either ascending or descending.

atonal not written in any key or mode.

C

cadence the close of a musical phrase.

cadenza a virtuoso solo passage, usually near the end of a movement of a concerto.

chamber music music written for a small group of instruments.

chord a group of notes sounded together, as a basis of harmony.

chromatic scale one ascending or descending by semitones.

coda the concluding passage of a piece or movement, usually forming an addition to the basic structure.

coloratura elaborate ornamentation of singing, especially by a soprano.

Musical Notation

Values of notes and rests

notes   rests

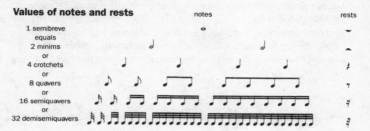

1 semibreve
equals
2 minims
or
4 crotchets
or
8 quavers
or
16 semiquavers
or
32 demisemiquavers

Some common symbols

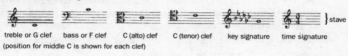

treble or G clef   bass or F clef   C (alto) clef   C (tenor) clef   key signature   time signature   } stave

(position for middle C is shown for each clef)

sharp (single & double)   flat (single & double)   natural   staccato   legato   tie   dotted note (value increased by half)   pause   repeat

The circle of fifths

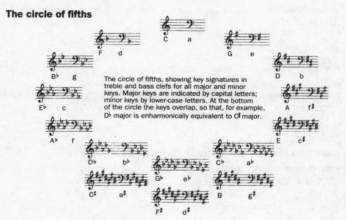

The circle of fifths, showing key signatures in treble and bass clefs for all major and minor keys. Major keys are indicated by capital letters; minor keys by lower-case letters. At the bottom of the circle the keys overlap, so that, for example, D♭ major is enharmonically equivalent to C♯ major.

compound time music with more than one group of simple time-units in each bar.

concert pitch the internationally agreed pitch whereby the A above middle C = 440 Hz.

continuo an accompaniment providing a bass line and harmonics indicated by figures, usually played on a keyboard instrument.

counterpoint a melody or melodies played in conjunction, according to fixed rules.

D

descant an independent treble melody sung or played above the basic tune.

diapason 1 the compass of a voice or musical instrument. 2 a fixed standard of musical pitch. 3 **open** or **stopped** diapason; either of two main organ-stops extending through the organ's whole compass. 4 a harmonious combination or melodious succession of notes.

diatonic scale one involving only notes proper to the prevailing key.

dominant the fifth note of any diatonic scale.

double stopping the sounding of two strings at once on a violin etc.

E

embouchure the mode of applying the mouth to a brass or wind instrument.

F

flat 1 below true or normal pitch. 2 lowered a semitone below natural pitch.

fundamental note the lowest note of a chord in its original uninverted form.

G

grace-note an extra note as an inessential embellishment.

ground bass a short theme in the bass constantly repeated, with the upper parts of the music varied.

I

interval the difference in pitch between two sounds.

K

key a system of notes definitely related to each other, based on a particular note, and predominating in a piece of music.

keynote the note on which a key is based.

L

leitmotif a recurrent theme associated throughout a musical work with a particular person, idea, or situation.

ligature a slur; a tie.

M

major 1 (of a scale) having intervals of a semitone between the third and fourth, and seventh and eighth degrees. **2** (of an interval) greater by a semitone than a minor interval.

mediant the third note of a diatonic scale.

minor 1 (of a scale) having intervals of a semitone between the second and third, fifth and sixth, and seventh and eighth degrees. **2** (of an interval) less by a semitone than a major interval.

mode 1 each of the scale systems that result when the white notes of the piano are played successively over an octave. **2** each of the two main modern scale systems, major and minor.

mordent an ornament consisting of one rapid alternation of a written note with the one immediately above or below it.

N

natural 1 (of a note) not sharpened or flattened. **2** (of a scale) not containing any sharps or flats.

O

octave 1 a series of eight notes occupying the interval between (and including) two notes of which one has twice or half the vibration frequency of the other. **2** the two notes at the extremes of this interval.

P

pentatonic scale one consisting of five notes.

pitch the degree of highness or lowness of a note.

polyphonic in two or more relatively independent parts; in counterpoint.

S

semitone half a tone; the smallest interval used in classical European music.

serial music music using a fixed arrangement of the twelve notes of the chromatic scale.

sharp 1 above the true or normal pitch. **2** raised a semitone above natural pitch.

sol-fa a system of associating each note of a scale with a particular syllable, *doh ray me*, etc.

syncopation displacement of the beats or accents, so that the strong ones become weak and vice versa.

T

tempo the speed at which music is to be played.

theme a prominent or recurring melody or group of notes in a composition.

tone an interval of a major second, e.g. C–D.

tonic the first degree of a scale, forming the keynote of a scale.

tremolo a tremulous effect produced by rapid reiteration of a note or alternation between two notes.

triple time that with three beats to the bar; waltz time.

V

vibrato a rapid slight variation in pitch, producing a tremulous effect.

Singing Voices

alto 1 contralto. **2** the highest adult male voice.

baritone the second lowest male voice.

bass the lowest adult male voice.

castrato the soprano or alto voice of an adult male singer who had been castrated in boyhood.

contralto the lowest female voice.

counter-tenor a male alto.

falsetto a method of voice production used especially by tenors to sing above their normal range.

mezzo-soprano a female voice between soprano and contralto.

soprano the highest voice of a female or boy singer.

tenor a male voice between baritone and alto, the highest of the ordinary adult male range.

treble soprano, especially with reference to a boy's voice.

Musical Instruments

Percussion

bongos a pair of small long-bodied hand drums.

castanets a pair of small concave discs held in the hands and clicked.

claves a pair of hardwood sticks struck together.

conga a tall, narrow, low-toned hand drum.

cymbal a concave metal plate, struck with a stick or with another cymbal.

glockenspiel a series of bells, bars, or tubes, mounted in a frame and struck by hammers.

kettledrum a large bowl-shaped drum that can be tuned.

maraca a hollow container filled with beans and usually shaken in pairs.

marimba a kind of deep-pitched xylophone.

side-drum a small double-handed drum.

snare drum a side-drum with wires stretched across one head.

tabla a pair of small Indian hand drums.

tambourine a hoop with parchment stretched on one side and jingling discs round the edge.

timpani a set of kettledrums.

tom-tom a traditional hand drum, now used in jazz bands etc.

triangle a steel rod bent into a triangle and struck with another steel rod.

tubular bells a row of hanging brass tubes struck with a hammer.

vibraphone a set of tuned metal bars with motor-driven resonators and metal tubes giving a vibrato effect.

washboard a ridged wooden board or metal sheet, played with the fingers.

xylophone a set of graduated bars struck with hammers.

Brass

bombardon a kind of valved bass tuba.

cornet an instrument like a short wide trumpet.

euphonium an instrument of the tuba family, used in bands.

flugelhorn a valved wind instrument, like the cornet but with a broader tone.

French horn a coiled wind instrument with a wide bell.

helicon a large spiral bass tuba that encircles the player's head.

sackbut an early form of trombone.

sarrusophone a metal wind instrument with a double reed like an oboe.

saxophone a keyed instrument in several sizes, used especially in jazz and dance music.

trombone a large wind instrument with a sliding tube.

trumpet a tubular or conical instrument with a flared bell.

tuba a low-pitched valved wind instrument.

Woodwind

alpenhorn a long wooden horn producing one note, used for calling cattle in the Alps.

bassoon a bass instrument of the oboe family, with a double reed.

clarinet a cylindrical instrument with one reed and a flared end.

contra-bassoon a bassoon pitched one octave below the normal one.

cor anglais an alto instrument of the oboe family.

fife a small shrill flute used with the drum in military music.

flageolet a small end-blown flute, like a recorder but with two thumb-holes.

flute a high-pitched wooden or metal instrument held across the body, with holes stopped by fingers or keys.

musette **1** a kind of small bagpipe with bellows, common in the French court in the 17th–18th centuries. **2** a small oboe-like double-reed instrument in 19th-century France.

oboe a double-reed instrument pitched below the flute and above the clarinet.

pan-pipes a musical instrument originally associated with the Greek rural god Pan, made of a series of short pipes graduated in length and fixed together with the mouthpieces in line.

piccolo a small flute pitched an octave above the normal one.

recorder an end-blown flute.

serpent an old S-shaped bass instrument made from leather-covered wood.

Strings

aeolian harp a stringed instrument that produces musical sounds when the wind blows through it.

balalaika a guitar-like Slav instrument, triangular and with 2–4 strings to be plucked.

cello, violoncello a bass instrument of the violin family, held upright on the floor.

double bass the largest and lowest-pitched member of the violin family.

dulcimer an instrument with strings stretched across a sounding-board to be struck with hammers.

guitar a usually 6-stringed instrument, played by plucking or with a plectrum.

harp a large upright instrument with vertical strings played by plucking.

kit a small fiddle once used especially by dancing-masters.

lute a pear-shaped guitar-like instrument, popular in the 14th–17th centuries.

mandolin an instrument like the lute but with paired metal strings.

sitar a long-necked Indian lute.

ukulele a small 4-stringed Hawaiian guitar.

viola an instrument like the violin but larger and of lower pitch.

violin an instrument with 4 strings of treble pitch, played with a bow.

Keyboard Instruments

accordion a portable instrument with reeds blown by bellows and played by means of keys and buttons.

celesta a small instrument like a glockenspiel, in which hammers strike hanging steel plates to give a bell-like sound.

clavicembalo a harpsichord.

clavichord a small keyboard instrument with a very soft tone.

clavier any keyboard instrument; a harpsichord, piano, etc.

dulcitone an instrument with steel tuning-forks struck with hammers.

fortepiano an early form of the pianoforte.

grand piano a piano on three legs, with the body, strings, and sounding-board arranged horizontally.

Hammond organ *trademark* an electronic organ like a small piano, whose sounds resemble those of a pipe organ.

harmonium a small organ in which the notes are produced by air driven through reeds by bellows operated by the feet.

harpsichord an instrument with horizontal strings plucked mechanically.

Moog synthesizer *trademark* an electronic keyboard instrument producing a wide variety of sounds.

organ a large instrument with pipes supplied with air by bellows and grouped into sets, each with a separate keyboard.

piano, pianoforte a large instrument whose keys cause hammers to strike metal strings, the vibration being stopped by dampers.

piano-accordion an accordion with a small vertical keyboard like a piano.

Pianola *trademark* a player–piano; one played automatically using an apparatus guided by perforated paper rolls.

portative organ a small portable medieval organ.

spinet a small wing-shaped harpsichord with oblique strings.

square piano an early kind of small oblong piano.

virginal a 16th–17th century form of spinet in a box.

vox angelica an organ-stop with a soft tremulous tone.

vox humana an organ-stop with a tone supposed to resemble a human voice.

Wurlitzer *trademark* an electronic organ once much used in cinemas.

Physics and Chemistry Terms

A

A ampere.

absolute zero a theoretical lowest possible temperature, at which the particles whose motion constitutes heat would be minimal, calculated as -273.15 C (or $0°$ K).

accelerator 1 an apparatus for imparting high speeds to charged particles. **2** a substance that speeds up a chemical reaction.

acid 1 any of a class of substances that liberate ions of the element hydrogen in water, are usually sour, and turn litmus red. **2** any compound or atom donating protons.

adsorb (usually of a solid) to hold (molecules of a gas or liquid or dissolved substance) to its surface, causing a thin film to form.

alcohol ethyl alcohol; a colourless volatile inflammable liquid forming the intoxicating element in wine, beer, spirits, etc.

aliphatic of or being organic compounds in which carbon atoms form open chains, not aromatic rings.

alkali 1 any of a class of substances that liberate ions of the element hydrogen in water, usually form caustic or corrosive solutions, and turn litmus blue. **2** any substance that reacts with or neutralizes hydrogen ions.

allotrope any of two or more physical forms in which an element can exist (*graphite, charcoal, and diamond are all allotropes of carbon*).

alpha particle a nucleus of the element helium, emitted by a radioactive substance, originally regarded as a ray.

alternating current an electric current that reverses its direction at regular intervals.

amino acid any organic compound containing the groups COOH and NH$_2$, occurring naturally in plant and animal tissues and forming the basic constituents of proteins.

ampere the SI base unit of electric current.

amphipathic having both a hydrophilic and a hydrophobic part.

amphoteric able to react as a base and an acid.

anion a negatively charged ion; one that is attracted to the anode in electrolysis (opp. CATION).

anode 1 the positive electrode in an electrolytic cell or electronic valve or tube. **2** the negative terminal of a battery etc. (opp. CATHODE).

antimatter matter composed solely of elementary particles with the same mass as given particles but opposite electric or magnetic properties.

aromatic (of compounds of carbon molecules) arranged in an unsaturated ring, especially containing a benzene ring.

atmosphere a unit of pressure equal to mean atmospheric pressure at sea level; 101, 325 pascals.

atom 1 the smallest particle of a chemical element that can take part in a chemical reaction. **2** this particle as a source of nuclear energy.

atomic number the number of protons in the nucleus of an atom, which is characteristic of a chemical element and determines its place in the periodic table.

atomic weight relative atomic mass.

B

bar a unit of pressure, 10 newton per square metre, approximately one atmosphere.

base a substance capable of combining with an acid to form a salt and water.

becquerel the SI unit of radioactivity, corresponding to one disintegration per second.

bel a unit used in the comparison of power levels in electrical communication or intensities of sound, corresponding to an intensity ratio of 10:1 (compare DECIBEL).

benzene ring the hexagonal unsaturated ring of six carbon atoms in the benzene molecule.

beta particle/ray a fast-moving electron emitted by radioactive decay of substances.

black body a hypothetical perfect absorber and radiator of energy, with no reflecting power.

boiling-point the temperature at which a liquid starts to boil.

bond linkage between atoms in a molecule or a solid.

breeder reactor a nuclear reactor that can create more fissile material than it consumes.

Brownian movement/motion the erratic random movement of microscopic particles in a liquid, gas, etc., as a result of continuous bombardment from molecules of the surrounding medium.

buffer a substance that slows down a chemical reaction, especially when a change is being made from acid to alcohol or vice versa.

butane a gaseous hydrocarbon used in liquid form as fuel.

C

C 1 the element carbon. **2** Celsius, Centigrade. **3** capacitance.

calorie 1 the amount of heat needed to raise the temperature of one gram of water through 1°C. **2** the amount needed to raise one kilogram of water through 1°C, often used to measure the energy value of foods.

candela the SI unit of luminous intensity.

capacitance 1 the ability of a system to store an electric charge. **2** the ratio of the change in an electric charge in a system to the corresponding change in its electric potential.

capacitor a device of one or more pairs of conductors separated by insulators, used to store an electric charge.

capillarity a phenomenon at liquid boundaries resulting in the rise or depression of liquids in narrow tubes.

carbohydrate any of the many energy-producing organic compounds containing the elements carbon, hydrogen, and oxygen, e.g. starch and sugars.

carbon a non-metallic element occurring naturally as diamond, graphite, and charcoal, and in all organic compounds.

catalyst any substance that, without itself undergoing any permanent chemical change, increases the rate of a reaction.

cathode 1 the negative electrode in an electrolytic cell or electronic valve or tube. **2** the positive terminal of a battery etc. (opp. ANODE).

cathode-ray tube a high-vacuum tube in which rays emitted from its cathode produce a luminous image on a fluorescent screen.

cation a positively charged ion; one that is attracted to the cathode in electrolysis (opp. ANION).

cd candela.

cellulose a carbohydrate forming the main constituent of plant-cell walls, used in the production of textile fibres.

Celsius scale/Centigrade a scale of temperature on which water freezes at 0° and boils at 100° under standard conditions.

centrifugal force an apparent force that acts outwards on a body moving about a centre.

centripetal force the force acting on a body causing it to move about a centre.

cgs centimetre-gram-second; a system using these as basic units of length, mass, and time.

chain reaction 1 a self-sustaining nuclear reaction, especially one in which a neutron from a fission reaction initiates a series of further reactions. **2** a self-sustaining molecular reaction in which intermediate products initiate further reactions.

chaos theory the study of those small changes in initial conditions which cause apparent randomness in the physical world.

charge 1 a property of matter that is a consequence of the interaction between its constituent particles and exists in a positive or negative form, causing electrical phenomena. **2** energy stored chemically for conversion into electricity.

cholesterol a naturally occurring alcohol found in most body tissues, including the blood, where high concentrations thicken and harden the arteries.

chromosome one of the threadlike structures, usually found in the cell nucleus, that carry the genetic information in the form of genes.

Ci curie.

colloid 1 a substance consisting of submicroscopic particles. **2** a mixture of such a substance with a second substance, especially to form a viscous solution.

conductor a thing that conducts or transmits heat or electricity, especially regarded in terms of its capacity to do this (*a poor conductor*).

conservation of energy/mass/momentum the principle that the total quantity of energy etc. of any system not subject to external action remains constant.

convection a transference of heat in a gas or liquid by upward movement of the heated and less dense medium.

copolymer a polymer with units of more than one kind.

cosmic rays/radiation radiations from space etc. that reach the earth from all directions, usually with high energy and penetrative power.

coulomb the SI unit of electrical charge, equal to the quantity of electricity conveyed in one second by a current of one ampere.

cryogenics the branch of physics dealing with the production and effects of very low temperatures.

crystal 1 an aggregation of molecules with a definite internal structure and the external form of a solid enclosed by symmetrically arranged plane surfaces. **2** a solid whose constituent particles are symmetrically arranged.

curie a unit of radioactivity corresponding to 3.7×10 disintegrations per second.

cusec a unit of flow (especially of water) equal to one cubic foot per second.

cyclotron an apparatus in which charged atomic and subatomic particles are accelerated by an alternating electric field while following an outward spiral or circular path in a magnetic field.

D

dB decibel.

decay **1** (of a substance etc.) to undergo change by radioactivity. **2** to undergo a gradual decrease in magnitude of a physical quantity.

decibel a unit (one-tenth of a bel) used in the comparison of two sound intensities, one of the pair usually being taken as a standard.

deliquesce to dissolve in water absorbed from the air.

detergent a cleansing agent, especially a synthetic substance (usually other than soap) used with water to remove dirt etc.

diamagnetic tending to become magnetized in a direction at right angles to the applied magnetic field.

dielectric insulating.

diffract (of the edge of an opaque body, a narrow slit, etc.) to break up (a beam of light) into a series of dark or light bands or coloured spectra, or (a beam of radiation or particles) into a series of alternately high and low densities.

diffraction grating a set of parallel wires, lines ruled on glass, etc. for producing spectra by diffraction.

diffusion the interpenetration of substances by the natural movement of their particles.

diode **1** a semiconductor with two electrodes, allowing the flow of current in only one direction. **2** a thermionic valve with two electrodes.

dioptre a unit of refractive power of a lens, equal to the reciprocal of its focal length in metres.

direct current an electric current flowing in one direction only.

discharge **1** the release of a quantity of electric charge from an object. **2** a flow of electricity through the air or other gas, especially when accompanied by the emission of light. **3** the conversion of chemical energy in a cell into electrical energy.

disperse **1** to distribute (small particles) uniformly in a medium. **2** to divide (white light) into its coloured constituents.

distil **1** to purify (a liquid) by vaporizing it with heat, then condensing it with cold and collecting the result. **2** to extract the essence of (a plant etc.) usually by heating it in a solvent.

DNA deoxyribonucleic acid; the self-replicating material present in nearly all living organisms, especially as a constituent of chromosomes, which is the carrier of genetic information.

Doppler effect/shift an increase (or decrease) in the frequency of sound, light, or other waves as the source and observer move towards (or away from) each other.

double bond a pair of bonds between two atoms in a molecule.

dynamics the branch of mechanics concerned with the motion of bodies under the action of forces (compare STATICS).

E

earth to connect (an electrical circuit) to the earth.

efficiency the ratio of useful work performed to the total energy expended or heat taken in.

effloresce 1 (of a substance) to turn to a fine powder on exposure to air. **2** (of salts) to come to the surface and crystallize on it. **3** (of a surface) to become covered with salt particles.

elastic (of a collision) involving no decrease of the energy of motion.

elastomer a natural or synthetic rubber or rubber-like plastic.

E-layer a layer of the ionosphere able to reflect medium frequency radio waves.

electrode a conductor through which electricity enters or leaves an electrolyte, gas, vacuum, etc.

electrolysis the decomposition of a substance by the application of an electric current.

electrolyte a substance which conducts electricity when molten or in solution, especially in an electric cell or battery.

electron a stable elementary particle with a charge of negative electricity, found in all atoms and acting as the primary carrier of electricity in solids.

electronics a branch of physics and technology concerned with the behaviour and movement of electrons in a vacuum, gas, semiconductor, etc.

electronvolt a unit of energy equal to the work done on an electron in accelerating it through a potential difference of one volt.

element 1 any of the hundred or so substances that cannot be resolved by chemical means into simpler substances. **2** a resistance wire that heats up in an electric heater etc.

elementary particle any of several subatomic particles supposedly not decomposable into simpler ones.

emulsion a fine dispersion of one liquid in another, especially as paint, medicine, etc.

entropy 1 a measure of the unavailability of a system's heat energy (owing to how widely the heat is spread out through the surrounding matter) for conversion into mechanical work. **2** a measure of the disorganization or degradation of the universe.

enzyme a protein acting as a catalyst in a specific biochemical reaction (*an enzyme in yeast changes sugar into alcohol*).

ester any of a class of organic compounds produced by combining an acid and an alcohol.

eV electronvolt.

F

Fahrenheit scale a scale of temperature on which water freezes at 32° and boils at 212° under standard conditions.

fallout radioactive debris caused by a nuclear explosion or accident.

farad the SI unit of capacitance, such that one coulomb of charge causes a potential difference of one volt.

fat any of a group of natural esters of glycerine and various fatty acids, existing as solids at room temperature.

fatty acid any of a group of organic compounds consisting of a hydrocarbon chain and an acid radical root at the end, especially those that are insoluble in water and related to the oils, waxes, etc.

fermentation the breakdown of substances by yeasts, bacteria, etc., usually in the absence of oxygen, especially of sugar to alcohol in making beers, wines, and spirits.

fibre optics optics employing thin glass fibres, usually for the transmission of light, especially modulated to carry signals.

fission nuclear fission.

flashpoint the temperature at which vapour from oil etc. will ignite in air.

fluid a substance, especially a gas or liquid, lacking definite shape and capable of flowing.

fluorescence the property of absorbing light of short (invisible) wavelengths, such as X-rays and ultraviolet light, and emitting light of longer (visible) wavelength.

fluorocarbon a compound formed by replacing one or more of the hydrogen atoms in a hydrocarbon with atoms of the element fluorine.

focal distance/length the distance between the centre of a mirror or lens and its focus.

force 1 an influence tending to cause the motion of a body. **2** the intensity of this, equal to the mass of the body and its acceleration.

fractional relating to the separation of parts of a mixture by using their different physical properties (*fractional crystallization; fractional distillation*).

free fall movement under the force of gravity only, as of the part of a parachute descent before the parachute opens.

free radical an unchanged atom or group of atoms which has one or more unpaired electrons and is therefore chemically incomplete.

freezing-point the temperature at which a liquid, especially water, freezes.

G

galvanize 1 to stimulate by electricity. **2** to coat (iron) with zinc (usually without the use of electricity) as a protection against rust.

gamma radiation radiation of very short wavelength emitted by some radioactive substances and dangerous to life.

gauss a unit of magnetic induction, equal to one ten-thousandth of a tesla.

Geiger counter a device for measuring radioactivity.

gel jelly formed from a colloidal suspension dispersed in a liquid.

glucose a simple sugar which is an important energy source in living organisms, and is found in honey and fruit and in the blood.

gluten the protein parts of flour and other cereals.

gravitation a force of attraction between any particle of matter in the universe and any other, causing the fall of bodies to the earth.

H

half-life the time taken for the radioactivity of a substance to decay to half its original value.

halogenated combined with a halogen (*halogenated rubber*).

halogens the chemical elements fluorine, chlorine, bromine, iodine, and astatine which, by simple union with a metal, form e.g. sodium chloride, common salt.

harmonic motion regular oscillation, such as the swing of a pendulum or the bouncing of a weight on the end of a spring.

heat pump a device for the transfer of heat from a colder to a hotter area, as in a refrigerator.

hertz the SI unit of frequency, equal to one cycle per second.

hologram a three-dimensional image formed by the interference of light beams.

hydraulics the science of the conveyance of liquids through pipes etc., especially as motive power.

hydrolysis the chemical reaction of a substance with water, usually resulting in decomposition.

hydrophilic dissolving easily in water; readily wettable.

hydrophobic not readily wettable.

Hz hertz.

I

inductance the property of an electric circuit that causes an electromotive force to be generated by a change in the current flowing.

induction 1 the production of an electric or magnetic state by the proximity (without contact) of something electric or magnetized. **2** the production of an electric current in a conductor by changing the magnetic field.

inertia the property by which matter remains motionless, or goes on moving in the same straight line, unless a force acts upon it.

infrared having a wavelength just greater than the red end of the visible light spectrum but less than that of radio waves.

inorganic chemistry the chemistry of all elements, and their compounds, other than carbon.

integrated circuit a small chip etc. of material replacing several separate components in a conventional electric circuit.

interference the combination of two or more wave motions to form a resultant wave in which the displacement may be strengthened or weakened.

ion 1 an anion; an atom that has gained one or more electrons and is negatively charged. **2** a cation; an atom that has lost one or more electrons and is positively charged.

isobar 1 a line on a map connecting places with the same atmospheric pressure at a given time. **2** an atom with different chemical properties but the same atomic weight as another.

isomer 1 a compound with the same molecular formula as another, but a different arrangement of atoms and different properties. **2** an atomic nucleus with the same atomic number and mass number as another but a different energy state.

isotope a form of an element differing from another in atomic mass, and in nuclear but not chemical properties.

J

joule the SI unit of work or energy, equal to the work done by a force of one newton when its point of application moves one metre in the direction of action of the force, equivalent to a watt-second.

K

K 1 kelvin. **2** the element potassium.

kelvin the SI unit of thermodynamic temperature, equal to the degree Celsius.

kinetics 1 dynamics. **2** the branch of physical chemistry concerned with the rates of chemical reactions.

L

laminar flow smooth flow of air or water over surfaces.

laser a device that generates an intense beam of infrared, visible, or ultraviolet light by stimulated emission of radiation.

latent heat the further heat required to melt a solid at melting-point, or to boil a liquid at boiling-point, without change of temperature.

lens a device for focusing or otherwise modifying the direction of movement of light, sound, electrons, etc.

litmus a dye obtained from lichens that is red under acid conditions and blue under alkaline conditions.

lm lumen.

lumen the SI unit that measures the flow of light from a source or on to a surface.

lux the SI unit of illumination, equal to one lumen per square metre.

lx lux.

M

Mach number the ratio of the speed of a body to the speed of sound.

macromolecule a molecule containing a very large number of atoms.

magnetic field a region of variable force around magnets, magnetic materials, or conductors.

magnetism magnetic phenomena, or the property of producing them.

maser a device using stored radio energy to detect and strengthen radio signals.

mass the quantity of matter a body contains (compare WEIGHT).

mass number the total number of protons and neutrons in a nucleus.

mass spectrometer a device employing electrical detection to separate isotopes, molecules, and molecular fragments according to their masses.

mechanics the branch of applied mathematics dealing with motion and the action of forces.

microwave a very short radio wave that can be used to heat or cook food.

mole, mol the SI unit of amount of substance.

molecular weight relative molecular mass.

molecule the smallest unit (usually a group of atoms) of a chemical compound that can take part in a chemical reaction.

moment the turning effect produced by a force acting at a distance on an object.

momentum the quantity of motion of a moving body, measured as the product of its mass and speed.

N

N newton.

natural gas an inflammable gas found in the earth's crust, not manufactured.

neutron an elementary particle of about the same mass as a proton but with no electric charge, present in all atomic nuclei except those of ordinary hydrogen.

newton the SI unit of force that, acting on a mass of one kilogram, increases its velocity by one metre per second per second.

noble gas any of a group of gaseous elements that almost never combine with other elements.

NTP normal temperature and pressure.

nuclear fission a nuclear reaction in which a heavy nucleus splits spontaneously or on impact with another particle, with the release of energy.

nuclear fusion a nuclear reaction in which lighter nuclei fuse to form a heavier nucleus, with the release of energy.

nucleon a proton or neutron.

nucleus the positively charged central core of an atom, containing most of its mass.

nylon a synthetic fibre with a protein-like structure and tough, elastic properties.

O

octane a colourless inflammable hydrocarbon whose presence in petrol affects the performance of an internal combustion engine.

ohm the SI unit of electrical resistance.

optics the scientific study of sight and the behaviour of light.

orbit the curved path of one body round another, e.g. of a planet round a star or an electron round an atomic nucleus.

organic (of a compound etc.) containing carbon.

osmosis the passage of a solvent through a membrane, from a weaker to a more concentrated solution.

oxidize 1 to combine with the gaseous element oxygen. **2** to make or become rusty. **3** to (cause to) undergo a loss of electrons.

ozone a colourless unstable gas with a strong smell and powerful oxidizing properties.

ozone layer a layer of ozone in the stratosphere that absorbs most of the sun's ultraviolet radiation.

P

pascal the SI unit of pressure, equal to one newton per square meter.

periodic table an arrangement of elements in order of their atomic number, in which those of similar chemical properties are grouped accordingly.

permeability a quantity measuring the influence of a substance on the flow of magnetism surrounding it.

peroxide a compound of oxygen with another element, containing the greatest possible proportion of oxygen (*hydrogen peroxide*).

phase a stage in a periodically recurring sequence, especially of alternating electric currents or light vibrations.

phosphates salts of phosphoric acid (from the element phosphorus) used as fertilizers.

piezoelectricity electricity produced by the application of pressure, especially to certain crystals.

plasma a gas so hot as to consist of positive ions and free electrons, with an approximately equal positive and negative charge.

plastics various synthetic polymeric substances that can be moulded into shape.

pneumatics the science of the mechanical properties of gases.

polarize 1 to restrict the vibrations of (a wave, especially light) to one direction. **2** to give (a substance or body) the quality of having magnetic poles.

pole 1 each of the two opposite points on the surface of a magnet at which magnetic forces are strongest. **2** each of two terminals (positive and negative) of an electric cell or battery etc.

polyester any of a group of polymers used to form synthetic fibres or to make resins.

polymer a large molecule formed by joining many smaller molecules of the same kind.

positron an elementary particle with a positive charge equal to the negative charge of an electron and of the same mass as an electron.

power 1 the capacity for exerting mechanical force or doing work. **2** the rate of energy output.

propane a gaseous hydrocarbon used as bottled fuel.

protein any of a group of organic compounds composed of chains of amino acids and forming an essential part of all living organisms.

proton a stable elementary particle with a positive electric charge equal in magnitude to that of an electron, and occurring in all atomic nuclei.

Q

quantum mechanics/theory a system or theory using the assumption that energy exists in discrete units.

R

rad a unit of absorbed radiation producing ions (e.g. from a radioactive substance) corresponding to the absorption of 0.1 joule per kilogram of absorbing material.

radiation the emission of energy, especially invisibly, as electromagnetic waves or as moving particles.

radical 1 a free radical. **2** an atom or group of atoms normally remaining unchanged and acting as a unit in various chemical compounds.

radioactivity the spontaneous breaking up of atomic nuclei, with the emission of usually penetrating radiation or particles.

radio-frequency the frequency band of telecommunication, about 10,000 or more cycles per second.

radio telescope a directional radio receiver with a very large aerial, for analysing radio waves from stars etc.

reagent a substance that causes a chemical reaction and may be used to detect another substance.

rectify 1 to purify (a liquid) by repeated distillation. **2** to convert (alternating current) into direct current.

reduce 1 to combine with the element hydrogen. **2** to (cause to) undergo addition of electrons. **3** to convert (oxide etc.) to metal by removing oxygen (*reduce iron oxide to iron*).

reflector a reflecting telescope; one that uses a mirror to produce images.

refractor a telescope using a lens to produce an image.

relative atomic mass the number of times one atom of an element is heavier than an atom of hydrogen.

relative molecular mass the number of times one molecule of an element or compound is heavier than an atom of hydrogen.

relativity 1 the special theory of relativity; a theory based on the principle that all motion is relative and that light has constant velocity, regarding space-time as a four-dimensional continuum. **2** the general theory of relativity; the extension of this to gravity and accelerated motion.

resin 1 a viscous secretion of certain plants, used for varnish etc. **2** a solid or liquid organic polymer used in plastics etc.

resistance the (measurable) property of hindering the conduction of electricity, heat, etc.

resonance **1** the property of a molecule whose structure is best represented by two or more forms rather than by a single formula. **2** a short-lived elementary particle that is an excited state of a more stable particle.

S

salt a chemical compound produced by the interaction of an acid with a base, when all or part of the hydrogen in the acid is replaced by a metal or metal-like radical.

scintillation a flash produced in a material by a particle converting into an ion.

second the SI unit of time, based on the natural periodicity of an atom of the element caesium.

semiconductor any solid substance (e.g. the element germanium) whose power of conducting electricity is partway between that of a metal and of an insulator.

SI the international system of units of measurement.

solenoid a cylindrical coil of wire acting as a magnet when carrying electric current.

spectrum **1** the band of colours, as seen in a rainbow etc., arranged in a progressive series according to their wavelength. **2** a similar band of the entire range of radio waves, X-rays, etc.

statics the science of bodies at rest or of forces in equilibrium, e.g. in the structure of a bridge (compare DYNAMICS).

strain **1** the condition of a body subjected to stress; molecular displacement. **2** a quantity measuring this, equal to the amount of deformation usually divided by the original dimension.

superconductivity the property of conducting electricity with no resistance, in some substances at very low temperatures.

suspension a mixture of particles floating throughout a fluid, as with mist or muddy water.

synthesis the artificial production of compounds from their constituents, as distinct from extraction from plants etc.

T

tesla the SI unit of magnetic flux density.

thermionic valve a device giving a flow of electrons at high temperature in one direction only, used in radio reception.

thermodynamics the science of the relations between heat and other (mechanical, electrical, etc.) forms of energy.

thermoplastic (of a substance) becoming repeatedly soft on heating and rigid on cooling.

thermosetting (of plastics) setting permanently when heated.

titrate to ascertain the amount of a constituent in (a mixture) by adding small measured quantities of a reagent of known strength until the reaction is completed.

torque the twisting force on a propellor etc.

transducer any device for changing a non-electrical signal into an electrical one, e.g. pressure into voltage.

transformer any apparatus for reducing or increasing the voltage of an alternating current.

transistor a semi-conductor device for controlling the flow of small electric currents, with three electrodes, capable of amplifying a signal as well as converting alternating to direct current.

trivial (of a name) popular; not scientific.

U

ultrasonic involving sound waves with a frequency above the upper limit of human hearing.

ultraviolet having a wavelength just above the violet end of the visible light spectrum.

unsaturated (of a chemical compound, especially a fat or oil) having double or triple bonds in its molecule, and therefore capable of joining with others to give further reaction.

V

valence electron an electron in the outermost shell of an atom involved in forming a chemical bond.

valency the power of an atom to join with other atoms, measured by the number of hydrogen atoms it can replace or combine with.

virtual relating to the points at which rays of light would meet if produced backwards (*virtual focus; virtual image*).

viscosity internal friction; resistance to flow.

volt the SI unit of force in an electric circuit; the pressure that would carry one ampere of current against one ohm of resistance.

W

watt the SI unit of power, measuring the rate at which electrical energy is used up or produced, equal to amperes multiplied by volts, or to one joule per second.

wavelength the distance between successive crests of a wave, especially of a sound wave, wave of visible light, radio wave, etc.

weight **1** the force experienced by a body as a result of the earth's gravitation (compare MASS). **2** any similar force with which a body tends to a centre of attraction.

work the exertion of force overcoming resistance or producing molecular change (*convert heat into work*).

X

X-rays radiation of very short wavelength, able to pass through opaque bodies.

Z

Z atomic number.

Psychology and Psychiatry Terms

A

aboulia the loss of will-power as a mental disorder.

abreaction the free expression and consequent release of a previously
repressed emotion.

aggression hostile or destructive tendency or behaviour.

alienation the sense of isolation and estrangement from friends,
society, etc.

amentia severe congenital mental deficiency.

amnesia a partial or total loss of memory.

anima the hidden personality (opp. PERSONA).

anoesis consciousness with sensation but without thought.

anorexia nervosa a psychological illness, especially in young women,
characterized by an obsessive desire to lose weight by refusing to eat.

anxiety a nervous disorder characterized by a state of excessive
uneasiness.

autism a mental condition, usually present from childhood,
characterized by complete self-absorption and a reduced ability to
respond to or communicate with the outside world.

aversion therapy treatment designed to make a subject averse to an
existing habit.

B

behaviour therapy the treatment of neurotic symptoms by training a
patient's reactions.

behaviourism the theory that human behaviour is determined by conditioning rather than by thoughts or feelings, and that psychological disorders are best treated by altering behaviour patterns.

Binet-Simon test a test used to measure intelligence, especially in children.

bulimia nervosa an emotional disorder in which bouts of extreme overeating are followed by depression and self-induced vomiting, purging, or fasting.

C

catatonia schizophrenia with intervals of catalepsy and sometimes violence.

catharsis the freeing of repressed emotion by association with the cause, and elimination by abreaction.

compensation the offsetting of a disability or frustration by development in another direction.

complex a related group of usually repressed feelings or thoughts which cause abnormal behaviour or mental states.

conditioned reflex a reflex response to a non-natural stimulus, established by training.

configuration gestalt.

convergent (of thought) tending to reach only the most rational result.

conversion the change of an unconscious conflict into a physical disorder or disease.

D

delirium tremens a mental derangement of chronic alcoholism, involving tremors and hallucinations.

delusion a false belief as a symptom of mental disorder.

dementia a disorder of the mental processes with memory disorders, personality changes, impaired reasoning, etc., due to brain disease or injury.

depersonalization the loss of one's sense of identity.

depression a state of extreme dejection; a mood of hopelessness and feelings of inadequacy, often with physical symptoms.

displacement 1 the substitution of one idea or impulse for another. **2** the unconscious transfer of unacceptable emotions from one object to another.

dissociated personality the pathological coexistence of two or more distinct personalities in the same person.

divergent (of thought) tending to reach a variety of possible solutions when analyzing a problem.

dyslexia abnormal difficulty in reading and spelling, caused by a condition of the brain.

E

ego the part of the mind that reacts to reality and has a sense of individuality.

Electra complex a daughter's subconscious sexual attraction to her father and hostility towards her mother.

encounter group a group of people seeking psychological benefit through close contact with one another.

exhibitionism a mental condition whereby one is compelled to display one's genitals indecently in public.

extroversion predominant concern with external things or objective considerations.

F

fixated having acquired an abnormal attachment to someone or something, owing to the arresting of part of the libido at an immature age.

frigidity sexual unresponsiveness in women.

fugue loss of awareness of who one is, often coupled with flight from one's usual environment.

G

gestalt an organized whole that is perceived as more than the sum of its parts.

guilt complex a mental obsession with the idea of having done wrong.

H

hypochondria 1 abnormal anxiety about one's health. **2** morbid causeless depression.

hypomania a minor form of mania.

hysteria a disturbance of the nervous system, of psychoneurotic origin and with no discernible organic cause.

I

id the inherited instinctive unconscious impulses of the individual.

imago an idealized mental picture of oneself or others, especially of a parent.

inferiority complex an unrealistic feeling of general inadequacy caused by actual or supposed inferiority in one sphere, sometimes marked by compensatory aggressive behaviour.

inhibition a self-imposed restraint on the direct expression of an instinct.

introversion predominant concern with one's own thoughts and feelings rather than with external things.

L

libido mental drive or energy, especially that associated with sexual desire.

limen the threshold below which a stimulus is imperceptible.

M

mania mental illness with periods of great excitement and violence.

manic-depressive *adj.* having a mental disorder with alternating periods of elation and depression.

melancholia a mental illness marked by depression and ill-founded fears.

N

neurosis a mental illness characterized by irrational or depressive thought or behaviour, caused by a disorder of the nervous system without organic change.

O

obsession a persistent idea or thought dominating the mind.

Oedipus complex a son's subconscious sexual attraction to his mother and hostility towards his father.

P

paranoia a mental disorder especially characterized by delusions of persecution and self-importance.

Pavlovian *adj.* of the work of the Russian physiologist I. P. Pavlov, especially on conditioned reflexes.

persona an aspect of the personality as shown to or perceived by others (opp. ANIMA).

phobia an abnormal or morbid fear or aversion.

projection 1 a mental image or preoccupation viewed as an objective reality. **2** the unconscious transfer of one's own impressions or feelings to external objects or people.

psychiatry the study or treatment of mental disease.

psychoanalysis a method of treating mental disorders by investigating the interaction of conscious and unconscious elements in the mind, and bringing repressed fears and conflicts into the conscious mind.

psychodrama a method of treating mental disorder in which patients act out events from their past.

psychopath 1 a person suffering from chronic mental disorder especially with abnormal or violent social behaviour. **2** a mentally or emotionally unstable person.

psychosis a severe mental derangement, especially with delusions and loss of contact with external reality.

psychosomatic *adj.* (of an illness) caused or aggravated by mental conflict, stress, etc.

psychotherapy the treatment of mental disorder by psychological means.

R

reflex an action performed in automatic response to a stimulus.

regression a return to an earlier stage of development, especially through hypnosis or mental illness.

repress to exclude actively (an unwelcome thought) from conscious awareness.

Rorschach test a personality test in which the subject is shown a standard set of ink-blots and asked to describe what they suggest or resemble.

S

schizophrenia a mental disease marked by a breakdown in the relation between thoughts, feelings, and actions, frequently accompanied by delusions and retreat from social life.

sublimation the diversion of the energy of a primitive, especially sexual, impulse into a culturally higher activity.

subliminal *adj.* (of a stimulus etc.) below the threshold of sensation or consciousness.

superego the part of the mind that acts as a conscience and responds to social rules.

superiority complex an undue conviction of one's own superiority to others.

T

threshold a limit below which a stimulus causes no reaction.

transactional analysis a method of treatment based on the attitudes revealed in transactions between the participants: parent, adult, and child.

transference the redirection of childhood emotions to a new object, especially to a psychoanalyst.

trauma emotional shock following a stressful event, sometimes leading to long-term neurosis.

Ships and
Nautical Terms

Ships and Boats

A

aircraft carrier a warship that carries and serves as a base for
aeroplanes.

Parts of a Ship

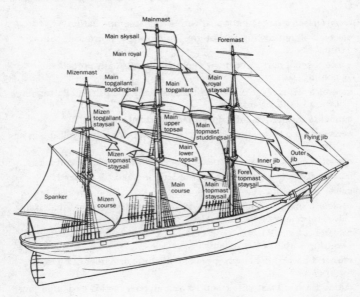

Mainmast

Main skysail

Foremast

Main royal

Mizenmast

Main topgallant studdingsail

Main topgallant

Main royal staysail

Mizen topgallant staysail

Main upper topsail

Main topmast studdingsail

Flying jib

Mizen lower topmast staysail

Main lower topsail

Outer jib

Inner jib

Fore topmast staysail

Spanker

Mizen course

Main course

Main topmast staysail

argosy a large medieval merchant ship, especially from Venice or Ragusa (now Dubrovnik).

B

barge 1 a long flat-bottomed boat for carrying freight on canals, rivers, etc. **2** a long ornamental boat used for pleasure or ceremony. **3** a boat used by the chief officers of a man-of-war.

barque a sailing-ship with the rear mast fore-and-aft rigged and the remaining (usually two) masts square-rigged.

barquentine a sailing-ship with the foremast square-rigged and the remaining (usually two) masts fore-and-aft rigged.

battle-cruiser a former type of heavy-gunned ship, faster and more lightly armed than a battleship.

battleship a warship with the heaviest armour and the largest guns.

bireme an ancient Greek warship, with two files of oarsmen on each side.

brig a two-masted square-rigged ship, with an additional lower fore-and-aft sail on the gaff and a boom to the mainmast.

brigantine a two-masted sailing-ship with a square-rigged foremast and a fore-and-aft rigged mainmast.

bum-boat any small boat plying with provisions etc. for ships.

C

cabin cruiser a large motor boat with living accommodation.

caique 1 a light rowing-boat on the Bosphorus. **2** a Levantine sailing-ship.

canoe a small narrow boat with pointed ends, usually propelled by paddling.

caravel a former type of light fast ship, chiefly Spanish and Portuguese of the 15th–17th centuries.

carrack a former type of large armed merchant-ship.

catamaran 1 a boat with twin hulls in parallel. **2** a raft of yoked logs or boats.

clipper a fast sailing-ship, especially one with raking bows and masts.

coble a flat-bottomed fishing-boat in Scotland and NE England.

collier a coal-ship.

coracle a small boat of wickerwork covered with watertight material, used especially on Welsh and Irish lakes and rivers.

corvette 1 a small naval escort-vessel. **2** a former type of flush-decked warship with one tier of guns.

cruiser 1 a warship of high speed and medium armament. **2** a cabin cruiser.

cutter 1 a small fast sailing-ship. **2** a small boat carried by a large ship.

D

destroyer a fast warship with guns and torpedoes, used to protect other ships.

dhow a lateen-rigged ship used on the Arabian sea.

dinghy 1 a small boat carried by a ship. **2** a small pleasure-boat. **3** a small inflatable boat, especially for emergency use.

dogger a two-masted Dutch fishing-boat with broad vertical bows.

dory *US* a flat-bottomed fishing-boat with high sides.

dreadnought a former type of battleship first launched in 1906, greatly superior in armament to all its predecessors.

dredger a boat containing a machine for dredging rivers.

drifter a boat used for drift-net fishing.

dromond a large medieval ship used for war or commerce.

duck an amphibious landing-craft.

F

factory ship a fishing ship with facilities for immediate processing of the catch.

felucca a small Mediterranean coasting vessel with oars or lateen sails or both.

flat boat, flat-bottomed boat one with a flat bottom for transport in shallow water.

freighter a ship designed to carry freight.

frigate 1 a British naval escort-vessel between a corvette and a destroyer in size. **2** *US* a similar ship between a destroyer and a cruiser in size. **3** a former type of warship next in size to ships of the line.

G

galleon 1 a former usually Spanish warship. **2** a large Spanish ship used in American trade. **3** a vessel shorter and higher than a galley.

galley 1 a low flat single-decked vessel which used sails and oars and was usually rowed by slaves or criminals. **2** an ancient Greek or Roman warship with one or more banks of oars. **3** a large open rowing-boat, e.g. that used by the captain of a man-of-war.

galliot 1 a Dutch cargo-boat or fishing-vessel. **2** a small, usually Mediterranean galley.

gig 1 a light ship's boat for rowing or sailing. **2** a rowing-boat, especially for racing.

gondola a light flat-bottomed boat used on Venetian canals, with a central cabin and a high point at each end, worked by one oar at the stern.

gunboat a small vessel of shallow draught and with relatively heavy guns.

H

houseboat a boat fitted up for living in.

hoy a former type of small vessel, usually rigged as a sloop, carrying passengers and goods, especially for short distances.

hydrofoil a boat fitted with planes for lifting its hull out of the water to increase its speed.

I

ice-boat 1 a boat on runners for travelling on ice. **2** a boat for breaking ice on rivers etc.

Indiaman a ship that was engaged in trade with India and the East Indies.

J

jolly boat a clinker-built ship's boat, smaller than a cutter.

junk a flat-bottomed sailing vessel used in the China seas, with a prominent stem and lugsails.

K

kayak 1 an Eskimo one-man canoe consisting of a light wooden frame covered with sealskins. **2** a small covered canoe resembling this.

keel a flat-bottomed vessel formerly used on the River Tyne etc. for loading coal-ships.

ketch a two-masted fore-and-aft-rigged sailing-boat, with a mizen-mast stepped forward of the rudder and smaller than its foremast.

L

launch 1 a large motor boat, used especially for pleasure. **2** a man-of-war's largest boat.

lifeboat 1 a specially constructed boat launched from land to rescue those in distress at sea. **2** a ship's small boat for use in emergency.

lighter a boat, usually flat-bottomed, for transferring goods from a ship to a wharf or another ship.

liner a ship carrying passengers on a regular line.

longboat a sailing-ship's largest boat.

long ship a long narrow warship with many rowers, used by the Vikings.

lugger a small ship carrying two or three masts with a lugsail on each.

M

man-of-war an armed ship, especially of a specified country.

minelayer a ship for laying mines.

minesweeper a ship for clearing away floating and submarine mines.

monitor a heavily armed shallow-draught warship.

mosquito-boat *US* a motor torpedo-boat.

N

narrow boat a British canal boat, especially one less than 7 ft. (2.1 metres) wide.

O

oil-tanker a ship designed to carry oil in bulk.

outboard a boat with an outboard engine, portable and attachable to the outside of the stern.

outrigger a boat fitted with outriggers, brackets bearing rowlocks projecting sideways.

P

packet a mail-boat or passenger-ship in former times.

paddle-boat, paddle steamer one propelled by a paddle-wheel, with boards round the edge to press backwards against the water.

pedalo a pedal-operated pleasure-boat.

pink a former type of sailing-ship, especially with a narrow stern and originally small and flat-bottomed.

pinnace a ship's small boat, now usually motor-driven, originally schooner-rigged and eight-oared.

piragua **1** a long narrow canoe made of one tree-trunk. **2** a two-masted sailing barge.

proa a Malay boat, especially with a large triangular sail and a canoe-like outrigger.

punt a long narrow flat-bottomed boat, square at both ends, used mainly for pleasure on rivers and propelled by a long pole.

Q

Q-ship an armed and disguised merchant ship, used as a decoy or to destroy submarines.

quinquireme an ancient Roman galley with five files of oarsmen on each side.

R

raft **1** a flat floating structure for conveying people or things. **2** a lifeboat or small (often inflatable) boat, especially for use in emergencies.

razee a ship reduced in height by the removal of her upper deck.

S

sampan a small boat usually with a stern-oar or two stern-oars, used in the far East.

schooner a fore-and-aft-rigged ship with two or more masts, the foremast being smaller than the others.

shallop **1** a large heavy sailing-boat; a sloop. **2** a dinghy.

shell a light racing-boat.

ship of the line a large battleship of former times, fighting in the front line of battle.

skiff a light rowing-boat or sculling-boat.

sloop 1 a small one-masted fore-and-aft-rigged vessel with mainsail and jib. **2** a **sloop-of-war**; a former type of small warship with guns on the upper deck only.

smack a single-masted sailing-boat for coasting or fishing.

submarine a vessel capable of operating under water and usually equipped with torpedoes, missiles, and a periscope.

supertanker a very large tanker ship.

T

tanker a ship for carrying liquids, especially mineral oils, in bulk.

tender a vessel attending a larger one to supply stores, convey passengers or orders, etc.

torpedo-boat a small fast lightly armed warship for carrying or discharging torpedoes.

tramp a merchant ship, especially a steamer, running on no regular route.

trawler a boat used for fishing with a trawl, a large wide-mouthed net dragged along the bottom.

trimaran a vessel like a catamaran, with three parallel hulls.

trireme an ancient Greek warship, with three files of oarsmen on each side.

tug a small powerful boat for towing larger boats and ships.

U

umiak an Eskimo skin-and-wood open boat propelled by women with paddles.

W

whaleboat a double-bowed boat of a kind used in whaling.

wherry 1 a light rowing-boat usually for carrying passengers. **2** a large light barge.

wind-jammer a merchant sailing-ship.

X

xebec a small three-masted Mediterranean vessel with lateen and usually some square sails.

Y

yawl 1 a two-masted fore-and-aft-rigged sailing-boat with the mizen-mast stepped far aft. **2** a small kind of fishing-boat. **3** a former kind of ship's jolly-boat with four or six oars.

Nautical Terms

A

abaft in the stern half of a ship.

abeam on a line at right angles to a ship's length.

after nearer the stern.

B

belay to fix (a running rope) round something to secure it.

belaying-pin a fixed wooden or iron pin for fastening a rope round.

bend to attach (a sail or cable) with a knot.

bilge 1 the almost flat part of a ship's bottom. **2** the filthy water that collects inside there.

bilge-keel a plate or timber fastened under a ship's bottom to prevent rolling.

board the side of a ship.

bull's-eye a hemisphere or thick disc of glass in a ship's deck or side to admit light.

bulwarks a ship's sides above deck.

C

careen to turn (a ship) on one side for cleaning, caulking, or repair.

carvel-built (of a boat) made with planks flush, not overlapping (compare CLINKER-BUILT).

cat to raise (an anchor) from the surface of the water to the cathead.

cathead a horizontal beam from each side of a ship's bow for raising and carrying the anchor.

centreboard (US **centerboard**) a board for lowering through a ship's keel to prevent leeway.

chains, channels the broad thick planks projecting horizontally from a ship's side abreast of the masts, used to widen the basis for the shrouds.

clinker-built (of a boat) made with external planks overlapping downwards (compare CARVEL-BUILT).

close-hauled (of a ship) with the sails hauled aft to sail close to the wind.

companion-ladder a ladder from a deck to a cabin.

companion-way a staircase to a cabin.

counter the curved part of a ship's stern.

cringle an eye of rope containing a metal ring for another rope to pass through.

D

dogwatch either of two short watches, 4–6 or 6–8 p.m.

dunnage mats, brushwood, etc. stowed under or among a ship's cargo to prevent wetting or chafing.

F

fiddle a contrivance for stopping things from rolling or sliding off a table in rough weather.

fore-and-aft (of a sail or rigging) set lengthwise, not on the yards.

freeboard the part of a ship's side between the waterline and the deck.

futtocks the middle timbers of a ship's frame, between the floor and the top timbers.

G

galley a ship's kitchen.

gangway 1 an opening in the bulwarks by which a ship is entered or left. **2** a bridge laid from ship to shore. **3** a passage on a ship.

garboard the first range of planks or plates laid on a ship's bottom next to the keel.

Genoa jib a large jib or foresail used especially on yachts.

gudgeon a socket at the stern of a boat, into which a rudder is fitted.

gunwales the upper edges of a boat's or ship's sides.

gybe (of a fore-and-aft sail or boom) to swing across in wearing or running before the wind.

H

half-deck the quarters of cadets and apprentices on a merchant ship.

hatchway an opening in a ship's deck for lowering cargo into the hold.

heads 1 the bows of a ship. **2** a ship's latrine.

heave to to bring or come to a standstill.

heel to lean or cause (a ship) to lean over owing to pressure of wind or an uneven load (compare LIST).

hold a cavity in the lower part of a ship, in which cargo is stowed.

K

kedge to move (a ship) by means of a hawser attached to a small anchor.

keelson a line of timber fastening a ship's floor-timbers to its keel.

killick a heavy stone used by small craft as an anchor.

L

lagan goods or wreckage lying on the bed of the sea, sometimes with a marking buoy etc. for later retrieval.

larboard port.

lateen sail a triangular sail on a long yard at an angle of 45° to the mast.

lazaret the after part of a ship's hold, used for stores.

list (of a ship, etc.) to lean over to one side, especially owing to a leak or shifting cargo (compare HEEL).

loran a system of long-distance navigation in which position is determined from the intervals between signal pulses received from widely spaced radio transmitters.

luff to steer (a ship) nearer the wind.

lugsail a quadrilateral sail which is attached to and hoisted from a yard.

M

marline a thin line of two strands.

marlinspike a pointed iron tool used to separate strands of rope or wire.

martingale a rope for holding down the jib-boom.

O

orlop the lowest deck of a ship with three or more decks.

P

painter a rope attached to the bow of a boat for tying it to a quay etc.

Plimsoll line a marking on a ship's side showing the limit of legal submersion under various conditions.

poop the stern of a ship; the aftermost and highest deck.

port the left-hand side, looking forwards, of a ship or boat.

promenade deck an upper deck on a passenger ship, where passengers may promenade.

prow the fore-part or bow of a ship.

Q

quarter-deck the part of a ship's upper deck near the stern, usually reserved for officers.

R

reach to sail with the wind abeam or abaft the beam.

reef each of several strips across a sail, for taking it in or rolling it up to reduce the surface area in a high wind.

riding-light a light shown by a ship at anchor.

roundhouse a cabin or set of cabins on the after part of the quarter-deck, especially on a sailing-ship.

rowlocks a pair of devices on a boat's gunwales which support the oars and give them leverage.

run (of a ship, etc.) to go straight and fast.

S

scupper a hole in a ship's side to carry off water from the deck.

skeg the after part of a ship's keel, or a projection from it.

spar a stout pole, especially used for a ship's mast, yard, etc.

spar-buoy a buoy made of a spar with one end moored so that the other stands up.

starboard the right-hand side, looking forwards, of a ship or boat.

stateroom a private compartment in a passenger ship.

stem the main upright piece at the bow of a ship, to which the ship's sides are joined.

stern the rear part of a ship or boat.

stern-post the central upright support at the stern, usually bearing the rudder.

strake a continuous line of planking or plates from the stem to the stern of a ship.

T

tack 1 the direction in which a ship moves regarded in terms of wind direction. **2** a temporary change of direction to take advantage of a side wind etc. **3** to change a ship's course by turning its head to the wind (compare WEAR).

thole-pins a pair of pins in a rowlock, on which the oar is supported.

thwart a rower's seat placed across a boat.

trim to arrange (sails) to suit the wind.

W

wardroom a room in a warship for the use of commissioned officers.

warp to haul (a ship) by a rope attached to a fixed point.

watch a four-hour spell of duty.

water-line the line along which the water surface touches a ship's side, marked on a ship for use in loading.

wear to change a ship's course by turning its head away from the wind (compare TACK).

wheel-house a steersman's shelter.

Y

yaw (of a ship) to fail to hold a straight course; go unsteadily, especially turning from side to side.

Winds and Weather

A

anticyclone a system of winds rotating outwards from an area of high pressure, producing fine weather.

B

bar a unit of pressure, 10^5 newton per square metre, approximately one atmosphere.

Beaufort scale a scale of wind speed ranging from 10 (calm) to 12 (hurricane).

berg wind a hot dry northerly wind blowing from the interior of S. Africa to coastal districts.

bise a keen dry northerly wind in Switzerland, S. France, etc.

bora a strong dry NE wind blowing in the upper Adriatic.

C

chinook **1** a warm dry wind which blows east of the Rockies. **2** a warm wet southerly wind west of the Rockies.

cirrus a form of white wispy cloud, especially at high altitude.

cold front the forward edge of an advancing mass of cold air.

convection the transfer of heat by the upward flow of hot air or downward flow of cold air.

cumulus a cloud formation consisting of rounded masses heaped above a horizontal base.

cyclone **1** a system of winds rotating inwards to an area of low pressure; a depression. **2** a violent hurricane of limited diameter.

D

depression a lowering of atmospheric pressure, especially the centre of a region of minimum pressure or the system of winds round it.

dew-point the temperature that is cool enough for dew to form.

doldrums an equatorial ocean region of calms, sudden storms, and light unpredictable winds.

dust devil *S. Afr.* a whirlwind visible as a column of dust.

F

föhn **1** a hot southerly wind on the northern slopes of the Alps. **2** a warm dry wind on the lee side of mountains.

G

geostrophic depending on the rotation of the earth.

greenhouse effect the trapping of the sun's warmth in the earth's lower atmosphere, caused by an increase in carbon dioxide, which is more transparent to solar radiation than to the reflected radiation from the earth.

greenhouse gas any of various gases, especially carbon dioxide, that contribute to the greenhouse effect.

H

haar a cold sea fog on the E. coast of Britain.

harmattan a parching dusty land-wind of the West African coast, occurring from December to February.

hurricane **1** a storm with a violent wind, especially a West Indian cyclone. **2** a wind of 65 knots (75 m.p.h.) on the Beaufort scale.

I

isobar a line on a map connecting places with the same atmospheric pressure at a given time or on average over a given period.

isohyet a line on a map connecting places with same amount of rainfall in a given period.

isotherm a line on a map connecting places with the same temperature at a given time or on average over a given period.

J

jet stream a narrow current of very strong winds encircling the globe several miles above the earth.

K

khamsin an oppressive hot south or SE wind occurring in Egypt for about 50 days in March, April, and May.

L

land breeze a breeze blowing towards the sea from the land, especially at night.

levanter a strong easterly Mediterranean wind.

M

microclimate the climate of a small local area, e.g. inside a greenhouse.

millibar one-thousandth of a bar.

mirage an optical illusion caused by atmospheric conditions, especially the appearance of a sheet of water in a desert or on a hot road from the reflection of light.

mistral a cold northerly wind that blows down the Rhone valley and S. France into the Mediterranean.

monsoon 1 a wind in S. Asia, especially in the Indian Ocean, blowing from the S.W. in summer (**wet monsoon**) and the N.E. in winter (**dry monsoon**). **2** the rainy season accompanying a wet monsoon. **3** any other wind with periodic alternations.

N

nimbus a rain-cloud.

O

occlusion a phenomenon in which the cold front of a depression overtakes the warm front, causing upward displacement of warm air between them.

P

pampero a strong cold SW wind in South America, blowing from the Andes to the Atlantic.

precipitation rain or snow etc. falling to the ground.

R

roaring forties stormy ocean tracts beteen latitudes 40° and 50° S.

S

sea breeze a breeze blowing towards the land from the sea, especially during the day.

serein a fine rain falling in tropical climates from a cloudless sky.

simoom a hot dry dust-laden wind blowing at intervals, especially in the Arabian desert.

sirocco 1 a Saharan simoom reaching the northern shores of the Mediterranean. **2** a warm sultry rainy wind in S. Europe.

stratus a continuous horizontal sheet of cloud.

T

thermal a rising current of heated air (used by gliders, balloons, and birds to gain height).

tornado a violent storm of small extent with whirling winds, especially in West Africa at the beginning and end of the rainy season, or in the US, etc. over a narrow path, often accompanied by a funnel-shaped cloud.

trade wind a wind blowing continually towards the equator, and deflected westward.

tramontana a cold N. wind in the Adriatic.

turbulence stormy conditions as a result of atmospheric disturbance.

typhoon a violent hurricane in E. Asian seas.

W

warm front an advancing mass of warm air.

waterspout a gyrating column of water and spray formed by a whirlwind between sea and cloud.

willy-willy an Australian cyclone or dust-storm.

Z

zonda a hot dusty N. wind in Argentina.

Part 4

The Lexicon

A Lexicon of Hard Words

The following words do not very obviously belong under any particular one of our list of Topics. Many or most of them will make interesting and useful additions to anyone's vocabulary; a few are so delightfully obscure that they should feature with advantage in quizzes and word games, and are frankly included here for fun.

A

aam a former liquid wine measure of 37 to 41 gallons; a cask.

abatis (also **abattis**) a defence made of felled trees with the boughs pointing outwards.

abecedarian 1 one occupied in learning the alphabet. **2** a teacher of the alphabet.

aberdevine a bird-fancier's name for the siskin, a small bird like a goldfinch.

aberrant diverging from the normal type or accepted standard.

abeyance a state of temporary disuse or suspension (*in abeyance*).

abiogenesis 1 the formation of living organisms from non-living substances. **2** the supposed spontaneous generation of living organisms.

ablation 1 the surgical removal of body tissue. **2** the evaporation or melting of part of the outer surface of a spacecraft, through heating by friction with the atmosphere.

abnegation 1 denial; the rejection or renunciation of a doctrine. **2** self-denial; self-sacrifice.

abomasum the fourth stomach of a ruminant.

abortifacient a drug or other agent that effects abortion.

abruption an interruption; a sudden break.

absell to descend a steep rock face by using a doubled rope coiled round the body and fixed at a higher point.

abstemious (of a person, habit, etc.) moderate, not self-indulgent, especially in eating and drinking.

abstruse hard to understand; obscure; profound.

abysmal 1 extremely bad (*abysmal weather; the standard is abysmal*). 2 profound, utter (*abysmal ignorance*).

acaricide a preparation for destroying mites.

acceptation a particular sense, or the generally recognized meaning, of a word or phrase.

accidie laziness, sloth, apathy.

accolade 1 the awarding of praise; an acknowledgement of merit. 2 a touch made with a sword at the bestowing of a knighthood.

accoutrements (*US* also **accouterments**) 1 equipment, trappings. 2 a soldier's outfit other than weapons and garments.

accretion 1 growth by organic enlargement or by slow additions of extraneous matter. 2 the product of such growing.

accrue to come as a natural increase or advantage, especially financial.

acculturate to (cause to) adapt to or adopt a different culture.

acerbic 1 astringently sour. 2 bitter in speech, manner, or temper.

acme the highest point or period (of achievement, success, etc.); the peak of perfection (*displayed the acme of good taste*).

acolyte 1 a person assisting a priest in a service or procession. 2 an assistant; a beginner.

acuity (of a needle, senses, understanding) sharpness, acuteness.

acumen keen insight or discernment, penetration.

adduce to cite as an instance or as proof or evidence.

adiaphorism religious or theological indifference; latitudinarianism.

adipose of or characterized by fat; fatty.

adit a horizontal entrance or passage in a mine.

adminicle 1 a thing that helps. 2 (in Scottish law) collateral evidence of the contents of a missing document.

adobe an unburnt sun-dried brick, or the clay used for making these.

adscititious adopted from without; supplementary.

adulate to flatter obsequiously.

adumbrate 1 to indicate faintly. 2 to represent in outline. 3 to foreshadow, typify. 4 to overshadow.

adventitious 1 accidental, casual. 2 added from outside or unexpectedly. 3 *Biol.* formed accidentally or under unusual conditions.

advowson (in British ecclesiastical law) the right of recommending a member of the clergy for a vacant benefice, or of making the appointment.

adze a tool for cutting away the surface of wood, like an axe with an arched blade at right angles to the handle.

aegis protection, defence (*under the aegis of* = under the protection of).

aegrotat **1** a certificate that a British university student is too ill to attend an examination. **2** an examination pass awarded in such circumstances.

aeolipyle an instrument by which steam produces circular motion.

aerotrain a train that is supported on an air cushion and guided by a track.

aestival (*US* **estival**) belonging to or appearing in summer.

afflatus a divine creative impulse; inspiration.

aficionado a devotee of a sport or pastime.

agape **1** a Christian feast in token of fellowship, especially one held by early Christians in commemoration of the Last Supper. **2** Christian fellowship, especially as distinct from erotic love.

agitprop the dissemination of Communist political propaganda, especially in plays, films, books, etc.

aglet **1** a metal tag attached to each end of a shoelace etc. **2** an aiguillette.

agnate **1** descended especially by male line from the same male ancestor. **2** descended from the same forefather; of the same clan or nation.

agora a place of public assembly, especially the market place.

agraffe a kind of hook on a ring, used as a clasp.

ahimsa in the Hindu, Buddhist, and Jainist tradition, respect for all living things, and avoidance of violence towards others both in thought and deed.

aigrette **1** the white plume of an egret. **2** a tuft of feathers or hair. **3** a spray of gems or similar ornament.

aiguillette a tagged point hanging from the shoulder on the breast of some uniforms.

aikido a Japanese form of self-defence making use of the attacker's own movements without causing injury.

ait (also **eyot**) *Brit.* a small island, especially in a river.

akimbo (of the arms) with hands on the hips and elbows turned outwards.

alcalde a magistrate or mayor in a Spanish, Portuguese, or Latin American town.

aleatoric **1** depending on the throw of a die or on chance. **2** involving random choice by a performer or artist.

alembic **1** an apparatus formerly used in distilling, an early kind of retort. **2** a means of refining or extracting.

aliment food.

allele (also **allel**) one of the (usually two) alternative forms of a gene.

alluvium a deposit of usually fine fertile soil left during a time of flood, especially in a river valley or delta.

almagest the astronomical treatise of Ptolemy; in the Middle Ages also other books of astrology and astronomy.

alopecia baldness.

altruism regard for others; unselfishness, concern for other people.

amah (in the Far East and India) a nursemaid or maid.

amanuensis a person who writes from dictation or copies manuscripts; a literary assistant.

ambagious roundabout; circuitous.

ambient surrounding.

ambit **1** the scope, extent, or bounds of something. **2** precincts or environs.

ambivalent having opposing feelings, especially love and hate, in a single context.

amice **1** a white linen cloth worn on the neck and shoulders by a priest celebrating the Eucharist. **2** a cap, hood, or cape worn by members of certain religious orders.

amnesty a general pardon, especially for political offences.

ampersand the sign & (= *and*).

amphibology **1** a quibble. **2** an ambiguous wording.

amphigoric of or being nonsense verses.

amphora a Greek or Roman vessel with two handles and a narrow neck.

ampoule (*US* **ampul** or **ampule**) a small capsule in which measured quantities of liquids or solids, especially for injecting, are sealed ready for use.

amygdaloid shaped like an almond.

anabasis **1** the march of the younger Cyrus into Asia in 401 BC, as narrated by Xenophon in his work *Anabasis.* **2** a military up-country march.

anabiosis revival after apparent death.

anadromous (of a fish) swimming up a river to spawn.

anaglyph **1** a composite stereoscopic photograph printed in superimposed complementary colours. **2** an embossed object cut in low relief.

analects (also **analecta**) a collection of short literary extracts.

analeptic (of a drug etc.) restorative.

analgesia the absence or relief of pain, especially without loss of consciousness.

anamnesis 1 recollection, especially of a supposed previous existence. **2** a patient's account of his or her medical history. **3** the part of the Eucharist recalling Christ's Passion, Resurrection, and Ascension.

anathema 1 a detested person or thing (*is anathema to me*). **2** a curse of the Church, excommunicating someone or denouncing a doctrine, or a person or thing so cursed.

anchorite a hermit; a religious recluse.

ancillary 1 (of a person, activity, or service) providing essential support to a central service or industry, especially the medical service. **2** subordinate or subservient (*to*).

andiron a metal stand for supporting logs in a fireplace; a firedog.

androgynous having both male and female sexual organs; hermaphrodite.

anfractuosity 1 circuitousness. **2** intricacy.

ankh a device consisting of a looped bar with a shorter crossbar, used in ancient Egypt as a symbol of life.

annular ring-shaped.

anodyne 1 able to relieve pain. **2** mentally soothing (*anodyne remarks*).

anomalous having an irregular or deviant feature; abnormal.

anomy (also **anomie**) lack of the usual social or ethical standards in an individual or group.

anopheles a genus of mosquitoes, many of which carry the malarial parasite.

anthelmintic any drug or agent that destroys tapeworms, roundworms, flukes, etc.

anthropomorphic (of a god, animal, or thing) having a human form or personality.

anti-hero a central character in a story or drama who noticeably lacks conventional heroic attributes.

antihistamine a substance used especially in the treatment of allergies.

antinomy 1 a contradiction between two reasonable beliefs or conclusions; a paradox. **2** a conflict between two laws or authorities.

anuran any tailless amphibian of the order that includes frogs and toads.

apatetic (of markings or colourings) deceptively resembling those of another species or of the environment.

apiculture bee-keeping.

aplomb assurance; self-confidence.

apodictic **1** clearly established. **2** of clear demonstration.

apophthegm (*US* **apothegm**) a terse saying or maxim; an aphorism.

aposematic *Zool.* (of coloration, markings, etc.) serving to warn or repel.

appanage (also **apanage**) **1** provision for the maintenance of the younger children of kings. **2** a perquisite. **3** a natural accompaniment or attribute.

appetence longing, desire.

apteryx a kiwi.

arachnid any arthropod of the class including scorpions, spiders, mites, and ticks.

arbalest (also **arblast**) a crossbow with a mechanism for drawing the string.

arboretum a botanical garden devoted to trees.

arcane mysterious, secret; understood by few.

archaism **1** the retention or imitation of the old or obsolete, especially in language or art. **2** an antiquated word or expression.

archetypical being a typical specimen or recurrent symbol.

archimandrite **1** the superior of a large monastery or several monasteries in the Orthodox Church. **2** an honorary title given to a monastic priest.

arcuate shaped like a bow; curved.

areola **1** a circular pigmented area, especially that surrounding a nipple. **2** any of the spaces between lines on a surface, e.g. of a leaf or an insect's wing.

argil clay, especially that used in pottery.

argol crude potassium hydrogen tartrate; a crusty deposit that builds up in vats during winemaking.

argute **1** sharp, shrewd. **2** (of sounds) shrill.

arisings the secondary or waste products of industrial operations.

armiger a person entitled to heraldic arms.

arrack (also **arak**) an alcoholic spirit, especially distilled from coconut sap or rice.

arraign **1** to indict before a tribunal; accuse. **2** to call (an action or statement) into question.

arras a rich tapestry, formerly hung on the walls of a room or to conceal an alcove.

arrogate **1** (often followed by *to* oneself) to claim (power, responsibility, etc.) without justification. **2** to attribute unjustly *to* a person.

arroyo *US* **1** a brook or stream. **2** a gulley.

arthropod any invertebrate animal of the phylum that has a segmented body, jointed limbs, and an external skeleton, e.g. an insect, spider, or crustacean.

ascesis the practice of self-discipline.

ashram a place of religious retreat for Hindus.

askari an East African soldier or policeman.

aspergillum a brush for sprinkling holy water.

assay to test (a metal, ore, or other substance) to determine its ingredients, concentration, etc.

assegai (also **assagai**) a slender iron-tipped spear, especially as used by South African peoples.

asseverate to declare solemnly.

asthenic 1 of lean or long-limbed build. **2** weakened and debilitated.

astral of or consisting of stars.

ataraxy (also **ataraxia**) calmness or tranquillity; imperturbability.

atavistic reverting to an earlier type, or to remote ancestors.

atheling a prince or lord in Anglo-Saxon England.

atoll a ring-shaped coral reef enclosing a lagoon.

atrabilious melancholy; ill-tempered.

attenuate to make thinner; dilute or reduce in force, value, or virulence.

auctorial of or pertaining to an author.

audile of the sense of hearing.

aumbry 1 a small recess in a church wall. **2** an old word for a cupboard.

aureole 1 a halo, especially round the head or body of a portrayed religious figure. **2** a corona round the sun or moon.

auscultation the act of listening, especially to sounds from the heart, lungs, etc., as a part of medical diagnosis.

austral 1 southern. **2** of Australia or Australasia.

autarky 1 self-sufficiency, especially as an economic system. **2** a state etc. run according to such a system.

autochthons the original or earliest inhabitants of a country; aboriginals.

autocross motor-racing across country or on unmade roads.

autodidact a self-taught person.

autonomous 1 having self-government. **2** acting independently or free to do so.

autotomy the casting off of a body part when threatened, e.g. the tail of a lizard.

avatar 1 in Hindu mythology, the descent of a deity or released soul to earth in bodily form. **2** incarnation; manifestation. **3** a manifestation or phase.

avid eager, greedy.

avionics electronics as applied to aviation.

avocation 1 a minor occupation. **2** a vocation or calling.

avuncular like or of an uncle; kind and friendly, especially towards a younger person.

axolotl an aquatic Mexican salamander which retains its larval form for life but can breed.

ayatollah a Shi'ite Muslim religious leader in Iran.

ayurvedic of or being traditional Hindu medicine.

azoth the alchemists' name for mercury.

B

baasskaap domination, especially of South African non-Whites by Whites.

babushka a headscarf tied under the chin.

baccalaureate 1 the university degree of bachelor. **2** an examination intended to qualify successful candidates for higher education.

bacchanalia drunken revelry.

bacchant riotous, roistering.

badinage humorous or playful ridicule.

bagatelle 1 a game in which small balls are struck into numbered holes on a board, with pins as obstructions. **2** a mere trifle; a negligible amount (and see MUSIC).

bagel a hard ring-shaped bread roll.

bagnio 1 a brothel. **2** an oriental prison.

bailiwick 1 the district or jurisdiction of a bailiff or bailie. **2** a person's sphere of operations or particular area of interest.

baklava a rich sweetmeat of flaky pastry, honey, and nuts.

baksheesh (also **backsheesh**) (in some oriental countries) a small sum of money given as a tip or in alms.

baldachin (also **baldaquin**) **1** a ceremonial canopy over an altar, throne, etc., or carried in a procession. **2** a rich brocade.

balderdash senseless talk or writing; nonsense.

baldric a belt for a sword, bugle, etc. that hung from the shoulder across the body to the opposite hip.

baleen whalebone.

ballista a catapult used in ancient warfare for hurling large stones etc.

balneal relating to bathing and medicinal springs.

baltimore (also **baltimore-oriole**) a North American bird of the starling family.

banausic 1 uncultivated or materialistic. **2** suitable only for artisans.

banderole (also **banderol**) **1** a long narrow flag flown at a masthead, or a similar streamer on a knight's lance. **2** a ribbon-like scroll.

banket the gold-bearing rocks of the Transvaal.

banneret 1 a knight who commanded his own troops in battle under his own banner. **2** a knighthood given on the battlefield for courage.

banshee an Irish or Scottish female spirit whose wailing warns of death in a house.

banzai 1 a Japanese battle-cry. **2** a form of greeting used to the Japanese emperor.

barbel any of the fleshy filaments growing from the mouth of a fish.

barbule a minute filament projecting from the barb of a feather.

Barmecide illusory, imaginary; such as to disappoint.

barracoon a rough barrack in which negro slaves, convicts, etc. were temporarily housed.

barre a horizontal bar at waist level used in dance exercises.

barrette 1 the crossbar of a fencing foil or hilt of a rapier. **2** a woman's hair ornament or bar for supporting the back hair.

barton 1 a farmyard. **2** the demesne lands of a manor.

bascule a type of drawbridge raised and lowered by counterweights.

basinet a light metal headpiece of medieval times, with a visor.

bastinado punishment by beating with a stick on the soles of the feet.

bat-fowling the catching of roosting birds at night.

bathos an unintentional lapse from the sublime to the absurd or trivial; a commonplace or ridiculous feature offsetting an otherwise sublime situation; an anticlimax.

bathysphere a spherical vessel for deep-sea observation.

batik cloth decorated with coloured designs produced by applying wax to the parts to be left uncoloured.

bayou a marshy offshoot of a river etc. in the southern US.

beatific 1 blissful (*a beatific smile*). **2** of blessedness, or making blessed.

bedizened gaudily decked out.

beedi an Indian cigarette made of a leaf rolled and tied with thread.

beestings the first milk (especially of a cow) after giving birth.

behemoth an enormous creature or thing.

behest a command; an entreaty (*went at his behest*).

bellicose eager to fight; warlike.

bell-wether 1 the leading sheep of a flock, on whose neck a bell is hung. **2** an absurd chief or leader.

belvedere a summer house or open-sided gallery usually at rooftop level.

benignant 1 kindly, especially to inferiors. **2** salutary, beneficial. **3** *Med.* (of a disease, tumour, etc.) benign; not malignant.

benison a blessing.

bergschrund a crevasse or gap at the head of a glacier or névé.

berserk wild, frenzied; in a violent rage (*went berserk*).

bestiary a moralizing medieval treatise on real and imaginary beasts.

bethel a chapel or nonconformist meeting-house.

bey (in the former Ottoman Empire) the title of the governor of a province.

bezel 1 the sloped edge of a chisel. **2** the oblique faces of a cut gem. **3** a groove or rim holding a watch-glass or gem.

bib-cock a tap with a bent nozzle fixed at the end of a pipe.

bibelot a small curio or artistic trinket.

bibliopole a seller of (especially rare) books.

bicuspid having two cusps, horns, or points (*bicuspid tooth*).

bifurcate to fork into two branches.

bight 1 a curve or recess in a coastline, river, etc. **2** a loop of rope.

bigot an obstinate and intolerant believer in a religion, political theory, etc.

bilboes an iron bar with sliding shackles formerly used for securing a prisoner's ankles.

biltong *S.Afr.* boneless meat salted and dried in strips.

biodegradable capable of being decomposed by bacteria or other living organisms.

bionic having artificial body parts or the superhuman powers resulting from these.

biretta a square usually flat cap with three flat projections on top, worn by (especially Roman Catholic) clergymen.

bisque 1 a rich shellfish soup, especially from lobster. **2** an advantage of scoring one free point in tennis, croquet, and golf, or of taking an extra turn or stroke. **3** fired unglazed pottery; biscuit.

bissextile leap year.

bistoury a surgical scalpel.

bistre (*US* **bister**) (the colour of) a brownish pigment made from the soot of burnt wood.

bitumen a tarlike mixture of hydrocarbons derived from petroleum, used for road surfacing and roofing.

blasé 1 unimpressed or indifferent because of overfamiliarity. **2** tired of pleasure; surfeited.

blatherskite a foolish chatterer.

bleachers (especially *US*) the outdoor uncovered bench seats at a sports ground, arranged in tiers and very cheap.

bleb 1 a small blister on the skin. **2** a small bubble in glass or on water.

blet the form of near-decay seen in over-ripe pears etc.

blunger a machine to mix clay etc. with water.

blurb a (usually eulogistic) description of a book, especially printed on its jacket, as promotion by its publishers.

bodega a cellar or shop selling wine and food, especially in a Spanish-speaking country.

boletus a large edible fungus, spongy underneath.

bolide a large exploding meteor; a fireball.

bolus 1 a soft ball, especially of chewed food. **2** a large pill.

bombazine (also **bombasine**) a twilled worsted dress material with or without some silk or cotton, especially when black.

bonzai 1 the art of cultivating ornamental artificially dwarfed trees and shrubs. **2** a tree or shrub grown in this way.

boondocks *US slang* rough or isolated country.

boondoggle *US slang* a trifling, useless, or wasteful undertaking.

borak *Austral. & NZ slang* banter, ridicule.

borborygmus a rumbling of gas in the intestines.

boreal of the North, or the north wind.

bosky wooded, bushy.

boules a French form of bowls, played on rough ground with usually metal balls.

bouleversement a violent inversion.

bowdlerize to remove objectionable matter from (a book etc.); expurgate.

brachial of or like an arm.

brad a thin flat nail with a narrow head.

braggadocio empty boasting; a boastful manner of speech and behaviour.

brandreth 1 a tripod or trivet. **2** a wooden framework supporting a cask, hay-rick, etc.

branks a scold's bridle; an iron framework for the head with a sharp metal gag.

brassage a mint charge levied to cover the expense of coining money.

brassard a band worn on the sleeve, especially with a uniform.

brasserie a restaurant, originally one serving beer with food.

brattice a wooden partition or shaft lining in a coal mine.

bravura 1 a brilliant or ambitious action or display. **2** a style of (especially vocal) music requiring exceptional ability.

braxy (*Scot*) an apoplectic disease of sheep.

brevet a document conveying a privilege from a sovereign or government, especially a rank in the army, without the appropriate pay.

breviary *RC Ch.* a book containing the service for each day, to be recited by those in orders.

brevier the name of a rather small type size.

brewis bread soaked in broth.

bridewell an old word for a prison or reformatory.

brimstone an old word for the element sulphur.

brindled (especially of domestic animals) brownish or tawny with streaks of other colour.

Brobdingnagian huge, immense, gigantic.

Brummagem cheap and showy and perhaps counterfeit (*Brummagem goods*).

bruxism the involuntary grinding or clenching of the teeth.

buccinator a flat thin cheek muscle.

buckler a small round shield that was held by a handle.

bucolic of shepherds, the pastoral life, etc.; rural.

buhl furniture etc. decorated with inlays of brass, tortoiseshell, etc. cut in patterns.

bulla 1 a watery blister on the skin. **2** a genus of deep-water molluscs.

bunraku the traditional Japanese puppet theatre.

bunt 1 the baggy centre of a sail or fishing net. **2** a disease of wheat. **3** (*verb*) **a** to butt with the head or horns. **b** to stop (a ball in US baseball) with the bat without swinging.

burette (*US* **buret**) a graduated glass tube with an end-tap for measuring small volumes of liquid in chemical analysis.

burgoo a thick oatmeal gruel or porridge used by sailors.

burin 1 a steel tool for engraving on copper or wood. **2** a flint tool of the Stone Age with a chisel point.

burke 1 to murder by suffocation or strangulation, or for the purpose of selling the victim's body for dissection. **2** to suppress quietly; to evade or shirk.

burlap 1 a coarse canvas, especially of jute, used for sacking etc. **2** a similar lighter material for use in dressmaking or furnishing.

bursa *Anat.* a fluid-filled cavity to lessen friction.

bushwhacker *US, Austral., & NZ* someone who clears woods and bush country, or lives and travels there.

buskins 1 thick-soled laced boots worn by ancient Athenian tragic actors to gain height. **2** medieval calf- or knee-high cloth or leather boots.

bustee an Indian shanty town; a slum.

butter-bump a dialect name for the bittern.

butyraceous like butter; buttery.

bwana (*Afr.*) master; sir.

C

cabal 1 a secret intrigue. **2** a political clique or faction.

caballero a Spanish gentleman.

cabbala 1 the Jewish mystical tradition. **2** mystic interpretation; any esoteric doctrine or occult lore.

caboose 1 a kitchen on a ship's deck. **2** *US* a guard's van; a car on a freight train for workmen etc.

cabotage 1 coastal navigation and trade. **2** the reservation to a country of (especially air) traffic operation within its territory.

cabriole a kind of curved leg characteristic of Queen Anne and Chippendale furniture.

cabriolet 1 a light two-wheeled carriage with a hood, drawn by one horse. **2** a car with a folding top.

cache a hiding place for treasure, provisions, ammunition, etc., or its contents.

cachet 1 a distinguishing mark or seal. **2** prestige. **3** *Med.* a flat capsule enclosing a dose of unpleasant-tasting medicine.

cachinnate to laugh loudly.

cachou a lozenge to sweeten the breath.

cacique 1 a West Indian or American Indian native chief. **2** a Spanish or Latin American political boss.

cacoethes an urge to do something undesirable.

cacography bad handwriting or spelling.

cadastral of or showing the extent, value, and ownership of land for taxation.

cadaver a corpse.

cadre 1 a basic unit, especially of servicemen, forming a nucleus for expansion when necessary. **2** a group of activists in a revolutionary party, or a member of such a group.

caduceus an ancient Greek or Roman herald's wand, especially as carried by Hermes or Mercury.

caesura 1 (in Greek and Latin verse) a break between words within a metrical foot. **2** (in modern verse) a pause near the middle of the line.

caisson 1 a watertight chamber in which underwater construction work can be done. **2** a floating vessel used as a floodgate in docks. **3** an ammunition chest or wagon.

cajole to persuade by flattery, deceit, etc. *into* or *out of*.

calabash 1 an evergreen tree of tropical America, *Crescentia cujete*. **2** a gourd from this tree, whose shell is used to carry water, make a tobacco pipe, etc.

calash 1 a light low-wheeled carriage with a removable folding hood. **2** *Canadian* a two-wheeled horse-drawn vehicle. **3** a woman's hooped silk hood.

calcaneus the bone forming the heel.

calefacient a substance producing a sensation of warmth.

calender a machine in which cloth, paper, etc. is pressed by rollers to glaze or smooth it.

calibrate 1 to mark (a gauge) with a standard scale of readings. **2** to correlate the readings of (an instrument) with a standard. **3** to determine the calibre of (a gun). **4** to determine the correct capacity or value of.

callipers compasses with bowed legs for measuring the diameter of convex bodies or internal dimensions.

callipygian having beautiful buttocks.

calotte a skullcap as worn by Roman Catholic clergymen.

caltrop (also **caltrap**) **1** a four-spiked iron ball that used to be thrown on the ground to impede cavalry horses. **2** a creeping plant of the genus *Tribulus*, with hard spines.

calumet a North American Indian peace pipe.

calumny slander; malicious misrepresentation.

cambist 1 one who deals in bills of exchange. **2** a manual of foreign exchanges.

camelopard an old word for a giraffe.

cameralistics the management of German state property.

campestral pertaining to fields or open country.

canard 1 an unfounded rumour. **2** an extra surface attached to an aeroplane forward of the main lifting surface, for extra stability or control.

cancellate marked with crossing lines.

cancroid 1 crablike. **2** resembling cancer.

cangue a broad heavy wooden frame worn round the neck as a former punishment in China.

cannelure the groove round a bullet.

cannula a small tube for inserting into the body to allow fluid to enter or escape.

Canopic urn/jar an urn for holding the entrails of an embalmed body in an ancient Egyptian burial.

cantankerous bad-tempered, quarrelsome.

canterbury a piece of furniture with partitions for holding music etc.

cantharides a preparation of dried beetles, causing blistering of the skin and formerly used in medicine and as an aphrodisiac.

canthus either corner of the eye, where the eyelids meet.

cantle the part that sticks up at the back of a saddle.

canto a division of a long poem.

canton a subdivision of a country, especially of Switzerland (and see HERALDRY).

cantor the leader of the singing in a church or synagogue.

cantoris (of music) to be sung by the north side of a church choir in antiphonal singing (compare DECANI).

caoutchouc raw rubber.

capitular 1 of a cathedral chapter. **2** of or being a lump on the end of a bone.

capote a long hooded cloak, formerly worn by soldiers and travellers.

capuche a monk's hood.

Capuchin 1 a Franciscan friar of the rule of 1529. **2** a cloak and hood formerly worn by women. **3** (**capuchin**) **a** a South American monkey with cowl-like head and hair. **b** a kind of pigeon with head and neck feathers like a cowl.

caracole a horse's half-turn to the right or left.

carapace the hard upper shell of a tortoise or crustacean.

caravanserai an Eastern inn with a central court where desert caravans may rest.

carboy a large globular glass bottle usually protected by a frame, for containing liquids.

carcanet an old word for a jewelled collar or headdress.

caret a mark (ʌ, ʌ) indicating a proposed insertion in printing or writing.

caries decay and crumbling of a tooth or bone.

carillon 1 a set of bells sounded either from a keyboard or mechanically. **2** an organ stop imitating a peal of bells.

carminative relieving flatulence.

carnet 1 a customs permit to take a motor vehicle across a frontier for a limited period. **2** a permit allowing use of a campsite.

carob an evergreen Mediterranean tree whose edible pods are sometimes used as a substitute for chocolate.

carpet-bagger 1 (especially *US*) a political candidate in an area where the candidate has no local connections. **2** an unscrupulous opportunist.

carrel a small cubicle for a reader in a library, or formerly for study in a cloister.

carronade a short ship's gun of large calibre, with a chamber for the powder like a mortar.

cartography the drawing of maps.

cartouche an oval ring usually enclosing a king's name in Egyptian hieroglyphics.

caruncle a fleshy excrescence such as a turkeycock's wattles, or a similar outgrowth on a plant.

casern a building in a town to accommodate troops; a barrack.

casque a helmet.

caste 1 any of the Hindu hereditary classes. **2** a more or less exclusive social class, or the position this confers.

castigate to rebuke or punish severely.

casuistry the resolving of moral problems with clever but false reasoning.

cataclysm 1 a violent, especially social or political, upheaval or disaster. **2** a great flood.

catafalque a decorative wooden framework to support a coffin during a funeral or when lying in state.

catamite a boy kept for homosexual practices.

catchpole 1 a Roman publican; a tax-gatherer. **2** a sheriff's officer or sergeant.

catechumen a Christian convert under instruction before baptism.

cateran a Highland irregular fighting man; a marauder.

catharsis 1 an emotional release in drama or art. **2** purging of the bowels.

catholicon a universal remedy; a panacea.

catoptric of or being a mirror, a reflector, or reflection.

caucus 1 a meeting of US political party members to decide policy; or a bloc of such members. **2** a secret meeting of a group within any larger organization; or such a group.

caudal of a tail, or the hind parts of the body.

caudillo (in Spanish-speaking countries) a military or political leader.

caul the inner membrane enclosing a foetus, a part of which is sometimes found on a child's head at birth.

cay a low insular bank or reef of coral, sand, etc.

cedilla 1 a mark written under the letter ç, especially in French, to show that it is sibilant (as in *façade*). **2** a similar mark under ş in Turkish and other oriental languages.

ceilidh *Ir. & Sc.* an informal gathering for conversation, music, dancing, songs, and stories.

cenacle a supping room; an upper chamber, especially that in which the Last Supper was held.

cephalic of the head.

cerecloth waxed cloth formerly used as a waterproof covering or (especially) as a shroud.

certitude a feeling of absolute certainty; conviction.

cerulean deep blue like a clear sky.

cerumen earwax.

cervelat a kind of smoked pork sausage.

cetacean any marine mammal with a streamlined hairless body and a blowhole on the back for breathing, including whales, dolphins, and porpoises.

chador (also **chador, chuddar**) a large cloth worn in some countries by Muslim women, wrapped around the body to leave only the face exposed.

chalcedony a type of quartz occurring in several forms, e.g. onyx, agate, tiger's eye, etc.

Chaldean 1 of ancient Chaldea or its people or language. **2** of or relating to astrology.

chalybeate (of mineral water etc.) impregnated with iron salts.

chamfer a bevelled surface at a right-angled edge or corner.

chanterelle an edible fungus with a yellow funnel-shaped cap and smelling of apricots.

chaplet 1 a garland for the head. **2** a string of beads used for counting prayers or as a necklace.

charisma 1 the ability to inspire followers with devotion and enthusiasm; great charm. **2** a divinely conferred power or talent.

charpoy a light Indian bedstead.

chasuble a priest's usually ornate loose sleeveless outer vestment.

chauvinism 1 exaggerated or aggressive patriotism. **2** excessive or prejudiced support for one's own cause or group or sex (*male chauvinism*).

chela 1 a prehensile claw of crabs, scorpions, etc. **2** in Buddhism, a novice or disciple.

cheongsam a Chinese woman's dress with a high neck and slit skirt.

cheval glass a tall mirror swung on an upright frame.

cheverel 1 kid leather. **2** pliable and yielding.

chibouk a long Turkish tobacco pipe.

chiliad 1 a thousand. **2** a thousand years.

chiliasm the doctrine of or belief in Christ's prophesied reign of 1,000 years on earth.

chimera (also **chimaera**) **1** a female monster in Greek mythology, with a lion's head, a goat's body, and a serpent's tail. **2** a fantastic product of the imagination; a bogy. **3** an organism formed out of different parts by grafting.

chirography handwriting, calligraphy.

chiropody the treatment of the feet and their ailments.

chiropteran any creature such as the bats and flying foxes, whose membraned limbs serve as wings.

chitin the hornlike substance in the shells of crustaceans etc.

chondrify to turn into cartilage.

chopine (also **chopin**) a woman's high-heeled clog.

chop-logic pedantic argument.

choragus (also **choregus**) **1** the leader of an ancient Greek chorus. **2** a choir leader.

chrestomathy a selection of passages used to help in learning a language.

chrism consecrated oil used especially for anointing in Catholic and Greek Orthodox rites.

chrisom a baby's white baptismal robe that was used as its shroud if it died within the month.

chthonic (also **chthonian**) of the underworld.

chutzpah *slang* shameless audacity; cheek.

chyle milky fluid consisting of lymph and absorbed food from the intestine after digestion.

cicerone a guide who gives information to sightseers.

cicisbeo the recognized male escort of a married woman.

cilice haircloth, or a garment made of this.

Cimmerian dark; densely gloomy.

cineaste a cinema enthusiast.

cingulum *Anat.* a girdle or similar structure, especially the ridge round the base of the crown of a tooth.

circinate *Bot. & Zool.* rolled up with apex in the centre, e.g. of young fronds of ferns.

circumspect wary, cautious; taking everything into account.

circumvent 1 to evade (a difficulty); find a way round. **2** to baffle, outwit.

clade *Biol.* a group of organisms evolved from a common ancestor.

clairschach the old Celtic harp strung with wire.

clandestine surreptitious, secret.

clapperdudgeon a term of insult for a beggar.

claque a group of people hired to applaud in a theatre etc.

claymore 1a an early Scottish broadsword. **b** a broadsword, often with a single edge, having a hilt with a basketwork design. **2** *US* a type of anti-personnel mine.

clemency mercy.

clepsydra an ancient time-measuring device worked by a flow of water.

clerihew a short comic or nonsensical verse in two rhyming couplets with lines of unequal length, about a famous person whose name usually provides one of the rhymes.

clerisy learned people as a body; scholars.

climacteric 1 *Med.* the period of life when fertility and sexual activity are in decline. **2** a supposed critical period in life (especially occurring every seven years).

cline a graded sequence of differences within a species etc.; a continuum.

clinquant glittering, as with tinsel or spangles.

cliometrics a method of historical research making much use of statistical information and methods.

cloaca the single genital and excretory passage in birds, reptiles, etc.

clone 1 a group of organisms produced asexually from one parent. **2** a person or thing regarded as identical with another.

cloture *US* the closure of a debate.

coalesce to come together and form one whole.

coaptation adaptation of parts to each other, e.g. the ends of a fractured bone.

cochleate shaped like a snail shell; spiral.

codex an ancient manuscript in book form.

coeliac of or affecting the belly.

coenobite a member of a monastic community.

coetaneous contemporary, simultaneous.

coeval 1 of the same age. **2** of the same duration. **3** existing at the same time.

cogent (of arguments, reasons, etc.) convincing, compelling.

cognomen 1 a nickname. **2** an ancient Roman's personal name or epithet, as in Marcus Tullius *Cicero*, Publius Cornelius Scipio *Africanus*.

cohere 1 (of parts or a whole) to stick together, remain united. **2** (of reasoning etc.) to be logical or consistent.

col a depression in a mountain ridge, generally affording a pass.

cold-short (of a metal) brittle in its cold state.

collogue to talk confidentially.

colloquium an academic conference or seminar.

collude to conspire, especially for a fraudulent purpose.

colophon 1 a publisher's device or imprint, especially on the title-page. **2** a tailpiece in a manuscript or book, often ornamental, giving the writer's or printer's name, the date, etc.

colophony rosin.

colostrum the first secretion from the mammary glands after giving birth.

colporteur an itinerant seller of (especially religious) books.

columbarium 1 a dovecote. **2** a vault with niches for funerary urns. **3** a hole left in a wall for the end of a beam.

comedo a blackhead.

commensurate having the same size, duration, etc.; coextensive or proportionate *with*.

commination the threatening of divine vengeance; the recital of divine threats against sinners.

commode 1 a chest of drawers. **2** a chamber-pot concealed in a chair with a hinged cover.

compliant disposed to comply; yielding, obedient.

complicity partnership in a crime or wrongdoing.

compunction the pricking of conscience; regret, scruples.

compurgation acquittal from a charge or accusation, formerly obtained by the oaths of witnesses.

concha *Anat.* any shell-like part, especially the outer ear.

concomitant going together; associated (*concomitant circumstances*).

concordance 1 agreement. **2** a book containing an alphabetical list of the important words used in a book or by an author, usually with citations of the passages concerned.

concordat an agreement, especially between the Roman Catholic church and a State.

concupiscence sexual desire.

condign (of a punishment etc.) severe and well-deserved.

condone 1 to forgive or overlook (an offence or wrongdoing). **2** to approve or sanction, usually reluctantly. **3** (of an action) to atone for (an offence); make up for.

conduit **1** a channel or pipe for conveying liquids. **2** a tube or trough for protecting insulated electric wires.

condyle (also **condyl**) a rounded projection at the end of a bone, forming a joint with another bone.

confluence **1** a place where two rivers meet. **2a** a coming together. **b** a crowd of people.

confrère a fellow member of a profession, scientific body, etc.

confute to prove (a person) to be in error or (an argument) to be false.

congeries a disorderly collection; a mass or heap.

connive **1** (followed by *at*) to disregard or tacitly consent to (a wrongdoing). **2** to conspire *with*.

connubial of marriage or the marital relationship.

conquistador a conqueror, especially one of the Spanish conquerors of Mexico and Peru in the 16th century.

consensus a general agreement of opinion, testimony, etc.; a majority view.

consign **1** to hand over; deliver to a person's possession or trust. **2** to commit decisively or permanently (*consigned it to the dustbin*).

consistory the council of Roman Catholic cardinals, or a court presided over by a bishop of the Church of England.

constrain **1** to compel, or bring about by compulsion. **2** to confine or restrict forcibly.

contentious **1** aggressive, quarrelsome. **2** likely to cause an argument; controversial.

contiguous touching, especially along a line; in contact *with*.

continuum anything seen as having a continuous, not discrete, structure (*space-time continuum*).

contrail a condensation trail, especially from an aircraft.

contumacious insubordinate; stubbornly disobedient, especially to a court order.

contumely insolent or reproachful language or treatment.

contusion a bruise.

conversant well experienced or acquainted *with*.

convoluted **1** coiled, twisted. **2** complex, intricate.

cony (also **coney**) a rabbit.

coprophagous *Zool.* dung-eating.

cordillera a system of parallel mountain ranges with intervening plateaux etc., especially of the Andes.

cordovan a kind of soft leather.

corniche a coastal road cut into the edge of a cliff.

corposant a luminous electric charge sometimes seen on a ship or aircraft during a storm.

corrida a bullfight.

corrigenda errors to be corrected in a printed book.

corsair a pirate, or pirate ship, especially formerly along the Barbary coast.

coruscate to sparkle; be brilliant.

corybantic wild, frenzied.

costive constipated.

coterminous having the same boundaries in space, time, or meaning *with*.

countervail to counterbalance; oppose forcefully and usually successfully.

couvade a custom by which a father appears to undergo labour and childbirth when his child is being born.

coven an assembly of witches.

cozen to cheat, defraud, beguile.

crambo a game in which a player gives a word or verse-line to which each of the others must find a rhyme.

cran a measure for fresh herrings ($37^1/_2$ gallons).

crapulent drunk, or resulting from drunkenness.

crepitate to make a crackling sound.

crepuscular **1** of twilight; dim. **2** appearing or active in twilight.

cromlech **1** a dolmen; a megalithic tomb. **2** a circle of upright prehistoric stones.

crosier a bishop's staff.

crural *Anat.* of the leg.

crux **1** the decisive point at issue. **2** a difficult matter; a puzzle.

cucking-stool a chair on which disorderly women were ducked as a punishment.

cudbear a purple dye derived from lichen.

culminate to reach the highest or final point (*the antagonism culminated in war*).

cuneiform the wedge-shaped writing impressed usually in clay in ancient Babylonian etc. inscriptions.

curmudgeon a bad-tempered person.

cursive (of writing) done with joined characters.

cursory hasty, hurried (*a cursory glance*).

cuspidor *US* a spitton.

cutaneous of the skin.

cwm a bowl-shaped hollow in the side of a hill.

D

dacha a Russian country house or cottage.

dacoit a member of a gang of armed robbers in India or Myanmar.

daedal 1 skilful; inventive. **2** (of the earth etc.) variously adorned.

dalmatic a wide-sleeved long loose ecclesiastical vestment.

daltonism colour-blindness, especially the inability to distinguish between red and green.

dariole a savoury or sweet dish cooked and served in a small cup-shaped mould.

dauphin the eldest son of the King of France.

deadlight 1 a shutter inside a ship's porthole. **2** *US* a skylight that cannot be opened.

deasil clockwise.

débâcle a sudden utter defeat or collapse.

debouch (of troops, a river, a road, etc.) to issue forth into an open area.

decanal of a dean or deanery.

decani (of music) to be sung by the south side of a church choir in antiphonal singing (compare CANTORIS).

deckle a device in a paper-making machine that limits the size of the sheet, leaving a rough edge.

decorticate to remove the bark, husk, or other outside layer from.

decretal a papal decree.

dedans the open gallery at the end of the service side of a real tennis court.

deemster a judge in the Isle of Man.

deeping each of the fathom-deep sections of a fishing net.

defalcation 1 misappropriation of money. **2** a shortcoming.

defeasance the act or process of rendering null and void.

defenestration the action of throwing (especially a person) out of a window.

defilade to secure (a fortification) against gunfire.

deft neatly skilful or dexterous; adroit.

deglutition the act of swallowing.

degust to taste attentively; savour.

deign to think fit; condescend.

deipnosophist a master of the art of dining.

delation reporting of an offence; impeachment.

delectation pleasure, enjoyment (*sang for his delectation*).

deleterious harmful to the mind or body.

demagogue **1** a political agitator appealing to the basest instincts of a mob. **2** a leader of the people in ancient times.

deme **1** a political or administrative division in both ancient and modern Greece. **2** a local population of closely related plants or animals.

demesne **1** a domain. **2** landed property attached to a mansion etc.

demiurge **1** according to Plato, the creator of the universe. **2** in Gnosticism etc., a heavenly being subordinate to the Supreme Being.

demivierge a woman of suspected unchastity who is still physiologically a virgin.

demography the study of the statistics of births, deaths, diseases, etc. in a community.

dendrite **1** a mineral with natural treelike markings. **2** a branching treelike crystal. **3** a branching outgrowth on a nerve cell.

denigrate to defame or disparage (someone's character); blacken.

denizen **1** a foreigner admitted to certain rights in the adopted country. **2** a naturalized word, animal, or plant.

deodand a personal chattel forfeited to the Crown for pious uses.

deontic of or relating to moral duty and obligation.

depilate to remove the hair from.

deploy **1** (of troops) to spread out from a column into a line. **2** to bring (arguments etc.) into effective action.

depredations despoiling, ravaging, or plundering.

deracinate to tear up by the roots.

dermabrasion the surgical removal of some layers of the skin with a revolving tool.

derogate (*from*) **1** to take away a part from; detract from (a merit, right, etc.). **2** to deviate from (correct behaviour etc.)

desalinate to remove salt from (especially sea water).

desiccate to dry out (especially food for preservation) (*desiccated coconut*).

desiderate to feel to be missing; regret the absence of; wish to have.

desist to abstain, cease (*please desist from interrupting*).

desuetude a state of disuse.

desultory going half-heartedly from one subject to another; unmethodical and superficial.

detent **1** a catch whose removal allows machinery to move. **2** a catch that regulates striking in a clock.

deuteragonist the second most important person in a drama.

Devanagari the alphabet used for Sanskrit, Hindi, and other Indian languages.

dewlap the loose fold of skin hanging from the throats of cattle, dogs, etc., or of old people.

dexter one of a small hardy breed of Irish cattle (and see HERALDRY).

dharma *Indian* **1** social custom; the right behaviour. **2** the Buddhist truth. **3** the Hindu social or moral law.

dhobi a washerman or washerwoman in India.

diacritical distinguishing; distinctive.

diaeresis (*US* **dieresis**) a mark (as in *naïve*) over a vowel to indicate that it is sounded separately.

dianetics the system of mental therapy associated with scientology.

diaphanous (of fabric etc.) light and delicate and almost transparent.

diaphoresis sweating, especially artificially induced.

diaphysis *Anat.* the shaft of a long bone.

Diaspora the dispersion of the Jews among the Gentiles, or any group of people similarly scattered.

diastema **1** an interval in ancient Greek music. **2** a space between two teeth.

diatribe a forceful verbal attack; a piece of bitter criticism.

dichotomy **1** a sharp division into two. **2** binary classification. **3** *Bot. & Zool.* repeated bifurcation.

dictum a formal utterance, saying, or maxim.

didicoy *slang* a gypsy; an itinerant tinker.

diktat a categorical decree, especially one imposed by a victor after a war.

dilatory given to or causing delay.

dilettante a person who studies a subject superficially.

dimity cotton fabric woven with stripes or checks.

dipnoan a fish with both gills and lungs.

dirigible a balloon or airship that can be guided.

discobolus a discus-thrower in ancient Greece.

discombobulate *US slang* to disturb, disconcert.

discrepancy difference; a failure to correspond; inconsistency.

discrete individually distinct; separate, discontinuous.

discursive **1** rambling or digressive. **2** based on argument or reasoning rather than on immediate insight.

disembogue (of a river etc.) to pour forth (waters) at the mouth.

disparage **1** to speak slightingly of; depreciate. **2** to bring discredit on.

disparity inequality; difference; incongruity.

disquisition a long or elaborate treatise or discourse on a subject.

distich a pair of verse lines; a couplet.

dittography a copyist's mistaken repetition of a letter, word, or phrase.

diuretic causing increased output of urine.

divot a piece of turf cut out, as by a golf club in making a stroke.

doge the chief magistrate of the former States of Venice or Genoa.

dolmen a prehistoric tomb with a large flat stone laid on two upright ones.

dolorous 1 distressing, painful; doleful, dismal. **2** distressed, sad.

dominie a Scottish schoolmaster.

dorsal 1 of or on the back. **2** ridge-shaped.

dortour (also **dorter**) a dormitory in a monastery.

do-se-do (also **do-si-do**) a figure in which two dancers pass round each other back to back and return to their original positions.

dotal pertaining to a woman's dowry.

dottle a remnant of burnt tobacco in a pipe.

doxology a hymn or verse of praise to God.

Draconian (of laws, etc.) very harsh or severe.

dragoman an interpreter or guide, especially in countries speaking Arabic, Turkish, or Persian.

drail a fish-hook or line weighted with lead for dragging below the surface of the water.

dressage the training of a horse in obedience and deportment, especially for competition.

drogue 1 a buoy at the end of a harpoon line, or a sea anchor. **2** a funnel-shaped fabric device used as a wind-sock, a target for gunnery, etc.

dryad in Greek mythology, a nymph inhabiting a tree; a wood nymph.

ductile 1 (of a metal) capable of being drawn into wire. **2** (of a substance) easily moulded. **3** (of a person) docile, gullible.

duenna an older woman acting as a governess or companion in charge of girls, especially in a Spanish family; a chaperone.

dugong a marine mammal of Asian seas; the sea cow.

dulcet (especially of a sound) sweet and soothing.

dundrearies long side-whiskers worn without a beard.

dunnock the common hedge sparrow.

dysphemism the substitution of an unpleasant or derogatory expression for a pleasant or harmless one (opp. EUPHEMISM).

dysphoria unease; mental discomfort.

dystopia an imaginary place or condition in which everything is as bad as possible (opp. UTOPIA).

E

eagre a high tidal wave rushing up a narrow estuary; a bore.

ebullient exuberant, high-spirited.

ecdysiast a strip-teaser.

echinoderm a marine invertebrate usually with a spiny skin, e.g. starfish and sea urchins.

eclectic 1 deriving ideas, tastes, style, etc. from various sources. **2** selecting one's beliefs etc. from various sources; attached to no particular school of philosophy.

eclogue a short poem, especially a pastoral dialogue.

ectoplasm the supposed semi-fluid substance issuing from the body of a spiritualistic medium during a trance.

ecumene a nuclear centre of dense population and high culture.

ecumenical seeking or promoting worldwide Christian unity.

edacious voracious; greedy.

effendi a former title of respect for a man of standing in Turkey.

effete 1 feeble and incapable. **2** worn out; exhausted of its essential quality or vitality.

efficacious (of a thing) producing or sure to produce the desired effect.

effluvium an unpleasant smell or exhaled substance affecting the lungs.

effulgent radiant; shining brilliantly.

egregious outstandingly bad; shocking (*egregious folly; an egregious ass*).

eidetic (of a mental image) having unusual vividness and detail, as if actually visible.

eidolon 1 a spectre; phantom. **2** an idealized figure.

eirenicon a proposal made as a means of achieving peace.

eisteddfod a congress of Welsh bards; a national or local festival for musical competitions etc.

elation high spirits.

eld old age.

electuary medicinal powder etc. mixed with something sweet.

eleemosynary 1 of alms; charitable. **2** gratuitous.

elucidate to throw light on; explain.

elude 1 to escape adroitly from (a danger, difficulty, pursuer, etc.); dodge. **2** to avoid compliance with (a law). **3** (of a fact, solution, etc.) to baffle (a person's memory or understanding).

emanate to issue or originate (*from*).

emasculate 1 to deprive of force or vigour; make feeble or ineffective. **2** to castrate.

embroil 1 to involve (a person) in conflict or difficulties. **2** to bring (affairs) into confusion.

emmetropia the normal condition of the eye; perfect vision.

emollient something that soothes and softens the skin.

empennage an arrangement of stabilizing surfaces at the tail of an aircraft.

empirical based on observation, not on theory; deriving knowledge from experience alone.

empyrean 1 the highest heaven, as the sphere of fire in ancient cosmology or as the abode of God in early Christianity. **2** the visible heavens.

emulate to try to equal or excel; imitate zealously.

encaenia an annual celebration in memory of founders and benefactors, especially at Oxford University.

enchiridion a handbook.

enclave 1 a part of a foreign country surrounded by territory of another (compare EXCLAVE). **2** a group of people who are culturally etc. distinct from those surrounding them.

encomium a formal or high-flown expression of praise.

encryption the conversion of data into code.

endemic (of a disease, plant, etc.) regularly or only found among a particular people or in a certain region.

endorphin any of a group of pain-reducing substances occurring naturally in the brain.

energumen an enthusiast or fanatic.

enfilade gunfire directed along a line from end to end at troops, a road, etc.

ensconce to establish or settle (oneself) comfortably, safely, or secretly.

entourage 1 the people attending an important person. **2** surroundings.

enzootic regularly affecting animals in a particular district or at a particular season.

Eonism transvestism, especially by a man.

eparchy a province of the Orthodox Church.

ephemeris an astronomical almanac.

epicene 1 having characteristics of both sexes or of neither; neuter. **2** effete, effeminate (and see LANGUAGE).

epigone one of a later and less distinguished generation; an inferior follower.

epitome a person or thing embodying a quality, class, etc.; a typical example.

eponymous of or being the person after whom something is named (*Macbeth is the eponymous hero of the play*).

epyllion a miniature epic poem.

equilibrist an acrobat, especially on a tightrope.

equilibrium **1** the state of physical balance. **2** mental or emotional equanimity. **3** a state in which the energy in a system is evenly distributed and forces, influences, etc. balance each other.

equivocate to use double meaning or inexactness to conceal the truth.

eremite a hermit or recluse.

erethism **1** excessive sensitivity to sexual stimulation. **2** abnormal mental excitement or irritation.

ergonomics the study of human efficiency in the working environment.

ergot a fungus causing a disease of cereals, used as a medicine to aid childbirth.

erinaceous of or like a hedgehog.

eristic (of an argument or arguer) aiming at winning rather than at reaching the truth; disputatious.

erogenous (especially of a part of the body) sensitive to sexual stimulation.

erubescence blushing.

eructation belching.

eschar a brown or black layer of dead skin, caused by a burn etc.

escheat in former times, the reversion of property to the State, or to a feudal lord, on the owner's dying without legal heirs.

esculent fit to eat; edible.

esemplastic moulding into unity; unifying.

esoteric intelligible only to the initiated or those with special knowledge.

espalier a lattice work along which trees or shrubs are trained to grow flat against a wall; or a tree or shrub grown in this way.

espièglerie frolicsomeness.

estovers necessaries formerly allowed by law to a tenant (e.g. fuel, or wood for repairs).

esurient **1** hungry. **2** impecunious and greedy.

eth the name of an old English and Icelandic letter, /ð/ = th.

ethereal **1** light, airy. **2** highly delicate, especially in appearance. **3** heavenly, celestial. **4** of or relating to ether.

ethos the characteristic spirit or attitudes of a community, people, or system, or of a literary work etc.

etiolated pale and sickly.

eupeptic of or having a good digestion.

euphoria a feeling of well-being, especially one based on over-confidence or over-optimism.

evanescent (of an impression or appearance etc.) quickly fading.

evince to make (a quality) evident (*evinced indignation*).

exacerbate **1** to make (pain, anger, etc.) worse. **2** to irritate (a person).

excerpt a short extract from a book, film, piece of music, etc.

exclave a part of one's own country surrounded by territory of another (compare ENCLAVE).

excoriate **1** to rub, strip, or peel off (skin). **2** to censure severely.

exculpate to free (a person) from blame; clear of a charge.

execrable abominable, detestable.

exegesis critical explanation of a text, especially of Scripture.

exemplar **1** a model or pattern. **2** a typical instance of something.

exigent urgent, pressing, exacting.

exiguous scanty, small.

exonerate **1** to free or declare free from blame etc. **2** to release from a duty.

exorbitant (of a price, demand, etc.) grossly excessive.

exorcize to drive out (a supposed evil spirit) by holy words, or free (a person or place) from such a spirit.

expedite to hasten (an action etc.); accomplish (business) quickly.

expiate to pay the penalty for (wrongdoing); make amends for.

expletive a swear-word used in an exclamation.

exponent a person who favours, promotes, or interprets something (and see MATHEMATICAL TERMS).

expunge to erase, remove (especially a passage from a book or a name from a list).

extenuate to lessen the seeming seriousness of (guilt) by showing some mitigating factor (*extenuating circumstances*).

extirpate to root out; destroy completely.

exordium the introductory part of a discourse or treatise.

exude **1** to (cause to) ooze out; emit, give off. **2** to display (an emotion etc.) freely (*exuded displeasure*).

eyas a young hawk, especially one taken from the nest for training in falconry.

eyot an ait.

eyrie (also **aerie**) a nest of an eagle or other bird of prey, built high up.

F

fabulist 1 a composer of fables. 2 a liar.

facetious intending to be amusing; flippant.

facile (of speech, writing, theories, etc.) easily achieved but of little value; fluent, glib.

factitious not genuine or natural.

factotum an employee who does all kinds of work.

famulus an attendant on a magician or medieval scholar.

fard make-up; cosmetics.

fartlek a method of training for running, mixing fast with slow work.

fasces 1 the bundle of rods with an axe, carried by a lictor in ancient Rome as a symbol of a magistrate's power. 2 the emblems of authority in Fascist Italy.

fascicle 1 a separately published instalment of a book. 2 a bunch or bundle of fibres etc.

fatwa an authoritative Islamic ruling on a religious matter.

faucal of the throat, especially guttural.

favela a Brazilian shack or slum.

faveolate honeycombed, cellular.

febrile of fever; feverish.

feculent murky; containing sediments or dregs.

feisty US slang aggressive, exuberant.

fenestra a small hole in a bone etc., especially in the inner ear.

fenks the fibrous parts of a whale's blubber.

feral 1 (of an animal or plant) wild, untamed, uncultivated. 2 (of an animal) living in a wild state after escape from captivity or domesticity. 3 brutal.

ferial (of a day) ordinary; not a religious festival or fast day.

Festschrift a collection of writings published in honour of a scholar.

fetlock part of the back of a horse's leg above the hoof where a tuft of hair grows.

fibrillate 1 (of a fibre) to split up. 2 (of a muscle, especially in the heart) to quiver.

filibuster 1 to obstruct progress in a legislative assembly by making long speeches. 2 (formerly) to engage in unauthorized warfare against a foreign State.

finocchio a kind of dwarf fennel.

fipple a plug at the mouth end of a wind instrument.

firkin a small cask for liquids, butter, fish, etc.

firmament the sky regarded as a vault or arch.

firman an oriental sovereign's edict, grant, or permit.

fisc the Roman emperor's privy purse.

fissile **1** capable of undergoing nuclear fission. **2** tending to split.

flaccid limp, flabby, drooping.

flagitious deeply criminal; utterly villainous.

fleer to laugh impudently or mockingly; sneer, jeer.

flense to cut up (a whale or seal).

flews the hanging lips of a bloodhound etc.

flocculent like tufts of wool; downy.

flume **1** an artificial channel conveying water etc. for industrial use. **2** a ravine with a stream.

flustra sea matweed.

fontanelle a membraneous space at the top of an infant's skull.

forensic used in connection with courts of law (*forensic medicine*).

formic relating to ants.

fortuitous due to chance; accidental, casual.

foudroyant **1** thundering or dazzling. **2** (of a disease) beginning suddenly and severely.

fouetté a quick whipping movement of the raised leg in ballet.

fox-fire *US* the phosphorescent light emitted by decaying timber.

fraise **1** a ruff, as worn in the 16th century. **2** a horizontal or sloping palisade for defence. **3** a tool for enlarging a round hole, or for cutting teeth in a wheel.

frass the refuse or excrement left by insects.

frenetic frantic, frenzied.

freshet **1** a rush of fresh water flowing into the sea. **2** the flooding of a river.

friable easily crumbled.

frisket a thin iron frame keeping the sheet in position during printing on a hand-press.

froward perverse; difficult to deal with.

frugivorous feeding on fruit.

fugacious fleeting, evanescent; hard to capture or keep.

fulguration the destruction of tissue (e.g. warts) by means of high-voltage electric sparks.

fuliginous sooty, dusky.

fulvous reddish-yellow, tawny.

fumarole an opening in a volcano, through which hot vapours emerge.

fumatory a place for smoking or fumigating purposes.

funambulist a rope-walker.

furcula a forked bone, e.g. the wishbone.

furuncle a boil.

fustanella a man's stiff white kilt worn in Albania and Greece.

futhorc the Scandinavian runic alphabet.

futon a Japanese quilted mattress rolled out on the floor for use as a bed.

fylfot a swastika.

fyrd the English militia before 1066.

G

gadroon a decoration on silverware etc., consisting of convex curves forming an edge like inverted fluting.

gaff 1 a hooked stick for landing large fish. **2** a spar to which the head of a fore-and-aft sail is attached.

gaffe a social blunder.

galliard a lively dance usually in triple time for two people.

galligaskins breeches or trousers, originally as worn in the 16th–17th centuries.

gallimaufry a heterogeneous mixture; a jumble.

gambade 1 a leap or bound of a horse. **2** a prank, freak, frolic.

gamelan an orchestra of SE Asia (especially Indonesia) with strings, woodwind, and many percussion instruments.

gammadion a decorative pattern formed of combinations of the Greek letter gamma.

ganglion 1 a nerve-nucleus, or assemblage of nerve-cells. **2** a cyst, especially on a tendon sheath.

gangue valueless earth etc. in which ore is found.

ganja marijuana.

garbanzo the chickpea.

Garda the State police force of the Irish Republic.

garrotte to strangle, especially with an iron or wire collar.

garth 1 an open space between cloisters. **2** an old word for a yard or garden.

gavage force-feeding with a pump and a tube passing into the stomach.

gavel an auctioneer's or chairman's hammer.

gavelkind 1 a Kentish form of land-tenure. **2** any of various ways of dividing up the property of a deceased man.

gazump (of a seller) to raise the price of a property after having accepted an offer from (an intending buyer).

geek an American fairground entertainer whose act often includes biting the head off a live chicken, snake, etc.

gelation solidification by freezing.

geminate combined in pairs.

gemot a judicial or legislative assembly in Anglo-Saxon England.

genuflect to bend the knee, especially in worship or as a sign of respect.

Georgic relating to agriculture.

germane relevant (*to*) a subject under consideration.

gerrymander to manipulate the boundaries of (a constituency etc.) to the undue advantage of a party or class.

gestate **1** to carry (a foetus) in the womb. **2** to develop (an idea etc.).

ghat **1** the steps leading down to an Indian river. **2** an Indian mountain pass or chain.

ghee Indian clarified butter.

gherao in India and Pakistan, coercion of employers, by which their workers prevent them from leaving the premises until certain demands are met.

ghyll a narrow mountain torrent in a ravine.

gibbous **1** convex, protuberant. **2** (of a moon or planet) between half and full.

gibus a man's tall collapsible hat.

gigot a leg of mutton or lamb.

gimmal a ring made of two linked rings.

gingili sesame seed or its oil.

gingivae the gums.

ginglymus a hingelike joint, as in the elbow or knee, with motion in one plane only.

ginnel a long narrow passage between houses.

girandole **1** a revolving cluster of fireworks. **2** a branched candlestick. **3** an earring or pendant with a large stone surrounded by small ones.

gismo *slang* a gadget.

glabrous hairless; smooth-skinned.

glacis a bank sloping down from a fort.

glair (also **glaire**) **1** white of egg. **2** glue made from this, used in bookbinding etc.

glaive a broadsword.

glasnost (in the former Soviet Union) the policy or practice of more open consultative government and wider dissemination of information.

glaucous 1 of a dull greyish green or blue. **2** covered with a powdery bloom as of grapes.

glebe a piece of land granted to a clergyman as part of his benefice.

glendoveer one of a race of beautiful sprites in Southey's quasi-Hindu mythology.

glossal of the tongue.

gluteal of the buttocks.

gnathic of the jaws.

gnomic of or using aphorisms; sententious.

gnomon the rod etc. on a sundial that shows the time.

gnosis knowledge of spiritual mysteries.

gobemouche a gullible listener.

gobo a portable screen used to deflect light in filming.

goety sorcery; necromancy.

gofer *US slang* someone who runs errands; a dogsbody.

goffer to crimp, make wavy (a lace edge, a trimming, etc.) with a hot iron.

goliard an educated medieval jester and author of loose or satirical Latin verses.

gombeen *Irish* usury.

gombroon a kind of Persian pottery.

gonfalon a banner, often with streamers, hung from a crossbar.

googly an off-break ball in cricket, deceptively bowled with apparent leg-break action.

gorget 1a a piece of armour for the throat. **b** a woman's wimple. **2** a patch of colour on the throat of a bird, insect, etc.

gorgonize to stare at so as to paralyse with fear.

grabble to sprawl on the floor and grope about to feel for something.

gradine 1 each of a series of low steps or a tier of seats. **2** a ledge at the back of an altar.

grallatorial of long-legged wading birds, e.g. flamingos.

gralloch to disembowel (a dead deer etc.).

graminivorous feeding on grass, cereals, etc.

grangerize to illustrate (a book) by sticking in pictures.

gravamen the most serious part of an argument or grievance.

greaves armour for the shins.

Greek Calends never.

gregarious fond of company.

grilse a young salmon that has returned to fresh water from the sea for the first time.

grommet a metal, plastic, or rubber eyelet fitted in a hole to protect a rope or cable etc.

groundling 1 a plant or animal that lives near the ground. **2** someone on the ground and not in an aircraft. **3** a spectator or reader of inferior taste.

grout a thin fluid mortar for filling gaps in tiling etc.

groyne a low wall built out from a shore to check erosion of a beach.

guacamole a salad or dip of mashed avocado mixed with onion, tomato, chilli, etc.

guano the excrement of sea-fowl, used as manure.

gubernatorial (especially *US*) of or relating to a governor.

guddle to catch fish with the hands.

gudgeon 1 a pivot working a wheel, bell, etc. **2** the tubular part of a hinge into which the pin fits to effect a joint. **3** a socket at the stern of a boat that holds the rudder.

guidon a pointed or forked pennant, especially one used as the standard of a regiment of dragoons.

guimpe a high-necked underblouse to be worn with a low-necked dress or pinafore dress.

gular of the throat or gullet.

gulosity gluttony.

gustatory of the sense of taste.

guttate having droplike markings; speckled.

guttler a glutton.

gymnotus an electric eel.

gynaecomastia enlargement of a man's breasts, usually due to hormone imbalance or hormone therapy.

H

haaf a deep-sea fishing ground.

habergeon a sleeveless coat of mail.

habile skilful, deft, dexterous.

hachures parallel lines used in hill-shading on maps, their closeness indicating the steepness of gradient.

hacienda (in Spanish-speaking countries) an estate or plantation with a dwelling-house, or a factory.

hagiography the writing of the lives of saints.

haik, haick an outer covering for head and body worn by Arabs.

haiku a Japanese three-part poem of usually 17 syllables.

hajji (also **haji**) a Muslim who has been to Mecca as a pilgrim.

haka a Maori ceremonial war dance accompanied by chanting.

halal to kill (an animal) as prescribed by Muslim law.

halitosis bad breath.

halitus vapour, exhalation.

hallux the big toe; or the corresponding digit in vertebrates.

hames the two curved iron or wooden pieces forming the collar of a draught-horse, to which the traces are attached.

haplography the accidental omission of letters when these are repeated in a word (e.g. *philogy* for *philology*).

haptic relating to the sense of touch.

hara-kiri ritual suicide by disembowelment with a sword, formerly practised by Samurai to avoid dishonour.

haras a breeding station for horses; a stud.

harbinger a forerunner that announces the approach of something (*crocuses are harbingers of spring*).

Harijan a member of the untouchable class in India.

harmala the plant wild rue.

harpy 1 (in Greek and Roman mythology) a monster with a woman's head and body and a bird's wings and claws. **2** a grasping unscrupulous person.

haruspex a Roman religious official who interpreted omens by inspecting animals' entrails.

haslet pieces of (especially pig's) offal cooked together and usually compressed into a meat loaf.

haulm (also **halm**) a stalk or stem of peas, beans, potatoes, etc.

havelock a covering for the cap, with a flap hanging over the neck as protection from the sun.

hebdomadal every week, weekly.

hebetude dullness.

hecatomb a great public sacrifice in ancient Greece or Rome, originally of 100 oxen.

heddle one of the sets of small cords or wires between which the warp is passed in a loom.

hedonism belief in pleasure as the highest good and mankind's proper aim.

hegemony leadership, especially by one State of a confederacy.

heinous (of a crime or criminal) utterly odious or wicked.

helot a serf, of a class in ancient Sparta.

helve the handle of a weapon or tool.

hemeralopia difficulty in seeing by daylight; day-blindness.

henge a prehistoric monument such as Stonehenge, consisting of a circle of massive uprights.

hepatic 1 of the liver. **2** dark brownish-red; liver-coloured.

heriot a tribute formerly paid to a lord on the death of a tenant, consisting of an animal, a chattel, etc.

herm a squared stone pillar with a head (especially of the god Hermes) on top, used by the ancient Greeks as a boundary marker etc.

hermeneutic concerning interpretation, especially of Scripture or literary texts.

hetman a Polish or Cossack military commander.

heuristic allowing or assisting to discover (and see COMPUTERS).

hiatus a break or gap in a series etc.

hibachi a portable Japanese pan or brazier in which charcoal is burnt for cooking or to heat a room.

hickwall the green woodpecker.

hidalgo a Spanish gentleman.

hidrosis perspiration.

hierophant an interpreter of sacred mysteries.

hilding 1 a worthless or vicious beast. **2** a contemptible or worthless person of either sex.

hinny (also **hinnie**) the offspring of a female donkey and a male horse.

hippocampus 1 a sea horse. **2** the elongated ridges on the floor of each lateral ventricle of the brain, thought to be the centre of emotion and the involuntary nervous system.

hippocras wine flavoured with spices.

hirsute hairy, shaggy.

hoggin a mixture of sand and gravel.

holistic 1 regarding the whole as greater than the sum of its parts. **2** giving medical treatment to the whole person rather than just to the symptoms of a disease.

holt 1 an animal's (especially an otter's) lair. **2** a wood or copse.

homily a sermon or tedious moralizing discourse.

hominid any member of the primate family Hominidae, including humans and their fossil ancestors.

homocentric having the same centre.

homunculus a little man, a manikin.

hone a whetstone, especially for razors.

hoplite a heavily armed foot soldier of ancient Greece.

horripilation goose-flesh.

hoveller an unlicensed boatman, especially on the Kentish coast.

howdah a seat for two or more, usually with a canopy, for riding on the back of an elephant or camel.

hoyden a boisterous girl.

hubble-bubble a rudimentary kind of hookah, the oriental tobacco pipe with a tube passing through water to cool the smoke.

hubris arrogant pride or presumption.

humectant a substance, especially a food additive, used to retain moisture.

humidor a room or container for keeping cigars or tobacco moist.

hurling an Irish game rather like hockey, played with broad sticks.

hustings 1 parliamentary election proceedings. **2** a platform from which, before 1872, parliamentary candidates were nominated and addressed electors.

hwyl an emotional quality inspiring impassioned eloquence, as in a Welsh poet.

hymeneal of or concerning marriage.

hyperborean of the extreme north of the earth.

hypnagogic inducing sleep, or accompanying the drowsy state leading to sleep.

hypocaust a hollow space under the floor of an ancient Roman house, into which hot air was sent for heating a room or bath.

hypocorism a pet name.

hypothecate to pledge, mortgage.

I

iatrogenic (of a disease etc.) caused by medical examination or treatment.

ichor in Greek mythology, fluid flowing like blood in the veins of the gods.

icon 1 a devotional painting or carving, usually on wood, of Christ or another holy figure, especially in the Eastern Church. **2** an image or statue.

iconoclastic destructive of holy images or of cherished beliefs.

ideogram a character symbolizing the idea of a thing without indicating the sequence of sounds in its name (e.g. a numeral, and many Chinese characters).

idiosyncrasy a mental constitution, view, feeling, or foible peculiar to a person.

idioticon a dictionary confined to a particular dialect, or containing words and phrases peculiar to one part of a country.

idolum a mental image; a phantom or fallacy.

ignominious **1** causing or deserving dishonour. **2** humiliating.

ikebana the art of Japanese flower arrangement.

illation a deduction or conclusion.

illicit unlawful, forbidden (*illicit dealings*).

illuminati people claiming to have special enlightenment.

imagism a movement in early 20th-century poetry which sought clarity of expression through the use of precise images.

imam **1** a leader of prayers in a mosque. **2** a title of various Muslim leaders, especially one succeeding Muhammad as leader of Islam.

imbricate to arrange (leaves, scales of a fish, etc.) so as to overlap like roof tiles.

imbroglio a confused or complicated situation.

imbrue to stain (one's hands, sword, etc.).

immanent **1** indwelling, inherent. **2** (of the supreme being) permanently pervading the universe (opp. TRANSCENDENT).

immarcescible unfading; incorruptible, imperishable.

immiscible that cannot be mixed.

immolate to kill or offer as a sacrifice.

immortelle a papery flower that keeps its shape and texture when dried.

impanate contained or embodied in bread.

impecunious having little or no money.

impedimenta **1** encumbrances. **2** travelling equipment, especially of an army.

impinge to make an impact, have an effect or encroach *on*.

implode to (cause to) burst inwards.

impost **1** a tax, duty, or tribute. **2** a weight carried by a horse in a handicap race.

imprest money advanced to someone for use in State business.

imprimatur an official licence by the Roman Catholic church to print a book.

impugn to challenge (a statement, action, etc.); call in question.

inane silly, senseless.

incarnate **1** embodied in flesh, especially in human form (*is the devil incarnate*). **2** represented in a recognizable or typical form (*folly incarnate*).

inchoate undeveloped, rudimentary.

incipient beginning; in an initial stage.

incivism lack of good citizenship.

incommunicado **1** without or deprived of the means of communication with others. **2** (of a prisoner) in solitary confinement.

incubus 1 an evil spirit supposed to lie on sleeping people, especially to have intercourse with sleeping women. **2** a nightmare, or something that oppresses like a nightmare.

inculpate 1 to involve in a charge. **2** to accuse, blame.

incunabula books printed very early, especially before 1501.

incursion an invasion or attack, especially when sudden or brief.

indite 1 to put (a speech etc.) into words. **2** to write (a letter etc.).

induct 1 to introduce formally into possession of a benefice. **2** to install (a person) into a room, position, etc.

indurate to harden.

ineffable 1 unutterable; too great for description in words. **2** too sacred to be uttered.

ineluctable unescapable.

infanta a daughter of the ruling monarch of Spain or Portugal, usually the eldest daughter who is not heir to the throne.

infarct a small localized area of dead tissue caused by an inadequate blood supply.

infibulation the fastening up of the sexual organs with a clasp etc., to prevent sexual intercourse.

inguinal of the groin.

insolation exposure to the sun's rays, especially for bleaching.

insouciant carefree, unconcerned.

inspissate to thicken, condense.

instauration restoration, renewal.

insurgent a rebel, a revolutionary.

integument a natural outer covering; a skin, rind, husk, etc.

intercalary (of a day or month) inserted in the calendar to harmonize it with the solar year, e.g. 29 February in leap years.

interim the time between two events (*in the interim he had died*).

internecine mutually destructive.

interregnum an interval between successive reigns or regimes, when the normal government is suspended.

intinction the dipping of the Eucharistic bread in the wine so that the communicant receives both together.

inveigh to speak or write with strong hostility *against*.

involute curled spirally, or rolled inwards at the edges.

irascible irritable; hot-tempered.

iridescent showing rainbow-like luminous or gleaming colours; shimmering.

irredentist a person, especially in 19th-century Italy, advocating the restoration to his or her country of any territory formerly belonging to it.

irrefragable 1 (of a statement, argument, or person) unanswerable, indisputable. **2** (of rules etc.) inviolable.

irrefutable impossible to refute or disprove.

irrision derision, mockery.

irrupt to enter forcibly or violently *into*.

isocheim a line on a map connecting places having the same average temperature in winter.

isomorphic having exactly the same form and relations.

istle fibre used for cord, nets, etc., obtained from the plant agave.

iterate to repeat; state repeatedly.

izard a chamois.

izzard an old name for the letter Z.

J

jabot an ornamental frill or lace ruffle on the front of a shirt or blouse.

jacobus an English gold coin struck in the reign of James I.

jacquerie the French peasants' revolt against the nobles in 1357–8.

jalousie a blind made of a row of angled slats.

janizary (also **janissary**) a member of the Turkish infantry forming the Sultan's guard in the 14th–19th centuries.

jarl a Norse or Danish chief.

jejune 1 (of ideas etc.) shallow, meagre, sparse. **2** (of the land) barren, poor.

jennet a small Spanish horse.

jeofail a mistake in a legal proceeding.

jeopardy danger, especially of severe harm or loss, or of conviction when on trial for a criminal offence.

jeremiad a doleful lamentation; a list of woes.

jeroboam a wine bottle of 4–12 times the ordinary size.

jerque to examine a ship's papers when checking the cargo for customs.

jeton a metal disc used, chiefly in France, instead of a coin for insertion in a public telephone box.

jihad (also **jehad**) a holy war undertaken by Muslims against unbelievers.

jingoism blustering patriotism in favour of war.

jocose 1 playful in style. **2** fond of joking; jocular.

jokul a permanently snow-covered mountain.

jugate having paired parts joined together.

juggernaut 1 a huge overwhelming force or object. **2** in Britain, a large heavy motor vehicle, especially an articulated lorry.

jugular of the neck or throat (*jugular vein*).

jugulate to kill by cutting the throat.

ju-ju a charm or fetish of some West African peoples.

jumbal a kind of sweet crisp cake.

junta a political or military group taking power after a revolution.

juxtapose to place side by side, especially for the sake of comparison.

jynx 1 a bird, the wryneck. **2** a charm or spell.

K

kabuki a form of popular traditional Japanese drama with highly stylized song, acted by males only.

kamikaze 1 a Japanese aircraft of World War II that was loaded with explosives and deliberately crashed on the target. **2** its suicide pilot.

kampong a Malayan enclosure or village.

kanaka a South Sea Islander, especially one of those formerly employed in forced labour in Australia.

kanga a patterned cotton cloth worn as a woman's garment in East Africa.

kaolin fine soft white clay used especially for making porcelain and in medicines; china clay.

kapok a firm fibrous cotton-like substance found surrounding the seeds of a tropical tree, *Ceiba pentandra*, used for stuffing things.

kaput *slang* broken, ruined, done for.

karma in Buddhism and Hinduism, the sum of a person's actions in previous lives, viewed as determining his or her future; one's fate or destiny.

kaross a sleeveless hairy mantle worn by Hottentots and other South African Negroid peoples.

kazoo a toy musical instrument that buzzes when the player sings or hums into it.

keelhaul 1 to drag (a person) under the keel of a ship as a punishment. **2** to scold severely.

keffiyeh an Arab headscarf.

keloid fibrous scar tissue.

kelp large broad-fronded brown seaweed suitable for use as manure.

kelpie a Scottish water-spirit, usually in the form of a horse, reputed to delight in the drowning of travellers.

kelt a salmon or sea trout after spawning.

kendo a Japanese form of fencing with two-handed bamboo swords.

kenning a compound expression in Old English and Old Norse poetry, e.g. *oar-steed* = ship.

kenosis the partial renunciation of the divine nature by Christ in the Incarnation.

kerf a slit made by sawing.

kibbutz a communal (especially farming) establishment in Israel.

kibitzer an onlooker at cards etc., especially a busybody who offers unwanted advice.

kiddle a barrier in a river fitted with nets to catch fish; or a similar arrangement of nets on stakes along the seashore.

kilderkin a 16- or 18-gallon cask for liquids.

kilim a pile-less woven Eastern rug or wall hanging.

kismet fate, destiny.

knag **1** a knot in wood. **2** a small dead branch. **3** a peg for hanging things on.

knobkerrie a short stick with a knobbed head used as a weapon, especially by South African tribes.

knout a scourge used in imperial Russia, often causing death.

koan a riddle used in Zen Buddhism to demonstrate the inadequacy of logical reasoning.

kohl a black powder used as eye make-up, especially in Eastern countries.

kris (also **crease, creese**) a Malay or Indonesian dagger with a wavy blade.

kukri a Gurka knife, curved and broadening towards the point.

kulak a peasant working for personal profit in Soviet Russia.

kymograph an instrument for recording variations in pressure, e.g. in sound waves or in blood within blood vessels.

L

laager **1** a camp or encampment in South Africa, especially one formed by a circle of wagons. **2** a park for armoured vehicles.

labial of, near, or using the lips.

labile unstable; liable to change.

labret a piece of shell, bone, etc. inserted in the lip as an ornament.

labrys the double-headed axe of ancient Crete.

lachrymal of or concerned with tears.

lachrymose given to weeping; tearful.

laconic (of speech or writing, or a speaker or writer) brief, concise, terse.

lactate (of mammals) to secrete milk.

lacuna a gap, blank, or cavity.

lacustrine of lakes; especially living or growing in lakes.

lagan goods or wreckage lying on the bed of the sea, sometimes with a marked buoy etc. for later retrieval.

lallation the pronunciation of *r* as *l*; or imperfect speech generally.

lama a Tibetan or Mongolian Buddhist monk.

lambaste 1 to thrash, beat. **2** to criticize severely.

lambent softly radiant.

lambrequin *US* a short piece of drapery hung over a door, window, or mantelpiece.

lamia a fabulous monster with a woman's body, supposed to prey on human beings.

lamina a thin plate of bone, stratified rock, vegetable tissue, etc.

lampion a usually coloured pot of oil with a wick, formerly used in illuminations.

lamprey an eel-like fish with a sucking mouth and horny teeth but no scales or jaws.

lanate woolly; covered with hairs like wool.

landau a four-wheeled enclosed carriage with a removable front cover and a back cover that can be raised and lowered.

langlauf cross-country skiing.

lansquenet 1 a German card game. **2** a German mercenary soldier in the 16th–17th centuries.

lanugo fine soft hair, especially that which covers a human foetus.

laparotomy a surgical incision into the abdominal cavity.

lapidary 1 concerned with, or engraved on, stone. **2** (of writing style) dignified and concise; suitable for inscriptions.

lapidate to pelt (someone) with stones.

lariat 1 a lasso. **2** a tethering-rope, especially used by cowboys.

lasque a flat piece of diamond.

lassitude 1 languor, weariness. **2** disinclination to exert or interest oneself.

latex the milky fluid found especially in the rubber tree and used for commercial purposes.

latifundia large estates or plantations.

latrant barking, snarling.

lauwine an avalanche.

lavabo 1 the ritual washing of the priest's hands at Mass. **2** a monastery washing trough.

lave 1 to wash, bathe. **2** (of water) to wash against; flow along.

laver bread a Welsh dish of boiled seaweed dipped in oatmeal and fried.

layette a set of clothing and equipment for a new baby.

lazaretto an isolation hospital or quarantine ship.

leach to remove (soluble matter) from bark, ore, ash, soil, etc. by the action of percolating liquid.

leat an open watercourse taking water to a mill.

lector 1 a reader, especially of lessons in church. **2** (*fem.* **lectrice**) a lecturer or reader, especially one employed in a foreign university to teach his or her native language.

lees the sediment of wine etc.

legerdemain sleight of hand; conjuring.

legume the seed pod of a pea, bean, etc. used as food.

lei 1 a Polynesian flower garland. **2** the plural of *leu*, the Romanian currency unit.

leister a pronged salmon-spear.

lemma 1 a proposition used in an argument or proof. **2** a heading indicating the subject of a literary composition, a dictionary entry, etc. **3** a motto appended to a picture etc.

lenitive soothing, palliative.

lenity mercy, gentleness.

lentigo a freckle or pimple.

lepidopterist an expert in or collector of butterflies and moths.

Lethe 1 in Greek mythology, a river in Hades producing forgetfulness of the past. **2** such forgetfulness.

leucoma a white opacity in the cornea of the eye.

levant *Brit. slang* to abscond or bolt, especially with betting or gaming losses unpaid.

levigate to reduce to smooth paste or powder.

levitate to (cause to) rise and float in the air (especially with reference to spiritualism).

lexigraphy a system of writing in which each character represents a word.

libation a drink-offering poured out to a god.

libidinous lustful.

lich-gate (also **lych-gate**) a roofed gateway to a churchyard where a coffin may be rested before a funeral.

Lilliputian tiny, diminutive.

limaceous of slugs or snails; snail-like.

limn to paint (especially a miniature portrait).

limpid (of water, eyes, etc.) clear, transparent.

linga a phallus, especially as the Hindu symbol of Shiva.

limpkin a water bird not unlike the cranes and rails.

lionize to treat as a celebrity.

lipography the omission of letters or words in writing.

lipper 1 a rippling of the sea. **2** a tool for forming the lip of a glass vessel.

lissom lithe, supple, agile.

littoral a region lying along the shore of the sea, a lake, etc.

llano a treeless grassy plain, especially in South America.

loblolly a thick gruel eaten especially by sailors.

lockage 1 the amount of rise and fall effected by canal locks. **2** a toll for the use of a lock. **3** the construction or use of locks.

logie *Scottish* the open space before a kiln fire.

logion a saying attributed to Christ, especially one not recorded in the recognized Gospels.

logistics the detailed planning and organization of an operation, especially of moving, lodging, and supplying troops and equipment.

logomachy a dispute about words; controversy turning on merely verbal points.

logorrhoea an excessive flow of words, especially in mental illness.

longanimity long-suffering; forbearance or patience under provocation.

loquacious talkative, chattering.

loricate having an armour of scales, plates, etc.

lorimer, loriner a maker of bits, spurs, and metal bridle mountings for horses.

loupe a small magnifying glass used by jewellers.

lovelock a curl or lock of hair worn on the temple or forehead.

lox *US* smoked salmon.

luau a feast with Hawaiian food and usually entertainment.

lubricious 1 slippery, smooth, oily. **2** lewd, prurient.

lucubration 1 nocturnal study. **2** pedantic or elaborate literary writings.

ludic of spontaneous play or games.

luge a light toboggan for one or two people, ridden in the sitting position.

lumbar of the lower back area.

lungi a length of cotton cloth, worn as a loincloth in India, or a skirt in Myanmar (where it is the national dress for both sexes).

lunula 1 the crescent-shaped area at the base of the fingernail. **2** a crescent-shaped Bronze Age ornament.

lustrate to purify by ceremonial sacrifice, washing, etc.

lustrum a period of five years.

lycanthrope a werewolf, or an insane person who thinks he or she is a wolf.

lycopod any of various clubmosses, especially of the genus *Lycopodium*.

lysis the disintegration of a cell.

M

macabre grim, gruesome.

macerate to make or become soft by soaking.

machete a broad heavy knife used in Central America and the West Indies as an implement and weapon.

machiavellian elaborately cunning; scheming, unscrupulous.

machismo exaggeratedly assertive manliness; a show of masculinity.

mackle a blurred impression in printing.

macramé the art of knotting string in patterns to make decorative articles.

macron a written or printed mark (ˉ) over a long or stressed vowel.

macroscopic **1** big enough to be visible to the naked eye. **2** regarded in terms of large units.

macula a dark spot, especially a permanent one, on the skin.

maelstrom **1** a great whirlpool. **2** a state of confusion.

maenad a female follower of the god Bacchus.

magnum a wine bottle of about twice the standard size.

magot **1** the tailless Barbary ape of Gibraltar. **2** a small grotesque Chinese or Japanese figure of porcelain, ivory, wood, etc.

maharishi a great Hindu sage or spiritual leader.

mahout in India etc. an elephant-driver or -keeper.

maieutic (of the Socratic mode of enquiry) serving to bring a person's latent ideas into clear consciousness.

maladroit clumsy; bungling.

malamute (also **malemute**) an Eskimo dog.

malediction a curse; cursing.

maleficent hurtful or criminal.

malign **1** (of a thing) injurious. **2** (of a disease) malignant. **3** malevolent.

malism the doctrine that the world is an evil one.

malversation corrupt behaviour in a position of trust, as by a public official.

mamilla (*US* **mammilla**) a nipple or teat.

mana 1 power, authority, prestige. **2** supernatural or magical power.

manacle a handcuff.

manciple an officer who buys provisions for a college, an Inn of Court, etc.

mandala a symbolic circular figure representing the universe in various religions.

mandor a foreman or overseer in Malaysia or Indonesia.

mandrel 1 a shaft in a lathe to hold work being turned. **2** a cylinder round which material is forged or shaped.

manes the deified souls of dead ancestors.

mangonel an ancient military engine for throwing stones, etc.

Manichee an adherent of a 3rd–5th century religious system representing Satan as in a state of everlasting conflict with God.

mansuetude meekness, docility, gentleness.

manumit to set (a slave) free.

marasmus a wasting away of the body.

marc brandy made from the refuse of pressed grapes.

marimba a xylophone played by natives of Africa and Central America, or a modern orchestral instrument derived from this.

marmoreal of or like marble.

marquois an apparatus for drawing equidistant parallel lines.

marram a kind of shore grass.

marshalsea a prison in Southwark abolished in 1842; also certain other London prisons.

martinet a strict (especially military or naval) disciplinarian.

martingale 1 a strap connecting a horses's noseband to the girth, to prevent rearing. **2** a gambling system of continually doubling the stakes.

martlet an old word for a swift or house-martin.

masochism 1 a form of (especially sexual) perversion characterized by pleasure derived from one's own pain or humiliation. **2** *colloq.* the enjoyment of what seems to be painful or tiresome.

mastaba 1 an ancient Egyptian tomb with sloping sides and a flat roof. **2** a bench outside a house in Islamic countries.

mastectomy the amputation of a breast.

matutinal of or in the morning.

maud a Scottish shepherd's grey striped plaid.

maudlin weakly or tearfully sentimental, especially in an effusive stage of drunkenness.

maulstick a light stick with a padded leather ball at one end, held by a painter in one hand to support the other.

maunder to talk or move dreamily or listlessly.

maverick **1** *US* an unbranded calf or yearling. **2** an unorthodox or independent-minded person.

mawkish sentimental in a feeble or sickly way.

maya *Hinduism* a marvel or illusion, especially perceptible to the senses.

meerschaum **1** a white clay-like mineral chiefly found in Turkey. **2** a tobacco pipe made of this.

megalopolis a great city.

megass the fibre left when sugar has been extracted from the cane.

megilp (also **magilp**) a mixture of mastic resin and linseed oil often added to oil paints in the 19th century.

melanin the dark pigment responsible for tanning the skin when exposed to sunlight.

melton cloth with a close-cut nap, used for overcoats etc.

menarche the onset of first menstruation.

menhir a tall upright usually prehistoric monumental stone.

mephitis a noxious emanation; a stench.

mercurial **1** sprightly, ready-witted, volatile. **2** of or containing mercury. **3** (**Mercurial**) of the planet Mercury.

meretricious **1** (of decorations, literary style, etc.) showily but falsely attractive. **2** of or befitting a prostitute.

merkin **1** false hair to cover the pudendum; a pubic wig. **2** a mop for cleaning out a cannon.

mesa *US* an isolated flat-topped hill with steep sides, found in landscapes with horizontal strata as in the south-west USA.

mestizo a Spaniard or Portuguese of mixed race, especially the offspring of a Spaniard and an American Indian.

metempsychosis the supposed transmigration of souls into a new body after death.

metheglin a kind of spiced mead, originally peculiar to Wales.

metopic of the forehead; frontal.

Mickey Finn a strong alcoholic drink adulterated with knockout drops.

micron one-millionth of a metre.

micturate to urinate.

mien a person's look or bearing, as showing character or mood.

mihrab a niche or slab in a mosque, used to show the direction of Mecca.

militate (of facts or evidence) to have force or effect *against* (*what you say militates against our opinion*).

milt **1** the spleen or spleen-like organ in vertebrates. **2** a sperm-filled reproductive gland of a male fish.

mimesis 1 deliberate imitation; mimicry. **2** *Biol.* a close external resemblance of an animal to another that is distasteful or harmful to predators of the first.

miniver (also **minever**) plain white fur used in ceremonial costume.

misandry the hatred of men.

miscegenation the interbreeding of races, especially of Whites and non-Whites.

miscreant a vile wretch; a villain.

misericord a shelving projection on the under side of a hinged seat in a choir stall serving (when the seat is turned up) to help support a person standing.

misogyny the hatred of women.

misprision 1 a misunderstanding. **2** failure to appreciate the value of something. **3** an old word for contempt.

mistigris a blank card used like a joker in a form of poker.

mithridatize to render proof against a poison by administering gradually increasing doses of it.

mitrailleuse a breech-loading 19th-century machine-gun.

mnemonic a phrase etc. designed to aid the memory, e.g. *face* for the musical notes F, A, C, E between the lines on the treble clef.

moiety each of two parts, especially halves, into which something is divided.

mollify to appease, pacify, soften.

moniker (also **monicker, monniker**) *slang* a person's name.

monition 1 a warning of danger. **2** a rebuke, admonishment.

monocoque an aircraft or vehicle structure in which the chassis is integral with the body.

monotreme any mammal of Australia and New Guinea, including the duckbill and spiny anteater, with a single opening for urine, faeces, and eggs.

monstrance in the Roman Catholic church, a vessel in which the Host is exposed for veneration.

mor humus formed under acid conditions.

mora 1a a delay. **b** a unit of time equal to the duration of a short syllable. **2** a game in which one player guesses the number of fingers held up by another. **3** a division of the Spartan army. **4** a tree of Guiana and Trinidad. **5** a footstool.

moratorium 1 a temporary prohibition or suspension of an activity. **2** a legal authorization to debtors to postpone payment.

mordant 1 (of sarcasm etc.) caustic, biting. **2** corrosive or cleansing.

mores the customs and conventions of a community.

morganatic (of a marriage) between people of different social ranks, the spouse and children having no claim to the possessions or title of the person of higher rank.

morion a kind of military helmet of the 16th and 17th centuries.

moshav a cooperative association of Israeli smallholders.

motile capable of motion.

moxibustion a Chinese and Japanese method of treating various conditions by burning a herbal mixture on part of the body.

muckluck (also **mukluk**) a high Eskimo boot made of sealskin, canvas, etc.

muezzin a Muslim crier who proclaims the hours of prayer usually from a minaret.

mugient lowing, bellowing.

mugwump US **1** a great man; a boss. **2** a person who holds aloof, especially from party politics.

mulct **1** to extract money from by fine or taxation. **2** to swindle, or obtain by swindling.

muliebrity **1** womanhood; the common characteristics of a woman. **2** softness, effeminacy.

multipara a woman who has borne more than one child.

mumchance silent; dumbstruck.

mummiform shaped like a mummy.

mumpsimus an ignorant opponent of reform; an old fogey.

mundungus bad-smelling tobacco.

murex a shellfish that gives a purple dye.

muscular stomach any organ that grinds and squeezes to aid digestion, such as a bird's gizzard.

musth (of a male elephant or camel) in a state of frenzy.

mutch a woman's or child's linen cap.

muzhik a Russian peasant of tsarist times.

myrmidon **1** a hired ruffian. **2** a base servant.

N

nacre mother-of-pearl.

naevus (US **nevus**) a birthmark or mole.

naiad **1** in Greek mythology, a water-nymph. **2** the larva of a dragon-fly etc.

nainsook a fine soft cotton fabric, originally Indian.

naker an old word for a kettledrum.

napalm a jellied petrol used in incendiary bombs.

nappa (also **napa**) a soft leather made by a special process from the skins of sheep or goats.

narcosis insensibility induced by drugs.

nascent just beginning to be; not yet mature.

natality birth rate.

natation swimming.

nattier blue a soft shade of blue.

neap tide a tide just after the first and third quarters of the moon, when there is least difference between low and high water.

Nearctic of the Arctic and the temperate parts of North America as a zoogeographical region.

nefarious wicked, iniquitous.

Negritude 1 the state of being a Negro. **2** the affirmation of the value of Negro culture.

nemesis downfall caused by retributive justice.

nenuphar a water-lily.

neonate a newborn child.

neophyte 1 a new convert, especially to a religious faith. **2** *RC Ch.* a novice of a religious order or newly ordained priest. **3** a beginner; a novice.

nepenthe a drug causing forgetfulness of grief.

nepotism favouritism shown to relatives in conferring appointments or privileges.

nereid in Greek mythology, a sea nymph.

nescience lack of knowledge; ignorance.

nether lower.

netsuke a carved button-like Japanese ornament, especially of ivory or wood, formerly worn to suspend articles from a girdle.

névé an expanse of granular snow not yet compressed into ice, at the head of a glacier.

nexus 1 a connected group or series. **2** a bond; a connection.

nictitate to blink or wink.

nidicolous (of a bird) bearing helpless young that remain in the nest until they can live without parental care.

nidifugous (of a bird) bearing well-developed young that leave the nest almost immediately.

niello a black composition of sulphur with silver, lead, or copper, for filling engraved lines in silver or other metal ornamental work.

nimbus a bright cloud or halo investing a deity or person or thing (and see WINDS AND WEATHER).

nimiety excess, redundancy.

niveous like snow; snowy.

nobiliary (of a preposition) forming part of a title of nobility (e.g. French *de*, German *von*).

nock a notch in a bow to hold the bowstring, or on an arrow to receive it.

noctambulist a sleepwalker.

noetic 1 of the intellect. **2** intellectual, speculative.

Noh traditional Japanese drama with dance and song, evolved from Shinto rites.

noisette a small round piece of meat etc.

nonage an old word for legal minority; immaturity.

nonce the time being (*for the nonce*).

nonchalant calm and casual, unmoved, unexcited, indifferent.

nonentity a person or thing of no importance.

nonpareil unrivalled or unique.

noria a Spanish and Eastern device for raising water, consisting of a revolving chain of pots or buckets which are filled below and discharged as they reach the top.

nostrum 1 a quack remedy. **2** a pet scheme, especially for political or social reform.

Notogæa the zoological region comprising Australia, New Zealand, and tropical and South America.

novena *RC Ch.* a devotion consisting of special prayers or services on nine successive days.

noyade execution by drowning.

nuance a subtle difference in or shade of meaning, feeling, colour, etc.

nubile (of a woman) marriageable or sexually attractive.

nuchal of or relating to the nape of the neck.

nugatory trifling, worthless, not valid.

nullify to make null; neutralize, invalidate.

numdah an embroidered felt rug from India etc.

numinous 1 indicating the presence of a god. **2** spiritual and awe-inspiring.

numismatics the study of coins and medals.

nyctalopia night-blindness.

nympholepsy ecstasy or frenzy caused by desire of the unattainable.

nymphomania excessive sexual desire in women.

O

oakum a loose fibre obtained by picking old rope to pieces and used especially in waterproofing the seams of boats.

oast a kiln for drying hops.

obdurate stubborn; hardened against persuasion.

obeah a kind of sorcery practised especially in the West Indies.

obfuscate to confuse or bewilder (a mind, topic, etc.).

obi a broad sash worn with a Japanese kimono.

objurgation scolding, chiding.

oblate a person dedicated to a monastic or religious life (and see MATHEMATICAL TERMS).

oblation something offered to a divine being, e.g. the offering of bread and wine to God in the Eucharist.

obloquy 1 the state of being generally ill spoken of. **2** abuse, detraction.

obol an ancient Greek coin equal to one-sixth of a drachma.

obsecration earnest entreaty.

obsequies funeral rites.

obstetric of childbirth and associated processes.

obstreperous turbulent, vociferous; noisily resisting control.

obtrude to thrust forward (oneself, one's opinion, etc.) unduly.

obviate to get round or do away with (a need, inconvenience, etc.).

Occident Europe and America as distinct from the Orient.

occiput the back of the head.

occlude to block up, close (an orifice).

ocellus 1 a simple (not compound) eye of some insects etc. **2** an eye-like marking, as on a butterfly's wing or peacock's tail.

oche the line behind which darts players stand when throwing.

octroi a duty levied in some European countries on goods entering a town.

od a hypothetical power once thought to pervade nature and account for various scientific phenomena.

odalisque an Eastern female slave or concubine, especially in the former Turkish Sultan's harem.

odontoid toothlike.

oestrus a recurring period of sexual receptivity in many female mammals; heat.

officinal 1 (of a medicine) kept ready for immediate dispensing. **2** (of a plant etc.) used in medicine.

ogdoad a group of eight.

ogham (also **ogam**) an ancient British and Irish alphabet of twenty characters formed by parallel strokes on either side of or across a continuous line.

oleaginous oily, greasy.

olfactory of the sense of smell.

oliver a hammer with its arm attached to an axle, worked with the foot by a treadle and used in shaping nails, bolts, etc.

omphalos 1 a conical stone (especially that at Delphi) representing the navel of the earth. 2 a centre or hub, such as the boss on a shield.

onager 1 a wild ass of Central Asia. 2 an ancient military engine for throwing rocks.

onanism 1 masturbation. 2 coitus interruptus.

oneiric of dreams or dreaming.

ontogenesis the origin and development of an individual.

opine to express as one's opinion.

oppidan a town-dweller.

oppugn to call into question; contradict.

opsimath a person who learns only late in life.

optophone an instrument converting light into sound, and so enabling the blind to read print etc. by ear.

opuscule a minor (especially musical or literary) work.

oracy the ability to express oneself fluently in speech.

ordinand a candidate for admission to holy orders.

ordnance mounted guns and other military weapons, ammunition, and equipment.

ordonnance the systematic arrangement especially of literary or architectural work.

ordure 1 excrement, dung. 2 obscenity; filth; foul language.

oread in Greek and Roman mythology, a mountain nymph.

orectic concerning desire or appetite.

oreide a kind of shiny brass used for imitation jewellery etc.

orgeat a cooling drink made from barley or almonds and orange-flower water.

orgulous haughty, splendid.

oriflamme 1 the sacred scarlet banner of St Denis carried into war by early French kings. 2 a principle or ideal as a rallying point in a struggle.

origami the Japanese art of folding paper into decorative shapes and figures.

ormolu gilded metal alloy used to decorate furniture, clocks, etc.

orotund 1 (of the voice or phrasing) full, round, imposing. **2** (of language) pompous, pretentious.

Orphic of the mysteries associated with the legendary Greek poet Orpheus; oracular, occult.

orphrey an ornamental stripe or border or separate piece of ornamental needlework, especially on ecclesiastical vestments.

orris any plant of the genus *Iris*, whose fragrant rootstock is used in perfumery.

ortanique a cross between an orange and a tangerine.

orthodontics the treatment of irregularities in the teeth and jaws.

orthodromy the art of sailing or flying on a great circle route, the most direct course.

ortolan a small European bird, eaten as a delicacy.

orts fragments of food; leavings.

oscitant yawning, drowsy.

osculate to kiss.

osmic of the sense of smell.

ossuary a place for the bones of the dead; a charnel-house.

osteal of bone.

ostler a stableman at an inn.

otiose serving no practical purpose; functionless.

ottoman an upholstered seat without a back or sides.

oubliette a secret dungeon with access only through a trapdoor.

ovation 1 an enthusiastic reception, especially spontaneous and sustained applause. **2** in ancient Rome, a lesser form of triumph.

oviparous egg-laying.

oxbow 1 a horseshoe bend in a river. **2** a lake formed when the river cuts across the narrow end of this.

oxytocic accelerating childbirth.

P

pabulum food, especially for the mind.

pachinko a Japanese form of pinball.

pachyderm a thick-skinned mammal, especially an elephant or rhinoceros.

paduasoy a strong corded silk fabric.

paean a song of praise or triumph.

paedophilia (*US* **pedo-**) sexual desire directed towards children.

paladin a knight errant; a champion.

palanquin (also **palankeen**) a covered litter for one passenger, used in the East.

palfrey an old word for a horse for ordinary riding, especially for women.

palimony *US colloq.* an allowance made to one's unmarried partner after separation.

palimpsest a manuscript on which the original writing has been effaced to make room for other writing.

palingenesis the reproduction of ancestral characteristics in the development of an individual.

palinode a poem in which the writer retracts a view expressed in a former poem.

palliate 1 to alleviate (disease etc.) without curing it. 2 to excuse, extenuate.

palmer a medieval pilgrim who had returned from the Holy Land with a palm branch or leaf.

palpebral of the eyelids.

palps the segmented feelers at the mouths of some shellfish and insects.

palstave a type of ancient chisel made of bronze etc. and shaped to fit into a split handle.

palter 1 to haggle or equivocate. 2 to trifle.

paludal 1 of a marsh; marshy. 2 malarial.

panache 1 assertiveness or flamboyant confidence of style or manner. 2 a tuft of feathers on a medieval headdress.

panada 1 a thick flour paste. 2 bread boiled to a pulp and flavoured.

pandect a complete body of laws; especially a compendium in 50 books of the Roman civil law made by order of Justinian in the 6th century.

pandemic an epidemic ranging over a whole country or the whole world.

pandour a former kind of soldier or mounted constable in the Balkans.

Pangæa the original vast supercontinent that split up into the land-masses of today.

panhandle *US* 1 a narrow strip of land extending from one State into another. 2 *verb* to beg for money in the street.

pannage 1 the right of pasturing swine in a forest. 2 the acorns etc. on which the swine feed.

pantheism the belief that God is identifiable with nature and natural forces.

pantheon 1 a building in which the illustrious dead are buried or commemorated. 2 all the deities of a people; or a temple dedicated to them.

panurgic able or ready to do anything; crafty and subtle.

paparazzo a freelance photographer who pursues celebrities to photograph them.

papilloma a wart, corn, or other usually benign tumour.

Paraclete the Holy Spirit as advocate or counsellor.

paradigm an example or pattern, especially a set of the inflections of a noun, verb, etc.

paramount 1 supreme; requiring first consideration; pre-eminent (*of paramount importance*). **2** in supreme authority.

parang a large heavy Malayan knife used for clearing vegetation etc.

paraph a flourish after a signature, originally as a precaution against forgery.

paraquat a quick-acting herbicide.

paravane a torpedo-shaped device towed by a ship to cut the moorings of submerged mines.

parbuckle a rope sling for raising or lowering casks and cylindrical objects.

pard an old word for a leopard.

parergon 1 work secondary to one's main employment. **2** an ornamental accessory.

parget to plaster (a wall etc.) especially with an ornamental pattern.

parison a rounded mass of glass formed by rolling immediately after taking it from the furnace.

parlay *US* to use (money won on a bet) as a further stake.

parlous dangerous or difficult.

Parousia the supposed second coming of Christ.

parr a young salmon in the freshwater stage.

parturition childbirth.

parvis (also **parvise**) **1** an enclosed area in front of a cathedral, church, etc. **2** a room over a church porch.

paschal of Easter or the Jewish Passover.

pasquinade a lampoon or satire, originally one displayed in a public place.

pastern the part of a horse's foot just above the hoof.

pastiche a picture, musical composition, or literary work either composed in the style of a well-known earlier creator or made up as a medley of various borrowed fragments.

patagium the wing-membrane of a bat, flying squirrel, etc.

patella the kneecap.

paterfamilias the male head of a family or household.

patrial having the right to live in the UK through the British birth of a parent or grandparent.

patrimony 1 property inherited from one's father or ancestor. **2** a heritage. **3** the endowment of a church etc.

patristic of the early Christian writers or their work.

patronymic a name derived from the first name of a father or ancestor, e.g. *Johnson, O'Brien, Ivanovitch.*

paucity smallness of number or quantity.

pavane (also **pavan**) a stately dance, formerly danced in elaborate clothing.

pavonine of or like a peacock.

pawl a lever to lock a capstan, the teeth of a wheel, etc.

paxwax the tendon in the nape of the neck of a horse, ox, sheep, etc.

peccadillo a trifling offence; a small sin.

peccant 1 sinning. **2** inducing disease.

peccary a kind of American wild pig.

pectin a soluble jelly-forming substance found in ripe fruit and used as a setting agent in jam.

peculation the embezzling of money.

pedagogue a schoolmaster; a teacher.

pederasty (also **paederasty**) anal intercourse between a man and a boy.

pedicular infested with lice.

peen the wedge-shaped or curved end of a hammer head.

peggle a dialect word for the fruit of the hawthorn; a haw.

peignoir a woman's loose dressing gown.

pelf money; wealth.

pellucid 1 (of water, light, etc.) transparent, clear. **2** (of style, speech, etc.) not confused; clear.

pemmican dried pounded meat mixed with melted fat and currants etc. for use by Arctic travellers etc.

penchant an inclination or liking (*has a penchant for old films*).

penetralia innermost shrines or recesses; secret hidden parts.

pennate feathery, winged.

pennill an improvised stanza sung to a harp accompaniment at an eisteddfod etc.

pensile hanging down; pendulous.

pentad the number five; a group of five.

pentagram a five-pointed star, formerly used as a mystic symbol.

Pentateuch the first five books of the Old Testament.

pentathlon an athletic event comprising five different events for each competitor.

penumbra 1 the partially shaded region round the shadow of an opaque body, especially that around the total shadow of the moon or earth in an eclipse. **2** a partial shadow.

peptic concerning or promoting digestion.

perdurable permanent; eternal; durable.

peregrination a journey or wandering, especially extensive.

peremptory dogmatic, imperious; admitting no refusal.

perfidy breach of faith; treachery.

perfunctory done merely superficially for the sake of getting through a duty (*a perfunctory kiss*).

periapt a thing worn as a charm; an amulet.

peripatetic 1 (of a teacher) working in more than one school or college etc. **2** going from place to place; itinerant. **3** (**Peripatetic**) Aristotelian (from Aristotle's habit of walking in the Lyceum while teaching).

peripheral 1 of minor importance; marginal. **2** on the fringe. **3** *Anat.* near the surface of the body, with special reference to the circulation and nervous system.

Perique a strong dark Louisiana tobacco.

peristalith a ring or row of ancient standing stones.

permafrost subsoil which remains frozen all the year round, as in polar regions.

peroration the concluding part of a speech, forcefully summing up what has been said.

perquisite 1 an extra profit additional to a main income. **2** a customary extra right or privilege; a perk.

persiflage light raillery, banter.

persimmon a usually tropical evergreen tree bearing edible tomato-like fruits.

perspicacity mental penetration; discernment.

perspicuity clearness of expression.

pertinent relevant to the matter in hand; to the point.

pertussis whooping cough.

pestilence a fatal epidemic disease, especially bubonic plague.

petard a small bomb used in former times to blast down a door etc.

petasus an ancient Greek hat, as worn by Hermes.

peterman a safe-breaker.

petroglyph a rock-carving, especially a prehistoric one.

pettitoes pigs' trotters, regarded as food.

pharos a lighthouse or beacon to guide sailors.

pheromone a chemical secreted by an animal to attract or warn others of the same species.

philander (of a man) to flirt, womanize.

philately stamp-collecting.

philippic a bitter verbal attack.

phillumeny the collecting of matchbox labels.

phlogiston a substance formerly thought to exist in all combustible bodies and to be released in burning.

phratry a tribal or kinship division; a clan.

phrenetic 1 frantic. **2** fanatic.

phylactery 1 a small leather box containing Hebrew texts, worn by Jewish men at prayer. **2** an amulet or charm.

phylum a taxonomic rank below kingdom, comprising a class or classes and subordinate groups.

phytotron a laboratory where plants can grow and be studied under controlled conditions.

piacular 1 atoning, especially for sacrilege. **2** needing atonement; sacrilegious.

piaffe (of a horse) to move as in a trot, but slower.

pibroch a series of martial or funerary variations for the bagpipes.

picador a mounted man with a lance who goads the bull in a bullfight.

picaresque (of a style of fiction) dealing with the episodic adventures of rogues etc.

piceous of or like pitch; black and glossy.

pichiciago (also **pichiciego**) a small South American armadillo.

piggin a wooden bucket with one long stave serving as a handle.

pikelet a thin kind of Northern English crumpet.

pilose (also **pilous**) hairy.

pinchbeck an alloy of copper and zinc used in cheap jewellery as imitation gold.

pinguid fat, oily.

pintle a pin or bolt, especially one on which some other part turns.

Pinyin a system of romanized spelling for transcribing Chinese.

pique ill-feeling; enmity, resentment.

piscatory of fishermen or fishing.

pismire a dialect word for an ant.

piste a ski run of compacted snow.

pizzle an animal's penis, especially that of a bull, formerly used as a whip.

placate to pacify, conciliate.

placebo a pill, medicine, etc. having no physiological effect, prescribed for psychological reasons or as a control in testing new drugs.

placer a deposit of sand, gravel, etc. in the bed of a stream etc., containing valuable minerals in particles.

placket a slit in a garment, for fastenings or access to a pocket.

planchette a small usually heart-shaped board on castors with a pencil that supposedly writes spirit messages when someone's fingers rest lightly on it.

plangent (of a sound) **1** loud and reverberating. **2** plaintive.

plantar of the sole of the foot.

plasma (also **plasm**) the colourless fluid part of blood, lymph, or milk (and see PHYSICS).

plaudit applause; emphatic approval.

pleach to entwine or interlace (especially branches to form a hedge).

plectrum a thin flat piece of plastic or horn etc. held in the hand to pluck the string of a guitar etc.

plenary **1** entire, unqualified (*plenary indulgence*). **2** (of an assembly) to be attended by all members.

plenitude fullness, completeness; abundance.

pleonastic using more words than are needed.

plethora an oversupply, e.g. an excess of any body fluid, or of red corpuscles in the blood.

plexor (also **plessor**) a small hammer used for testing reflexes and tapping the chest etc. for diagnosis.

pneuma the spirit or soul.

poco-curante careless, indifferent.

pogoniate bearded, unshaven.

pogrom an organized massacre (originally of Jews in Russia).

polder a piece of low-lying land reclaimed from the sea or a river, especially in the Netherlands.

polity **1** a form or process of civil government or constitution. **2** an organized society; a State as a political entity.

pollard **1** a hornless sheep, ox, or goat. **2** a tree, especially a riverside willow, whose branches have been cut off to encourage new growth.

pollex the thumb, or corresponding digit of a forelimb.

poltroon a spiritless coward.

polymath a person of much or varied learning; a great scholar.

polynya a stretch of open water surrounded by ice, especially in the Arctic seas.

pomace 1 the mass of crushed apples in cider-making, before or after the juice is pressed out. **2** the refuse of fish etc. after the oil has been extracted, generally used as a fertilizer.

pomander a spiced orange or ball of mixed aromatic substances to be placed in a cupboard etc.

pompadour a woman's hairstyle with the hair in a high turned-back roll round the face.

poniard a small slim dagger.

pontine of bridges.

porringer a small bowl, often with a handle, for soup, stew, etc.

posit to assume as a fact; postulate.

postprandial after dinner or lunch.

postulate to assume as a necessary condition; take for granted.

potable drinkable.

potamic of rivers.

poteen (also **potheen**) *Irish* alcohol distilled illicitly, usually from potatoes.

pother a noise; commotion; fuss.

potlatch among North American Indians, a ceremonial giving away or destruction of property to enhance status.

pragmatic dealing with matters with regard to their practical requirements or consequences.

praxis 1 accepted practice or custom. **2** the practising of an art or skill.

precedent a previous case or legal decision etc., taken as a guide for later cases or as a justification.

preclude to prevent, exclude, make impossible (*so as to preclude all doubt*).

predilection a preference or special liking.

pre-empt to forestall, acquire, or prevent by action in advance (*pre-empt an attack/my rival/the land*).

prehensile (of a tail, limb, elephant's trunk, etc.) capable of grasping.

premonition a forewarning; a presentiment.

prepuce the foreskin.

prequel a story, film, etc. whose events precede those of an existing work.

presbyopia long-sightedness, developing especially in middle and old age.

prescient having foreknowledge or foresight.

prestidigitation conjuring.

prevalent 1 generally occurring or existing. **2** predominant.

prevaricate to speak misleadingly; quibble.

priapic phallic; sexually licentious.

primogeniture the fact of being the first-born child, often with the consequent right of inheritance.

pristine in its original condition; unspoilt.

probang a flexible strip with a sponge or button at the end, for surgical introduction into the throat.

probity uprightness, honesty.

proclivity a tendency or inclination.

proem a preface, preamble, or prelude.

prognathous having a projecting jaw.

prognosis a forecast, as of the course of a disease etc.

prolegomena the introductory matter of a book etc., especially when critical or discursive.

prolepsis 1 the anticipation and answering of possible objections. **2** the representation of something as happening in advance, as in *he was a dead man when he entered.*

prolix (of speech, writing, etc.) lengthy; tedious.

promulgate 1 to make (a cause etc.) known to the public; disseminate, promote. **2** to proclaim (a decree, news, etc.)

prophylactic 1 a preventive medicine or course of action. **2** US a condom.

propitiate to appease (an offended person etc.)

proponent someone advocating a motion, theory, or proposal.

prorogue to discontinue the meetings of (a parliament etc.) without dissolving it.

proscribe 1 to banish, exile. **2** to reject or denounce (a practice etc.).

prosthesis an artificial leg, breast, tooth, etc. (and see LANGUAGE).

protean variable, versatile; taking many forms.

prothalamium a song or poem to celebrate a forthcoming wedding.

provenance the origin or history of especially a work of art.

pruritus severe itching of the skin.

psychokinesis the movement of objects supposedly by mental effort without the action of natural forces.

puce dark red or purple-brown.

pulchritude beauty.

pullulate 1 (of a seed, shoot, etc.) to bud, sprout, germinate. **2** (especially of animals) to swarm, throng, breed abundantly, abound.

pulmonary of the lungs.

pulverulent powdery, or likely to crumble.

punctate spotted, speckled.

punctilio petty overattention to ceremony and etiquette.

punty an iron rod used in glass-blowing.

purfle an ornamental border, especially on a violin etc.

purulent consisting of or discharging pus.

pusillanimous lacking courage; timid.

putative reputed, supposed.

putcher a conical basket or wicker trap for catching salmon.

puteal of a well or pit.

putsch an attempt at political revolution; a violent uprising.

pyknic (also **pycnic**) having a thick neck, large abdomen, and short limbs.

pyrexia fever.

pyx (also **pix**) **1** the vessel in which the bread of the Eucharist is kept. **2** a box at the Royal Mint in which specimen gold and silver coins are deposited for testing annually.

Q

quadrat a small area marked for ecological study.

quadrennium a period of four years.

quadroon a person with three White grandparents and one Negro one.

quagga an extinct zebra-like South African mammal with yellowish-brown stripes.

quandary a state of perplexity; a practical dilemma.

quant a punting-pole.

quantal composed of discrete units; varying in steps, not continuously.

quartan (of a fever etc.) recurring every fourth day.

quartile in statistics, one of three values of a variable dividing a population into four equal groups as regards the value of that variable.

quebracho any of several kinds of American trees, with very hard timber and medicinal bark.

quenelle a seasoned ball or roll of pounded fish or meat.

quern a hand-mill for grinding corn.

quiddity **1** the essence of a person or thing; what makes a thing what it is. **2** a quibble; a trivial objection.

quidnunc a newsmonger; a person given to gossip.

quietus **1** something which quiets or represses. **2** release from life; death, final riddance.

quincunx five objects (e.g. planted trees, or the five on a dice) set so that four are at the corners of a square or rectangle and the fifth is at its centre.

quintain a post set up as a mark for the medieval military exercise of tilting, often provided with a sandbag to swing round and strike an unsuccessful tilter.

quire 1 four sheets of paper folded to form eight leaves, as often in medieval manuscripts. **2** 25 (formerly 20) sheets of paper.

quittance 1 a release from something. **2** an acknowledgement of payment.

quodlibet 1 a topic for philosophical or theological discussion, as set for an exercise. **2** a light-hearted medley of well-known tunes.

R

rabid 1 furious, violent (*rabid hate; a rabid nationalist*). **2** (especially of a dog) affected with rabies.

rachitic suffering from rickets.

raddle the red ochre often used to mark sheep.

raddled worn out; untidy, unkempt.

rale an abnormal rattling sound as heard in unhealthy lungs.

ramose branched, branchy.

rancour (*US* **rancor**) inveterate bitterness, spitefulness.

raptor any bird of prey; an owl, falcon, etc.

raster a pattern of scanning lines for a cathode-ray tube picture.

rataplan a drumming sound.

ratiocination logical reasoning.

ratite a flightless bird, e.g. an ostrich, emu, or cassowary.

rattan (also **ratan**) the jointed pliable stem of an East Indian climbing plant, used for walking sticks, furniture, etc.

raucous harsh-sounding, loud and hoarse.

ravelin an outwork of early fortification, with two faces projecting outwards at an angle.

razzia a hostile incursion for conquest, plunder, capture of slaves, etc., as practised by the Muslim peoples in Africa.

realtor *US* an estate agent.

rebarbative repellent, unattractive.

rebato a kind of stiff collar worn by both sexes from about 1590 to 1630.

reboation a re-bellowing echo.

rebus a representation of a word or phrase (especially a name) by pictures etc. suggesting its parts, as in 'if the Gbmt put:' for 'if the grate be empty put coal on'.

recalesce to grow hot again (especially of iron allowed to cool from white heat, whose temperature rises at a certain point for a short time).

recension a particular form or version of a text resulting from revision.

recherché 1 carefully sought out; rare or exotic. **2** far-fetched, obscure.

recidivist a person who relapses into crime.

réclame popular fame, notoriety.

recondite abstruse; out of the way; obscure.

recoup 1 to recover or regain (a loss). **2** to compensate or reimburse (someone) for a loss.

recrudescence (of a disease or difficulty etc.) to break out again, especially after a dormant period.

recto 1 the right-hand page of a book. **2** the front of a page (opp. VERSO).

rectrix a bird's strong tail-feather directing flight.

recusant someone who refuses submission to an authority or compliance with a regulation; especially formerly, one who refused to attend services of the Church of England.

recuse to object, renounce; especially to object to (a judge) as prejudiced.

redact to put into literary form; edit for publication.

redound (of an action etc.) to make a great contribution (*it redounded to his credit*).

reflux 1 a backward flow. **2** a method of boiling a liquid so that any vapour is liquefied and returned to the boiler.

refulgent shining; gloriously bright.

regelate to freeze again (especially of pieces of ice etc. frozen together after temporary thawing of the surfaces).

regenerate 1 to bring or come into renewed existence. **2** to give or acquire new and better life; reform. **3** to regrow new tissue. **4** to restore to an initial state.

regimen 1 a prescribed course of exercise, way of life, and diet. **2** *archaic* a system of government.

regisseur the director of a theatrical production, especially a ballet.

regnant 1 reigning, not merely a consort (*Queen regnant*). **2** (of things, qualities, etc.) predominant, prevalent.

regulus 1 the purer or metallic part of a mineral that separates on reduction. **2** an impure metallic product formed during smelting.

reify to convert (a person, abstraction, etc.) into a thing; materialize.

reliquary a receptacle for a religious relic.

remontant blooming more than once a year.

remora any of various sea fish that attach themselves with sucker-like fins to other fish and to ships.

renal of the kidneys.

renege (also **renegue**) to go back on one's word; recant.

rennet curdled milk from the stomach of an unweaned calf (or a preparation made from its stomach-membrane) used in making cheese and junket.

repine to fret, be discontented.

rescind to abrogate (a law, contract, etc.); revoke, cancel.

respire **1** to breathe; inhale and exhale air. **2** to get rest or respite.

resurgent rising or arising again.

ret (also **rate**) **1** to soften (flax etc.) by soaking. **2** (of hay etc.) to be spoilt by wet or rot.

retiarius a Roman gladiator using a net and trident.

reticle a network of threads or lines in the focal plane of an optical instrument to help accurate observation.

retroussé (of a nose) turned up at the tip.

revanchism a political policy of seeking to retaliate, especially to recover lost territory.

revers the turned-up edge of a garment at a lapel or cuff, revealing the (often lined) under-surface.

revet to face (a rampart etc.) with masonry, especially in fortification.

rheum a watery discharge from the eyes or nose.

rhinal of a nostril or the nose.

rhonchus a snoring or whistling sound from the chest.

rhotacism excessive or peculiar pronunciation of the sound r.

rhumb **1** any of the 32 points of the compass. **2** the angle between two successive compass points.

rictus the gape of a mouth or beak.

rifampicin an antibiotic used to treat various diseases, especially pulmonary tuberculosis.

riffler a tool with a curved file-surface at each end, used by sculptors, metal-workers, and wood-carvers.

rile to anger, irritate.

rilletts a tinned preparation of minced ham, chicken, fat, etc.

rime frost, especially white frost deposited by cloud or fog.

rinderpest a virulent infectious disease of ruminants, especially cattle.

riparian of or on a river bank (*riparian rights*).

riprap US a collection of loose stones as a foundation for a structure.

risible laughable, ludicrous.

rivière a gem necklace, especially of more than one string.

roborant a strengthening drug.

roc a gigantic bird of Eastern legend.

rodomontade boastful bragging talk or behaviour.

roil to make (a liquid) muddy by stirring it.

Romany 1 a Gypsy. 2 the language of the Gypsies.

rondavel a South African round tribal hut usually with a thatched conical roof.

rondeau a poem of ten or thirteen lines with only two rhymes throughout and with the opening words used twice as a refrain.

roquelaure a man's knee-length cloak of the 18th and early 19th centuries.

rosarium a rose garden.

rotund 1 (of a person) large and plump, podgy. 2 (of language) sonorous, impressively highfalutin.

roué a debauchee, especially an elderly one; a rake.

rouleau 1 a cylindrical packet of coins. 2 a coil or roll of ribbon etc., especially as trimming.

rowen US a second growth of hay; an aftermath.

rubicund (of a face, or person in this respect) ruddy, rosy, high-coloured.

ruche a frill or gathering of lace, etc. as a trimming.

ruminate 1 to meditate; ponder. 2 (of ruminants) to chew the cud.

runagate a deserter, fugitive, runaway.

rundale a system by which land is divided into strips or patches of which several, not adjoining each other, are cultivated by each holder.

runt 1 a small pig, especially the smallest in a litter. 2 a weak undersized person. 3 a large domestic pigeon. 4 an ox or cow of various small breeds.

S

sabot a shoe hollowed out of a block of wood.

sabulous sandy, granular.

sacerdotal of priests; priestly.

sachem 1 the supreme chief of some American Indian tribes. 2 US a political leader.

saffian a leather made from goatskins or sheepskins dyed in bright colours.

saggar (also **sagger**) a protective fireclay box enclosing ceramic ware while it is being fired.

salangane a kind of swallow that makes edible nests.

salicylism aspirin poisoning.

salientian a frog or toad.

salmagundi 1 a salad of chopped meat, anchovies, eggs, onions, etc. **2** a general mixture; miscellaneous collection.

saltation 1 the act of leaping or dancing; a jump. **2** a sudden transition.

samite a rich medieval dress-fabric of silk sometimes interwoven with gold.

samizdat a system of underground publishing of banned literature in the former USSR.

samp *US* coarse maize porridge.

sandiver liquid scum formed in glass-making.

sanguinary delighting in bloodshed; bloodthirsty.

sans-culotte 1 a lower-class Parisian republican in the French Revolution. **2** an extreme republican or revolutionary.

sans serif (also **sanserif**) a form of printing type without serifs, the projections finishing off the strokes of the letters.

saponaceous of soap, soapy.

Sapphic 1 of the Greek poetess Sappho. **2** lesbian.

sardonic grimly jocular; bitterly mocking or cynical.

sartorial of tailoring, or men's clothes.

sastrugi wave-like irregularities, caused by winds, in the surface of hard polar snow.

satrap 1 a provincial governor in the ancient Persian empire. **2** a subordinate ruler, colonial governor, etc.

saturnine 1 sluggish, gloomy; dark and brooding. **2** an old word referring to the metal lead, or to lead poisoning.

satyagraha passive resistance; originally the policy of resistance to British rule advocated by Gandhi.

savannah (also **savanna**) a grassy plain in the tropics or subtropics.

sawder flattery, blarney.

scabrous 1 rough, scurfy. **2** indecent, salacious.

scapular 1 a monk's short cloak. **2** a bandage for the shoulders. **3** a bird's feather near the shoulder.

scaramouch an old word for a boastful coward.

scarify 1 to slit or scrape (the skin). **2** to hurt by severe criticism. **3** to loosen (soil) with a spiked tool.

scatophagous feeding on dung.

schlock *US colloq.* inferior goods; trash.

sciamachy (also **skiamachy**) fighting with shadows; imaginary or futile combat.

scintilla 1 a trace. **2** a spark.

sciolist a superficial pretender to knowledge.

scofflaw (especially *US*) one who treats the law with contempt, especially a person who avoids various kinds of not easily enforceable laws.

scorbutic of, or affected with, scurvy.

Scouse the dialect of Liverpool.

scrannel thin, meagre.

screeve **1** to write. **2** to draw coloured pictures on the pavement.

scrimshank *Brit. slang* to shirk duty.

scrimshaw shells, ivory, etc. adorned with carved or coloured designs as a sailors' pastime at sea.

scry to divine by crystal-gazing.

scut the short tail of especially a hare, rabbit, or deer.

scutage money formerly paid by a feudal landowner instead of personal service.

scuttlebutt **1** a water-butt on the deck of a ship, for drinking from. **2** *colloq.* rumour, gossip.

sebaceous fatty, oily.

sedulous persevering, painstaking, diligent.

seg a protective stud on the toe or heel of a boot.

seigniorage (also **seignorage**) a profit made by issuing currency, especially by issuing coins rated above the value of their metal.

seine a large fishing net with floats at the top and weights at the bottom edge.

seismic of earthquakes.

selvedge (also **selvage**) the edge of a cloth along the warp.

seminal **1** of seeds or semen. **2** (of ideas etc.) providing the basis for future development (*a seminal book*).

sempiternal eternal, everlasting.

seneschal the steward of a medieval great house.

sententious pompously moralizing; given to the use of maxims.

seppuku Japanese ritual disembowelment; hara-kiri.

sequacious **1** inconsequent, incoherent. **2** dependent, servile.

sequelae complications following a disease.

serac one of the tower-shaped masses into which a glacier is divided at steep points by crevasses crossing it.

serang the head of a crew of East Indian seamen.

sere (of leaves etc.) dried up, withered.

serendipity the faculty of making happy and unexpected discoveries by accident.

serialism the composing of music using a fixed arrangement of the twelve notes of the chromatic scale.

sericulture the breeding of silkworms.

sesquipedalian 1 (of a word or expression) of many syllables. **2** half a yard high or long.

setiferous (also **setigerous**) bristly.

sett 1 a badger's burrow. **2** a granite paving block.

shaddock the largest citrus fruit, with a thick yellow skin and bitter pulp.

shadoof a pole with a bucket and counterpoise, used especially in Egypt for raising water.

shagreen 1 a kind of rough untanned leather. **2** rough sharkskin used for rasping and polishing.

shaman a witch doctor or priest claiming to communicate with gods, etc.

shard 1 a broken piece of pottery or glass. **2** a beetle's wing-case.

sheading each of the six administrative divisions in the Isle of Man.

shibboleth a long-standing formula, doctrine, or phrase etc., held to be true by a party or sect (*must abandon outdated shibboleths*).

shikar hunting in India.

shillelagh a thick stick of blackthorn or oak, used in Ireland especially as a weapon.

shirr 1 to gather (fabric) with especially elastic parallel threads. **2** *US* to bake (eggs) without their shells.

shive a thin flat cork for a wide-mouthed bottle, or bung for a cask.

shofar a ram's-horn trumpet used in Jewish religious ceremonies and as an ancient battle-signal.

shoji a sliding paper-covered screen door in a Japanese house.

siccative a substance causing drying, especially mixed with oil-paint etc.

sigmoid crescent-shaped or S-shaped.

simony the buying or selling of ecclesiastical privileges.

simulacrum an image or likeness of something, often deceptive.

simulate 1 to pretend to have or feel or be. **2** to imitate, counterfeit (*simulated fur*).

simulcast simultaneous transmission of the same programme on radio and television.

singultus hiccups.

sjambok in South Africa, a rhinoceros-hide whip.

skald (also **scald**) in ancient Scandinavia, a composer and reciter of poems honouring the deeds of heroes.

skean-dhu a dagger worn in the stocking as part of Highland costume.

skerry *Scot.* a reef or rocky island.

skewbald (of an animal) with irregular patches of white and another colour, properly not black.

skilly a thin broth or gruel, usually of oatmeal flavoured with meat.

slalom **1** a ski race down a zigzag course between artificial obstacles. **2** an obstacle race for canoes, cars, skateboards, or water-skis.

slivovitz a plum brandy made especially in the Balkans.

slurry semi-liquid mud, cement, or manure.

smallage any of several kinds of celery or parsley.

smegma an oily secretion in the folds of the skin, especially of the foreskin.

snaffle a horse's simple bridle-bit, without a curb and usually with a single rein.

snood an ornamental net to hold a woman's back hair.

sobriquet (also **soubriquet**) **1** a nickname. **2** an assumed name.

sodality a confraternity or association, especially a Roman Catholic religious guild or brotherhood.

softa a Muslim student of sacred law and theology.

solarium a room with sun-lamps, or large glass areas, for sunbathing.

solidus an oblique stroke (/) used in writing fractions ($^3/_4$), or to denote alternatives (*and/or*) or ratios (*miles/day*).

solipsism the philosophical view that the self is all that exists or can be known.

somatic of the body, especially as distinct from the mind.

somite each body-division of an animal divided into similar segments.

somniferous inducing sleep; soporific.

somniloquent talking in one's sleep.

sophism a false argument, especially one intended to deceive.

sophomore *US* a second-year university or high-school student.

sorites a series of logical propositions in which the predicate of the first is the subject of the second, as in *all A = B, all B = C, therefore all A = C.*

sororal by or of a sister; sisterly.

sorority a female students' society in an American university or college.

sortilege divination by lots.

souk a market place in Muslim countries.

soutane a priest's cassock.

southpaw a left-handed person, especially in boxing.

spall a splinter or chip of rock.

spatchcock a chicken or especially game bird split open and grilled.

spatterdash a cloth or leather legging, formerly worn to protect the legs from mud etc.

spatulate broad with a rounded end (*a spatulate finger/leaf*).

speculum **1** a surgical instrument for stretching body cavities for inspection. **2** a mirror, especially of polished metal in a reflecting telescope. **3** a lustrous coloured area on the wing of especially ducks.

spermaceti a white waxy secretion from a sperm whale's head, used in making candles, ointments, etc.

speys thick woodland.

sphagnum a moss growing in bogs and peat, used in packing, as fertilizer, etc.

sphragistics the study of engraved seals.

spikenard a costly perfumed ointment, made in former times from an Indian plant.

spindrift spray blown along the surface of the sea.

spiracle an external vent for breathing, in insects, whales, and some fish.

spitchcock an eel split and broiled.

splanchnic of the viscera; intestinal.

splenetic ill-tempered; peevish.

spline a ridge fitting into a groove in the hub or shaft of a wheel to allow longitudinal play.

spoor the track or scent of an animal.

sporadic occurring only here and there or occasionally; separate, scattered.

sprocket each of several teeth on a wheel engaging with links of a chain, e.g. on a bicycle.

squamous scaly.

stacte a sweet spice used by the ancient Jews in making incense.

stanchion **1** a post or pillar; an upright support. **2** a bar or pair of bars for confining cattle in a stall.

stannary a tin-mine.

steatopygous having fat buttocks.

stein a large earthenware beer mug, typically with a lid.

stellate arranged like a star; radiating.

stentorian (of a voice or speech) very loud.

stercoraceous **1** consisting of dung or faeces. **2** living in dung.

sternum the breastbone.

sternutation sneezing.

stertorous (of breathing etc.) heavy; sounding like snoring.

stevedore a person employed in loading and unloading ships; a docker.

stichomythia in classical Greek drama, dialogue in alternate lines.

stigmata in Christian belief, marks corresponding to those left on Christ's body by the Crucifixion, said to have been impressed on the bodies of St Francis of Assisi and others.

stirk a yearling bullock or heifer.

stirps a classificatory group in biology (and see LEGAL TERMS).

stochastic 1 determined by a random distribution of probabilities. **2** governed by the laws of probability.

stoma 1 a small mouthlike opening in some lower animals, e.g. a hookworm. **2** a small orifice made surgically in the stomach (and see BOTANICAL TERMS).

stomatic good for diseases of the mouth.

stoush *Austral. & New Zealand* to fight with, attack.

stover winter food for cattle.

strabismus a squint.

strappado a form of torture in which the victim is secured to a rope and made to fall from a height almost to the ground and then stopped with a jerk.

strath a broad mountain valley in Scotland.

stricture a critical or censorious remark.

stridulate (of insects, especially the cicada and grasshopper) to make a shrill sound by rubbing the legs or wing-cases together.

strigil a skin-scraper used by ancient Greek and Roman bathers after exercise.

struma goitre.

struthious of or like an ostrich.

stultify to make useless or futile, especially as a result of tedious routine (*stultifying boredom*).

stupa a round usually domed building erected as a Buddhist shrine.

Stygian dark, gloomy, indistinct.

stylite an ancient or medieval ascetic living on top of a pillar.

suave 1 (of a person, especially a man) smooth; polite; sophisticated. **2** (of a wine etc.) bland, smooth.

subereous of cork; corky.

sublunary of this world; earthly.

suborn to induce by bribery etc. to commit perjury or any other unlawful act.

subreption the obtaining of something by surprise or misrepresentation.

subrogation the substitution of one party for another as creditor, with the transfer of rights and duties.

subsume to include (an instance, idea, category, etc.) within a larger class.

subvention a grant of money from a government etc.; a subsidy.

succedaneum a substitute, especially for a medicine or drug.

succotash a dish of green maize and beans boiled together.

succour (US **succor**) aid, assistance.

succubus a female demon believed to have intercourse with sleeping men.

succumb 1 to be forced to give way; be overcome (*succumbed to temptation*). **2** to be overcome by death (*succumbed to his injuries*).

succuss to shake (a patient) vigorously so as to hear any splashing sound in the lungs.

sudd floating vegetation impeding the navigation of the White Nile.

sudorific causing sweating.

sulcus a groove or furrow, especially on the surface of the brain.

sullage filth, refuse, sewage.

sumo a style of Japanese wrestling, in which a participant is defeated by touching the ground with any part of the body except the soles of the feet or by moving outside the marked area.

supererogation the performance of more than duty requires.

superfetation a second conception during pregnancy, giving rise to embryos of different ages.

supernal 1 heavenly, divine. **2** of or concerning the sky. **3** lofty.

supine 1 lying face upwards. **2** inert, indolent; morally inactive.

surcingle a band round a horse's body usually to keep a pack etc. in place.

surrogate a substitute, deputy.

suspire 1 to sigh, or utter with a sigh. **2** to breathe.

sussuration a sound of whispering or rustling.

sutler a person in the past who followed an army and sold provisions to the soldiers.

suture 1 the stitching of a wound or incision, or the thread or wire used for this. **2** the seamlike junction of two bones, especially in the skull.

suzerain 1 a feudal lord. **2** a sovereign or State having some control over another State that is internally autonomous.

swami a Hindu male religious teacher.

swarf fine chips or filings of stone, metal, plastic, etc. removed by cutting.

swatch a sample, especially of cloth.

swinge to strike hard, beat.

swingletree a pivoted crossbar to which the traces are attached in a cart, plough, etc.

sybarite a self-indulgent person; one devoted to sensuous luxury.

sycophant a servile flatterer; a toady.

syllabub a dessert made of cream or milk flavoured, sweetened, and whipped.

symbiosis an interaction between two different organisms living in close physical association, usually to the advantage of both.

synaesthesia (*US* **synesthesia**) **1** the production of a mental sense-impression relating to one sense by the stimulation of another sense, as when a sensation of colour is aroused by a smell. **2** a sensation produced in one part of the body by stimulation of another part.

syncretism the process of attempting to unify differing schools of thought (and see LANGUAGE).

synergism the combined effect of drugs, organs, etc. that exceeds the sum of their individual effects.

syphilophobia an abnormal fear of being infected with syphilis.

syrinx the song-organ of birds (and see MUSIC).

T

tabard **1** a herald's official coat bearing the arms of the sovereign. **2** a woman's sleeveless jerkin. **3** a medieval knight's short tunic bearing his arms and worn over armour.

tabouret (*US* **taboret**) **1** a low seat usually without arms or back. **2** an embroidery frame.

tacit understood or implied without being stated (*tacit consent*).

taciturn reserved in speech; saying little; incommunicative.

tactile of or perceived by the sense of touch.

tahina (also **tahini**) a paste of sesame seeds originally from the Middle East.

taiga coniferous forest lying between tundra and steppe, especially in Siberia.

taint a corrupt condition or trace of decay.

tampion (also **tompion**) a stopper or plug, e.g. for the muzzle of a gun or an organ-pipe.

tangential only slightly relevant; peripheral.

tangram a Chinese puzzle square cut into seven pieces to be combined into various figures.

tanist the heir apparent to a Celtic chief, usually his most vigorous adult relation, chosen by election.

tantalus a stand in which spirit-decanters may be locked up but visible.

tantamount (*to*) equivalent to (*was tantamount to a denial*).

tarantella a rapid whirling Southern Italian dance.

tare 1 an allowance made for the weight of the packing round goods. **2** the weight of an unladen goods vehicle without fuel.

tarot cards a pack of cards for fortune-telling, with symbolic pictures.

taw the game of marbles, a large marble, or the line from which players throw marbles.

taws (also **tawse**) a thong with a slit end formerly used for punishing children in Scottish schools.

taxidermy the art of stuffing and mounting the skins of animals.

taxonomy the science or practice of classifying living or extinct organisms.

tazza a saucer-shaped cup, especially one mounted on a foot.

tectonics 1 the production of practical and beautiful buildings. **2** the study of large-scale geological features.

telekinesis the movement of objects at a distance supposedly by mental powers.

telergy the supposed force operating in telepathy and directly affecting the brain or human organism.

tellurian of or inhabiting the earth.

telpher a system for transporting goods by cable-cars.

temporal 1 worldly rather than spiritual; secular. **2** of time. **3** of the temples of the head, between forehead and ear.

tenable that can be defended against attack (*a tenable position/theory*).

tendentious (of writing etc.) calculated to promote a particular cause or controversial viewpoint; having an underlying purpose.

tenebrous dark, gloomy.

tensile 1 of tension. **2** capable of being drawn out or stretched.

tenson (also **tenzon**) a contest in verse-making between troubadours.

teraph a small image as a domestic deity or oracle of the ancient Hebrews.

tercel a male hawk, especially a peregrine or goshawk to be used in falconry.

tergiversate 1 to change one's party or principles. **2** to equivocate; make conflicting or evasive statements.

tergum the back or upper surface of an articulated creature, e.g. a crayfish.

termitarium a termites' nest.

ternary composed of three parts.

Terpsichorean of dancing.

terret each of the rings on a harness-pad for the driving-reins to pass through.

tesseract a four-dimensional hypercube; extension of a cube into the fourth dimension.

testudo a overhead protection, either in the form of a portable screen or of their overlapping shields, for besieging troops in ancient Roman warfare.

Tetragrammaton the Hebrew name of God written in four letters, articulated as *Yahweh* etc.

thalassic of the sea or seas, especially small or inland seas.

thaumatrope a disc or card with two different pictures on its two sides, which merge into one when the disc is rapidly twirled.

thaumaturgy the working of miracles.

thegosis tooth-grinding in animals to sharpen the teeth.

theodicy the vindication of divine providence in view of the existence of evil.

theophany a visible manifestation of God or a god to man.

theriomorphic (especially of a deity) having an animal form.

thespian of tragedy or drama.

thimblerigger a trickster who uses sleight of hand in a game involving three inverted thimbles or cups, which are moved about, contestants having to spot which one has a pea or other object under it.

thrall 1 a slave. **2** a state of slavery; bondage (*in thrall*).

thrasonical bragging, boastful, vainglorious.

threnody a lamentation or song of lamentation, especially on a person's death.

thurible a container for burning incense in; a censer.

thurifer an acolyte carrying a vessel of incense in a service or procession.

thyrsus in Greek and Roman antiquity, a staff tipped with an ornament like a pine-cone, an attribute of Bacchus the god of wine.

tick-tack-toe *US* noughts and crosses.

tilde a mark (˜) put over a letter, e.g. over a Spanish *n* when pronounced *ny* (as in *señor*).

tine a prong of a fork.

tipcat a game with a short piece of wood tapering at the ends and struck with a stick.

tippet 1 a stole for the shoulders formerly worn by women. **2** a similar garment worn as part of some official uniforms, especially by the clergy.

tiro, tyro a beginner or novice.

tisane a tea-like infusion of dried herbs etc.

titillate 1 to excite pleasantly. **2** to tickle.

titivate (also **tittivate**) to adorn, smarten.

tomalley the fat of the North American lobster, which becomes green when cooked.

tong a Chinese guild, association, or secret society.

tonsorial of a hairdresser or hairdressing.

tontine an annuity shared by subscribers to a loan, the shares increasing as subscribers die till the last survivor gets all, or until a specified date when the remaining survivors share the proceeds.

toper an excessive (especially habitual) drinker.

topiary the art of clipping shrubs and trees into ornamental shapes.

tor a hill or rocky peak, especially in Devon or Cornwall.

torchère a tall stand with a small table for a candlestick etc.

torque a necklace of twisted metal, especially of the ancient Gauls and Britons (and see PHYSICS).

torsade a twisted fringe or ribbon decorating a hat etc.

torus a solid in the shape of a ring doughnut or tyre (and see ARCHITECTURE, BOTANY).

toupee (also **toupet**) a wig to cover a bald spot.

tournedos a small round thick cut from a fillet of beef.

toxophilite an archer, or lover of archery.

traduce to speak ill of; misrepresent.

transient of short duration; momentary, passing, impermanent (*of transient interest; transient guests*).

transilient passing from one thing or condition to another.

translucent allowing light to pass through diffusely; semi-transparent, as with frosted glass.

transmogrify to transform, especially in a magical or surprising manner.

transvestite a person who likes to wear the clothes of the opposite sex, especially as a sexual stimulus; a cross-dresser.

trapunto a kind of quilting in which the design alone is padded.

trave a timber or wooden beam or enclosure of bars.

trebuchet (also **trebucket**) **1** a military machine formerly used for throwing stones etc. in siege warfare. **2** a tilting balance for accurately weighing light articles.

trematode a parasitic flatworm, especially a fluke.

trepan 1 a cylindrical saw formerly used by surgeons for removing part of the skull bone. **2** a borer for sinking shafts.

triage **1** the act of sorting out according to quality. **2** the assignment of degrees of urgency to decide the order of treatment of wounds, illnesses, etc.

tribade a woman who takes part in a simulation of sexual intercourse with another woman.

triskelion a symbolic figure of three legs or lines from a common centre, e.g. the Manx emblem.

triturate **1** to grind to a fine powder. **2** to masticate thoroughly.

triumvirate a ruling group of three men, especially in ancient Rome.

troche a small usually circular medicated tablet or lozenge.

troglodyte **1** a cave-dweller. **2** a wilfully obscurantist or old-fashioned person.

troika **1** a Russian vehicle with three horses harnessed abreast. **2** a group of three people, especially as an administrative council.

trommel a revolving cylindrical sieve for cleaning ore in mining.

trounce **1** to defeat heavily. **2** to beat, thrash.

truculent aggressively defiant; pugnacious.

trudgen a swimming stroke like the crawl, with a scissors movement of the legs.

trunnion a supporting pin on each side of a cannon or mortar, on which it can pivot.

tucket a flourish on a trumpet; a fanfare.

tumbril (also **tumbrel**) **1** an open cart that carried prisoners to the guillotine during the French Revolution. **2** a cart that tips to discharge its load, especially a dung cart.

tumescent becoming inflated; swelling.

tumid **1** (of parts of the body etc.) swollen, inflated. **2** (of a style etc.) inflated, bombastic.

tunicate clothed in concentric layers.

turbary the right of digging turf or peat.

turpitude baseness, depravity, wickedness.

twill a fabric so woven as to have a surface of diagonal parallel ridges.

U

ubiquitous present everywhere simultaneously; often encountered.

uhlan a cavalryman who was armed with a lance, especially in the former German army.

uhuru national independence of an African country.

ukase **1** an arbitrary command. **2** an edict of the Tsarist Russian government.

ulema a body of Muslim doctors of sacred law and theology.

ullage the amount by which a cask etc. falls short of being full, by evaporation or leakage.

ulotrichan having tightly curled hair, especially denoting a human type.

ultra-crepidarian going beyond one's proper province; giving opinions on matters beyond one's knowledge.

ululate to howl, wail; make a hooting cry.

umbles the edible offal of deer etc.

umbo **1** the boss of a shield. **2** a rounded knob.

umbrageous **1** shady; affording shade. **2** (of persons) suspicious, jealous.

umlaut a mark (¨) used over a vowel, especially in Germanic languages, to indicate a vowel change.

unau the South American two-toed sloth.

uncinate hooked, crooked.

unction **1** the act of anointing for religious or medical purposes. **2** the oil or ointment so used. **3** excessive or overfervent words.

ungulate hoofed; having hooves.

uniparous producing one offspring at a birth.

upcast a shaft through which air leaves a mine.

Uranian **1** celestial, heavenly. **2** of the planet Uranus. **3** homosexual.

urticate to sting like a nettle.

usquebaugh (*especially Irish & Scot.*) whisky.

uxorious greatly or excessively fond of one's wife.

V

vaccinia a virus used as vaccine against smallpox.

vacillate **1** to fluctuate in opinion or resolution. **2** to move from side to side; oscillate; waver.

vandyke each of a series of large points forming a border to a lace collar etc.

vaporetto a canal motor-boat in Venice, used for public transport.

vaquero a cowboy or herdsman in Spanish America.

variorum **1** (of an edition of a text) having notes by various editors or commentators. **2** (of an edition of an author's works) including variant readings.

variola smallpox.

vasectomy the surgical sterilization of a man by cutting the spermatic ducts.

vatic prophetic or inspired.

vavasour a vassal who owed allegiance to a great lord and had other vassals under him.

vedette 1 a mounted sentry positioned beyond an army's outposts to watch the enemy. **2** a motor launch. **3** a stage or film star.

vegan a vegetarian who also avoids milk and eggs.

vehmgericht a form of secret tribunal which exercised great power in Westphalia from the 12th–16th centuries.

velar 1 of a veil or membrane. **2** (of a sound) pronounced with the back of the tongue near the soft palate.

velleity a low degree of volition; a slight wish or inclination.

velodrome a track, often banked, for cycle-racing.

venatic of hunting.

venation 1 the arrangement of veins in a leaf or an insect's wing etc. **2** the system of venous blood vessels in an organism.

ventage a finger-hole on a wind instrument.

veracity 1 truthfulness, honesty. **2** accuracy (of a statement etc.).

verbatim in exactly the same words; word for word (*repeated it verbatim; a verbatim report*).

verglas a thin coating of ice or frozen rain.

veridical (of visions etc.) coinciding with reality.

verisimilitude the appearance of being true or real.

verjuice an acid liquor obtained from crab-apples, sour grapes, etc., and formerly used in cooking and medicine.

vernal of or in spring (*vernal equinox; vernal breezes*).

verso 1 the left-hand page of a book. **2** the back of a page, or of a coin (opp. RECTO).

vesicant a blistering agent.

vesicle a small bladder, bubble, or hollow structure.

vespertine (of flowers, insects, etc.) opening, or active, in the evening.

vespiary a wasps' nest.

vexillum 1 an ancient Roman military standard. **2** the vane of a feather.

viatical of a road or journey.

vibrissae 1 the stiff coarse hairs near the mouth of most mammals (e.g. a cat's whiskers) and in the human nostrils. **2** bristle-like feathers near the mouth of insect-eating birds.

vicarious 1 done or experienced through another person. **2** deputed, delegated.

vicegerent someone exercising delegated power; a deputy.

vicuña a South American mammal like a llama, or its fine silky wool.

videlicet viz.; namely, that is to say.

vignette 1 a short description or brief incident in a book, film, etc. **2** an illustration or decorative design, especially on the title-page of a book.

vinaceous wine-red.

viniculture the cultivation of grapevines.

virago a fierce or abusive woman.

virelay a short (especially old French) lyric poem with two rhymes to a stanza variously arranged.

virgule **1** a slanting line used to mark division of words or lines. **2** the stroke (/) used in writing fractions etc.; a solidus.

virid green, verdant.

viscid glutinous, sticky.

vitellus the yolk of an egg.

vivarium a place for keeping animals in (nearly) their natural state indoors.

viviparous bringing forth young alive, rather than laying eggs.

volar of the palm of the hand or sole of the foot.

volition **1** the exercise of the will. **2** the power of willing (*by one's own volition*).

vomer the small thin bone separating the nostrils in man and most vertebrates.

vomitory each of the passages to the seats in an ancient Roman theatre or amphitheatre.

voyeurism the obtaining of sexual satisfaction from observing others' sexual actions or organs.

W

wadi (also **wady**) a rocky watercourse in North Africa etc., dry except in the rainy season.

wainwright a wagon-builder.

wale **1** a ridge on a woven fabric, e.g. corduroy. **2** a stout horizontal timber along a ship's sides, supporting the piles of a dam, etc. **3** a strong band round a woven basket.

wampum shell beads used as money, decoration, or aids to memory by North American Indians.

wapentake a former division of a British shire in areas of England with a large Danish population; a hundred.

warlock a sorcerer; a male witch.

water-gall **1** a boggy tract in a field. **2** a secondary or imperfectly-formed rainbow. **3** a watery bubble in the liver of swine. **4** a flaw in an article caused by the settling of water.

wayzgoose an annual summer dinner or outing held by a printing-house for its employees.

welkin the sky; the upper air.

wether a castrated ram.

whitlow an inflammation near a fingernail or toenail.

widdershins (also **withershins**) anticlockwise.

windage 1 the friction of air against the moving part of a machine. **2** the effect of the wind in deflecting a missile. **3** the difference between the diameter of a gun's bore and that of its projectile.

windrow a row in which hay, peats, sheaves of corn, etc. are laid for drying.

winze a shaft connecting levels in a mine.

withe (also **withy**) a tough flexible shoot of willow or osier, used for tying a bundle of wood etc.

wittol a man aware of his wife's infidelity; a complaisant cuckold.

woggle a leather ring fastening a Scout's or Guide's neckerchief.

wok a bowl-shaped frying-pan used in especially Chinese cookery.

X

xanthochroid having light-coloured hair and a pale complexion.

xenoglossia the faculty of using intelligibly a language one has not learnt.

xeric having dry conditions, as of a desert.

xiphoid sword-shaped.

xystus 1 a covered portico where ancient Greek athletes exercised. **2** a garden walk or terrace in ancient Rome.

Y

yahoo a coarse bestial person.

yang in Chinese philosophy, the active male principle of the universe (compare YIN).

yapp a form of bookbinding with a limp leather cover projecting to fold over the edges of the leaves.

yare ready, prompt, brisk.

yarmulke (also **yarmulka**) a skullcap worn by Jewish men.

yean to bring forth (a lamb or kid).

yeti the Abominable Snowman; an unidentified manlike or bearlike animal said to exist in the Himalayas.

yin in Chinese philosophy, the passive female principle of the universe (compare YANG).

ylem the primordial matter of the universe, conceived as a gas of neutrons.

yogh a middle English letter used for certain values of *g* and *y*.

Z

ziggurat a rectangular stepped tower in ancient Mesopotamia, with a temple on top.

zillah an administrative district in India.

zoetrope an old-fashioned optical toy in the form of a picture-lined cylinder producing moving images when revolved and viewed through a slit.

zymosis fermentation.

zymurgy the branch of applied chemistry dealing with the use of fermentation in brewing etc.